Unemployment, Recession and Effective Demand

To Wendy, Brunella, Cati and Emma

Unemployment, Recession and Effective Demand

The Contributions of Marx, Keynes and Kalecki

Claudio Sardoni

Professor of Economics, Sapienza University of Rome, Italy

Edward Elgar

Cheltenham, UK • Northampton, MA, USA

Published by
Edward Elgar Publishing Limited
The Lypiatts
15 Lansdown Road
Cheltenham
Glos GL50 2JA
UK

Edward Elgar Publishing, Inc.
William Pratt House
9 Dewey Court
Northampton
Massachusetts 01060
USA

A catalogue record for this book
is available from the British Library

Library of Congress Control Number: 2011924300

MIX
Paper from
responsible sources
FSC® C018575

ISBN 978 1 84844 969 5 (cased)

Typeset by Cambrian Typesetters, Camberley, Surrey
Printed and bound by MPG Books Group, UK

Contents

Figures

Foreword

Unemployment, Recession and Effective Demand: The Contributions of Marx, Keynes and Kalecki is a revised, updated edition of Claudio Sardoni's *Marx and Keynes on Economic Recession* (1987). I wrote the Foreword to that volume; I emphasised the author's originality, scholarship and relevance in the sense of examining greats of the past within their own contexts and times and then drawing out their insights for contemporary problems and times. I stressed the value of his approach to analytical history, that it provided definitive understanding of what had gone before and why, and was framed in such a way as to make it suitably useful and valuable for contemporary analysis.

The second edition exhibits all these characteristics, matured and enriched by the years in between. In the new volume, Marx's and Keynes's lasting contributions (as well as limitation and errors) are thoroughly (but succinctly) re-examined. There is now much more on Kalecki's contributions, the framework for which came from Marx. This enabled Kalecki both to avoid some pitfalls of Keynes's analysis and to correct and then build on, Marx's own analysis. Finally Claudio Sardoni sets out the principal propositions of modern macroeconomics, especially those of the New Keynesians and the New Classical Macroeconomists. He compares them, often to their disadvantage, with the corresponding analyses of Marx, Keynes and Kalecki and his own synthesis of the propositions of these three authors.

Claudio Sardoni is never a bigot or a zealot – he looks for the positive aspects in the writings of the authors examined. He calls for tolerance and open-mindedness, a willingness to learn from those with whom you disagree, and to examine their writings always within their own contexts in order to see what is worthwhile and helpful to take on in your own approach. Most of all, he calls for dialogue and a willingness to frame analysis and arguments in such a way that comprehension and communication are possible and new lessons may be learnt.

Unemployment, Recession and Effective Demand is a fine example of how critical analysis and debate about fundamental issues should be carried out. Claudio Sardoni does not pull his punches, but he criticises with courtesy in a learned and fair-minded way. His writings are a role model of proper procedure allied with cumulative persuasion through weight of evidence, sound scholarship and argument.

G.C. Harcourt
Cambridge, July 2010

Preface

The present book is a largely revised version of my previous book *Marx and Keynes on Economic Recession* (Sardoni, 1987). When the book was published in the late 1980s, mainstream economics was not too worried about economic recessions. By and large, macroeconomics was still dominated by the New Classical approach, with its concern for equilibrium characterized as the outcome of maximizing behaviour in a competitive framework.

In the midst of the current world economic crisis, several economists have claimed the necessity to return to the Marxian and Keynesian traditions to better understand the dynamics and the contradictions of market economies. This book is a step in that direction as it tries to single out and discuss the elements of Marx's, Keynes's and Kalecki's theories that can contribute to the understanding of the world in which we live.

This book, therefore, is not a mere exercise in the history of economic thought. But neither is it an attempt at analysing and modelling the current crisis. The main intent of the present work is to provide a critical examination of the foundations of macroeconomics as developed in the tradition of Marx, Keynes and Kalecki. A book concerned with these economists may be, hopefully, of interest to a larger portion of the profession, beyond historians of thought and Marxist, Keynesian and Post Keynesian economists.

Marx was one of the first economists who provided a thorough analysis of the recurrent crises to which market economies are prone; Keynes wrote *The General Theory* by drawing from the experience of the great depression of the 1930s. Kalecki solved some analytical problems left unsolved by Marx and Keynes, and developed his analysis by considering an economy in which markets are not perfectly competitive.

The current mainstream in macroeconomics is also characterized by carrying out the analysis under the hypothesis that the economy works under some form of imperfect or monopolistic competition. Thus, the book looks at the relationship between the Kaleckian approach and the mainstream, with respect to the problem of market forms and their relevance for macroeconomics.

The book has undergone several changes from its 1987 edition. All chapters have been revised and updated; new chapters have been added to take account of theoretical developments occurring in the last 10–15 years in the field of macroeconomics. This new edition of the book comes after a long time during which I kept on working on many of the topics that it covers. During such time I benefitted from comments, criticisms and suggestions from so many people that it would be too long to thank them all. However, I would like to mention and thank Geoff Harcourt and Fabrizio Patriarca for their more recent comments and suggestions. Part of the work for this edition of the book has been carried out within a research project on macroeconomics and market forms funded by Sapienza University of Rome (project C26A09PP8H, 2009). Of course, I am alone responsible for any errors.

Rome, October 2010

1. Introduction

INTENT AND MOTIVATION OF THE BOOK

This book is mainly focused on the works of Marx, Keynes and Kalecki, three great economists of the past, but its object is not to provide a historical reconstruction of their thought. The book aims at giving an analytical contribution to the development of a viable alternative to the current mainstream in economics, macroeconomics in particular, by drawing from the founding fathers of two important alternative approaches to economics, the Marxist and the Post Keynesian traditions.[1] Such a declaration of intent, however, requires a number of clarifications and delimitations in order to avoid vagueness and excessive boldness.

First of all, it is necessary to explain why the book concentrates on Marx's, Keynes's and Kalecki's original works rather than on more recent contributions inspired by them. The basic reason for this choice is that Marxists and Post Keynesians have never showed much interest in the study of the analytical relationship among Marx's, Keynes's and Kalecki's original works, in particular in the relationship between the works of Marx and Keynes.[2] But to look directly at their works can be very helpful to better understand which are the elements of similarity between the two traditions and, hence, to develop an alternative based on common grounds. In this sense, considering Kalecki's contribution is of central importance, not only because he represents a sort of 'bridge' between the Marxian and Keynesian traditions but also because he gave answers to several important analytical problems left unsolved by both Marx and Keynes.

It is also necessary to clearly spell out that the book is not concerned with the relationships among the three economists at the ideological and political level. Marx's, Keynes's and Kalecki's ideologies were very different and far from one another, especially in the case of Marx and Keynes. Taking account of their different ideologies would require dealing with problems and issues well beyond the realm of economic analysis, in which the book is situated. The book is concerned only with some economic problems; more precisely, it concentrates on a specific, though very important, issue: the problem of unemployment and effective demand.

We argue that Marx and Keynes come close to one another in dealing with money and the role it plays in the explanation of situations in which the economy generates a level of effective demand that is insufficient to ensure the full employment of labour as well as the full use of the existing productive capacity. But, in dealing with these issues, Marx and Keynes also exhibit important differences.

Keynes could provide an analytical explanation of 'underemployment equilibria', that is to say, situations in which the economy suffers the underuse of its capacity and unemployment of labour, and there are no forces at work that push it towards full employment. Such situations are not necessarily characterized by significant market perturbations. Marx's analytical framework can only provide the explanation of crises, that is significant market perturbations, during which there is unemployment and unused capacity, but not of underemployment equilibria. The economy recovers from crises in a relatively short time and its process of growth starts again.

Studying Marx's and Keynes's different analytical conclusions, and why they arrived at them, also allows us to realize that there are some flaws in both economists' reasoning. In fact, we argue that neither was able to provide a fully satisfactory treatment of the problem of effective demand and unemployment. A solution to some of the difficulties encountered by Marx and Keynes may be found in the work of Kalecki who, starting from the Marxian tradition, was able to produce results that are similar to Keynes's but based on more solid foundations.

Taking into consideration Kalecki's work brings to the fore the problem of the kind of markets that prevail in the economy. Whereas Marx and Keynes based their analyses on a hypothesis of perfect or, more correctly, free competition, Kalecki abandoned such an assumption and based his analysis on the hypothesis that most markets operate in conditions of non-perfect competition.

In the book, the problem of market forms receives considerable attention. This is not only because it is argued that abandoning the competitive hypothesis helps solve several of the problems encountered in Marx's and Keynes's analyses, but also because the approach to macroeconomics under the assumption of non-perfectly competitive markets is a distinctive feature of the current mainstream. It is therefore interesting to contrast the Kaleckian approach with the mainstream in order to better understand their differences and possible similarities.

The remaining sections of this chapter outline the points and problems mentioned above to introduce the reader to the more thorough treatment in the following chapters.

KEYNES'S REVOLUTION AND MARX'S ANTICIPATIONS

Keynes tried to demonstrate that a market capitalist economy does not necessarily achieve a full-employment equilibrium. In order to achieve this result, it was crucial for him to criticize and reject Say's Law, according to which it is impossible to have underemployment equilibria due to insufficient aggregate demand, at least in the long term.

Keynes pointed out that the law could hold good only in an economy with characteristics far removed from those of a real capitalist economy. In particular, in order for the law and all its corollaries to apply, the analysis has to refer to a postulated 'non-monetary economy', in which money is never kept idle, so that all savings are invested.

For Keynes, however, the characteristics of a capitalist economy are such that a demand for idle money can exist, and this can prevent the system as a whole from achieving full employment. Keynes regarded his criticism and rejection of Say's Law as a radical break with the whole previous tradition in economic thought.

> From the time of Say and Ricardo the classical economists have taught that supply creates its own demand. ... As a corollary of the same doctrine, it has been supposed that any individual act of abstaining from consumption necessarily leads to, and amounts to the same thing as, causing the labour and commodities thus released from supplying consumption to be invested in the production of capital wealth. ... The doctrine is never stated to-day in this crude form. Nevertheless it still underlies the whole classical theory which would collapse without it.[3] (Keynes, 1936, pp. 18–9)

For Keynes, only Malthus and a few other minor economists, questioned – though not very successfully – the validity of Say's Law. Ricardo 'conquered England as completely as the Holy Inquisition conquered Spain'. As for Marx, Keynes recognized that the 'great puzzle of Effective Demand' lived furtively in Marx's underworld, but he much preferred Gesell's work to Marx's theory of capitalism (Keynes, 1936, p. 355).

Keynes's interpretation of economic theory before the *General Theory* is neither accurate nor correct. On the one hand, he failed to see that there were significant differences between the classical approach of Ricardo and the marginalist approach of Marshall, Pigou and others. On the other hand, Keynes overestimated the analytical relevance of Malthus's attempts to reject Say's Law, while he underestimated Marx's contribution. Marx's critique and rejection of Say's Law are based on the introduction and use of analytical concepts that bring him much closer to Keynes than Malthus.[4]

Marx argued that Ricardo could consider Say's Law valid only because of his inadequate concept of money and its role in a capitalist economy. Ricardo held that money is a mere means of circulation. In so far as this concept is accepted, Ricardo's reasoning is correct: supply necessarily creates its own demand, and effective aggregate demand can never fall short of aggregate supply. But in a capitalist economy, for Marx, money is not a mere means of circulation.

Money is also a store of value and as such can be hoarded and kept idle. The very logic of the capitalists' behaviour may induce them to hoard money instead of using it to start productive processes and to invest. If this happens, aggregate demand falls short of supply and, as a result, the economy suffers the simultaneous existence of unused productive capacity and unemployed labour; that is, it experiences a general overproduction crisis. Thus, in criticizing Ricardo, Marx had already introduced analytical concepts that very closely resemble those used by Keynes.

Marx was able to offer an explanation of unemployment that is different from the Ricardian explanation. In Ricardo's theory unemployment is never due to insufficient effective demand, but to a rate of growth lower than the rate of growth of population, or to technical progress. In both cases, however, the existing productive capacity is fully used. Marx too, as is well known, was very much concerned with the problem of technological unemployment, and in his analysis he was certainly influenced by Ricardo. Here, however, we do not deal with technological unemployment in Marx's theory in order to emphasize his other explanation of unemployment, which is closer to the Keynesian explanation.

THE DIFFERENCES BETWEEN MARX AND KEYNES

Both Marx and Keynes rejected Say's Law and held that it is possible to have unemployment of labour along with underuse of productive capacity. However, for Marx and Keynes, such a phenomenon may occur in significantly different ways.

Within the Marxian analytical framework, one can show that unemployment of labour can coincide with underutilization of capacity only during, and as a consequence of, a general overproduction crisis, that is to say a relevant market perturbation. In Marx's theory it is not possible to demonstrate that we can have underemployment equilibria, that is situations in which there are no automatic forces at work pushing the economy towards the full use of its capacity and the corresponding level of employment.

This result of Marx's theory is due to the specific micro-framework that he adopted. The economic system works under conditions of free competition and firms, in order to maximize their profits, tend to produce and invest at the highest possible rates, in that they have flat short-period cost curves (up to capacity) and the expected return on investment is not a decreasing function of the level of investment itself. Under such conditions the economy normally tends to the full use of its productive capacity and the corresponding level of employment, which, however, is not necessarily the full employment of labour, because the existing capacity could be insufficient to employ the total labour force.

When aggregate demand falls short of aggregate supply, a general over-production crisis occurs, and both labour and capacity remain partly idle. But, for Marx, crises are not permanent. The economy as a whole overcomes the crisis, and a new upward phase begins towards the full use of capacity, associated with an increase in employment.

Marx's results are different from Keynes's analytical conclusions. In Keynes's theory, general overproduction crises are not necessary to produce a situation of unemployment combined with unused productive capacity. Underemployment equilibria are possible. Keynes could achieve these results because he based his analysis on different microfoundations, strongly influenced by Marshall.

Keynes's microfoundations postulate competitive markets in which firms are characterized by increasing short-period cost curves and downward-sloping investment functions. In such a case it is possible to have underemployment equilibria: firms maximize their profits, while the economy as a whole experiences less than full employment. There is no force at work that pushes the economy towards full employment.

Marx's theory of effective demand allows us to demonstrate that capitalist economies are subject to fluctuations. The process of accumulation and growth is interrupted by crises which imply a temporary underutilization of capacity and an increase in unemployment. Keynes's theory of effective demand allows us to achieve another relevant analytical result. Not only do capitalist economies experience fluctuations around their equilibrium positions (Keynes, of course, recognized the existence of cycles) but the equilibrium position itself is not necessarily found at full employment. Such a result allows us to give an account of protracted periods of low employment, low output and unused capacity.

FLAWS IN MARX'S AND KEYNES'S ANALYSES. KALECKI'S SOLUTION

The divergence between Marx's and Keynes's results is largely explained by their differing microfoundations. Therefore, this topic receives considerable attention in the book. I argue that, on the whole, Marx's hypothesis about short-period returns and cost curves is more satisfactory than Keynes's assumption of decreasing returns. Moreover, I argue that Keynes's theory of investment is flawed.

But another issue arises. On the one hand, we have Marx's more acceptable micro-framework that yields analytical results partly inconsistent with reality. On the other hand, Keynes's analytical results seem to be more consistent with observed reality, but they are founded on a micro-framework that proves to be either unrealistic or inconsistent. Once Keynes's mistakes and inconsistencies are eliminated, we are left with an analytical framework not widely divergent from that of Marx – one in which it is no longer possible to demonstrate the possibility of underemployment equilibria.

It was Kalecki who offered the solution to this paradox. Kalecki, on the one hand, criticized Keynes's microfoundations and adopted a micro-framework that, on the whole, is closer to Marx's but, on the other hand, he was able to provide a demonstration of the possibility of underemployment equilibria. From this point of view, Kalecki's abandonment of the hypothesis of free or perfect competition, which both Marx and Keynes made, is crucially important.

Kalecki postulated a capitalist economy characterized by non-perfect competition and oligopoly. Within this context, firms are not necessarily spurred either to produce to capacity, despite constant returns, or to invest at the highest possible rate, even though new investment would lower production costs (increasing returns to scale). The obstacles to firms' growth are demand (downward-sloping demand curves) and 'imperfections' in financial markets that prevent them from obtaining any desired amount of capital.

Marx and Keynes criticized and rejected their predecessors by claiming that their theories were based upon assumptions and hypotheses which were too far removed from the essential characteristics of the actual capitalist economic system. Both Marx and Keynes rejected the previous theories of money, as based upon a concept that failed to correspond to the real role of money in a capitalist economy. Neither, however, was able to push his innovative developments far enough to give a fully satisfactory analysis of the problem of effective demand and unemployment. Kalecki went further in this direction, by grounding his theory on a still more realistic and adequate set of assumptions and abstractions.

MARX, KEYNES AND KALECKI IN RELATION TO MODERN MAINSTREAM ECONOMICS

It is possible to perceive similarities between the line of reasoning followed in the book and the development of the debate within the mainstream since the demise of the Keynesian revolution of the 1930s; in both cases, the problem of the microfoundations of macroeconomics is central. Keynes and the (old) Keynesians were accused of grounding their macroeconomic analyses on weak, if not altogether wrong, microfoundations. More precisely, the Keynesian results were seen to contradict the basic principles of microeconomics, characterized by rational maximizing agents operating in conditions of perfect competition.

New Classical Macroeconomics, in the wake of Monetarism, provided the most radical and self-consistent response to the Keynesian revolution. The alleged contradiction between micro and macro theory was eliminated by transforming macroeconomics into a mere exemplification of neoclassical microeconomics. Not surprisingly, New Classical Macroeconomics produced results radically different from Keynes and the Keynesians, but also quite incapable of yielding a tenable explanation of the phenomena of the world in which we live.

The New Keynesian approach, which today is the mainstream in macro-economics, is the reaction to the failures of new classical macroeconomics. The New Keynesians, though accepting the New Classical challenge to provide coherent and rigorous microfoundations of macroeconomic analysis, have developed models that are said to be able to give Keynesian results.

The Keynesian nature of the results obtained from New Keynesians' models is open to discussion. Many Post Keynesians have strongly criticized such models by emphasizing their neoclassical nature and the distance from Keynes's own approach to economic theory. However, it is also significant that the New Keynesian models are based on hypotheses of imperfect competition, with firms that are demand-constrained. The hypotheses of non-perfect competition are regarded as more adequate to deal with the actual economy.

In this respect, the New Keynesian approach seems to show a certain degree of similarity with the Kaleckian approach. Keynesian results are also obtained in Kalecki in a context characterized by non-perfectly competitive markets. It is then interesting to look at the theoretical and analytical relation-ships between the New Keynesian mainstream and the Kaleckian alternative approach. It is worth considering the extent to which the two notions of (imperfect) competition are really similar to one another. We argue that the distance between the two theoretical systems remains large. However, we also hold that the mainstream's attempt to develop a more realistic analysis of the actual economy may open the possibility to establish more productive and fruitful relations between the two approaches.

SOME POINTS OF CLARIFICATION

In this introduction, many of the concepts introduced have not been discussed or presented in a detailed way. The following chapters will deal with them more fully. However, it seems necessary at this point to provide further clarification on a number of issues, in order to eliminate some possible misunderstandings right at the outset.

First of all, it may be helpful to clarify the sense in which both classical and neoclassical economists accepted Say's Law. For classical political economists, the acceptance of the law did not imply that they held that the economy necessarily experiences the full employment of labour. The equality between aggregate demand and aggregate supply implies no more than the full use of existing productive capacity at any time. Moreover, the equality between investment and saving is assumed, not ensured by some adjustment process. Instead, Say's Law in its neoclassical formulation implies that the economy achieves a full-employment equilibrium and that equality between investment and saving is ensured by the working of an adjustment process (changes in the rate of interest).

Marx, of course, criticized Say's Law in its classical formulation and he was never concerned with the problem of full employment. His critique rather aimed to show that the economy can generate insufficient levels of effective demand, which bring about crises characterized by unused capacity and higher unemployment than would be the case if the entire productive capacity were used. Keynes's concern was different: his critique of the neoclassical version of Say's Law seeks to demonstrate that the economy may well experience involuntary unemployment; specifically, that full employment is not necessarily ensured by market processes, like changes in the interest rate and/or the wage rate.

Another issue is the analytical relevance of the concept of equilibrium for Marx's, Keynes's and Kalecki's analyses. The book argues that a satisfactory approach to the problem of effective demand and unemployment must be able to provide the demonstration that underemployment equilibria are possible. This requires some elucidation to avoid misunderstandings.

An underemployment equilibrium position (or 'rest state') is a position in which aggregate demand and aggregate supply are equal at levels of employment and capacity use which are below full employment and full-capacity use, and from which the economy does not tend to move away unless changes occur in the relevant variables determining this position. At any given time, the economy may find itself out of its equilibrium position because of accidental disturbances, but it will tend towards it unless in the meantime there are changes in the determinant variables. Equilibrium positions represent, as it were, 'centres of gravitation'.

It is in this sense that Keynes's analysis was more realistic than Marx's. Keynes's results are more consistent with observed reality in so far as real economies do not seem to show any inherent tendency towards full employment and full use of capacity. Quite to the contrary, market economies tend to experience protracted periods of low employment and low output without significant market perturbations. Violent market perturbations (crises) are much less frequent phenomena. It is from this point of view that to show the existence of underemployment equilibria is crucial. Unless one can show it, the conclusion has to be that the economy tends, although fluctuating, to the full use of its capacity and to the corresponding level of employment.

Finally, some remarks about the interpretation of Keynes's theory that is presented here. As it will become clear in Chapters 4 and 5, the interpretation of Keynes in this book can be regarded as Post Keynesian. But there are also other interpretations of Keynes's theory. Much of Keynesian economics after the Second World War has developed within the IS-LM framework first adopted in the 1930s by Hicks (1937).[5] In particular, underemployment equilibrium positions have been explained by the existence of wage rigidities rather than by the specific characteristics of investment expenditure in a capitalist economy. [6] However, to provide a detailed comparison of these alternative interpretations with the one adopted here and to explain why the latter is preferred, is well beyond the scope of this book.

PLAN OF THE BOOK

The book is organized into eight chapters plus this introduction. Chapters 2 and 3 are concerned with Marx's analysis of money, effective demand and overproduction crises. Chapters 4 and 5 deal with Keynes's analysis. Chapter 4 concentrates on those aspects of Keynes's approach more similar to Marx's (money and Say's Law in particular). Chapter 5 deals with the issues where the differences from Marx are more evident. Particular attention is given to the problem of Keynes's Marshallian microfoundations, which gave him the possibility to have short-period underemployment equilibria.

Chapters 6 and 7 are mainly devoted to criticism of Keynes's microfoundations and to Kalecki's contribution. Chapter 6 deals with Kalecki's position on short-period returns and his criticism of Keynes's theory of investment. Chapter 7 delineates a basic Kaleckian macroeconomic model.

Finally, Chapter 8 is concerned with modern macroeconomics, concentrating on the problem of market forms and their relationship with the Kaleckian approach. Chapter 9 concludes with some considerations that are mainly methodological.

NOTES

1. There are several traditions of thought that are alternative to the current mainstream in economics. Among these, the Marxian and the Post Keynesian traditions probably are the most significant. Many surveys of the alternative approaches to the mainstream, in fact, pay much attention to them; see, for example, Hamouda and Harcourt (1988), Lavoie (2006) and Harcourt (2006).
2. There are, of course, exceptions. Joan Robinson certainly is the Keynesian economist who paid most attention to the relations between Marx and Keynes; see, for example, Robinson (1951, 1960b, 1965a,b, 1973b, 1980b). In the years immediately following the publication of *The General Theory*, some attempts to compare the two economists in a systematic way were

made; see, for example, Fan-Hung (1939) and Alexander (1940). For more recent contributions, see Dasgupta (1983), Dillard (1984) and Hein (2006).
3. For Keynes, as is well known, 'classical economists' included also Marshall and Pigou (Keynes, 1936, p. 3n).
4. For critical analyses of the relationship between Malthus and Keynes, see, for example, Corry (1959), Hollander (1962) and Garegnani (1978).
5. Which, however, became much less popular with Hicks than many other economists (see Hicks, 1982a,b).
6. Some considerations on the role of wage rigidities in Keynes's analysis are presented in section 5.5 of Chapter 5 and in Appendix B.

2. The Marxian notion of a monetary economy and the critique of Say's Law

2.1 INTRODUCTION

In Marx's analysis of the functioning of market economies, money plays a fundamental role. Money is the means through which all commodities express their exchange value; it is the universal equivalent. Any economic system based on the exchange of products through the market needs a universal equivalent in terms of which all the commodities can express their values. Otherwise, exchange itself could not take place.[1]

But in Marx's analysis the role of money is also crucial to understand the possibility and the actual occurrence of economic crises due to an insufficient level of effective demand (general overproduction crises). It is Marx's notion of money that allows him to criticize and reject Say's Law, according to which such crises are impossible.

Marx criticized Say's Law in the form in which it was expressed by Ricardo. Ricardo's version of the law, in turn, is strictly related to his theory of money and money prices. The next section is devoted to a brief exposition of Ricardo's views, while section 2.3 deals with Marx's critique.

Central to Marx's criticism of Ricardo and the rejection of Say's Law is the notion of money hoards, that is to say the possibility that money is demanded to be kept idle, as a store of value, rather than being demanded exclusively as a means of circulation. Sections 2.4 to 2.6 look at Marx's analysis of money hoards and the reasons why the demand for them can increase in a capitalist economy. Section 2.7 concludes and outlines the problems raised by Marx's approach to money and crises that are dealt with in Chapter 3.

2.2 SAY'S LAW AND THE THEORY OF MONEY IN RICARDO

Marx's theory of money and his notion of a monetary economy can be best understood starting from his critique of Ricardo's theory of money and his version of Say's Law. The law aimed to demonstrate the impossibility of general overproduction crises ('general gluts') due to an excess of aggregate supply over aggregate demand, claiming that supply itself would create the required level of demand. Ricardo expressed the law in the following terms:

> M. Say has ... most satisfactorily shewn, that there is no amount of capital which may not be employed in a country because demand is only limited by production. No man produces, but with a view to consume or sell, and he never sells, but with an intention to purchase some other commodity, which may be immediately useful to him, or which may contribute to future production. By producing, then, he necessarily becomes either the consumer of his own goods, or the purchaser and consumer of the goods of some other person. It is not to be supposed that he should, for any length of time, be ill-informed of the commodities which he can most advantageously produce, to attain the object which he has in view, namely, the possession of other goods; and, therefore, it is not probable that he will continually produce a commodity for which there is no demand. (Ricardo, 1951, p. 290)

Within Ricardo's analytical framework, for every sale there is a corresponding purchase. Therefore, it is impossible for production and investment to be limited by insufficient effective demand. In such a framework, money has no relevant role to play. It is merely a device to facilitate the exchange of commodities. In fact, exchange through money is not different conceptually from barter: 'productions are always bought by productions, as by service; money is only the medium by which the exchange is effected' (Ricardo, 1951, pp. 291–2).

The money income that is earned by selling commodities is never kept idle. In Ricardo's world, people do not obtain any utility from keeping money idle but draw utility from the commodities that it can buy. If capitalist producers as a whole are able to supply those commodities for which there is a demand, not only can each producer sell all their commodities but each producer also spends all the money income on commodities, assuming they are actually able to satisfy their needs (directly or indirectly).

This concept of money has an implication for Ricardo's theory of money prices: there exists a direct relationship between the quantity of money in the economy and the level of money prices. If we suppose that gold is money, the velocity of circulation of money (V) is given and the outputs of all commodities are given as well, the quantity of money that is required to exchange the whole national product is

$$M_T = \frac{1}{V} \sum_{i=1}^{n} X_i p_i \qquad (2.1)$$

where p_i is the price (expressed in terms of the price of gold) and X_i is the quantity of the i–*th* commodity.

If, for any reason, the actual quantity of gold in the economy changes, and differs from M_T in (2.1), the result, for Ricardo, is that all prices (and the money wage rate) change as well. If, for example, the quantity of money increases, people own a larger quantity of money which, by assumption, is not kept idle but spent on commodities. The money value of the aggregate demand therefore increases. Since the outputs X are given, the necessary result is that all prices must increase in proportion to the increase in the quantity of money.[2] Ricardo's theory of money can be denoted as a 'quantity theory of money'.

2.3   MARX'S CRITIQUE OF RICARDO AND SAY'S LAW

For Marx, it is not possible to deal with the problem of demand and Say's Law in a meaningful way if the analysis is carried out by ignoring the essential characteristics of capitalism.

> In order to prove that capitalist production cannot lead to general crises, all its conditions and distinct forms, all its principles and specific features – in short capitalist production itself – are denied. In fact it is demonstrated that if the capitalist mode of production had not developed in a specific way and become a unique form of social production, but were a mode of production dating back to the most rudimentary stages, then its peculiar contradictions and conflicts and hence also their eruption in crises would not exist. (Marx, 1968, p. 501)

Ricardo, by regarding the capitalist exchange of commodities as equivalent to barter, denied an essential feature of this mode of production and, hence, could deny the possibility of crises.

> The only circumstance which could prevent overproduction in all industries simultaneously is ... the fact that commodity exchanges against commodity – i.e. recourse is taken to the supposed conditions of barter. But this loophole is blocked by the very fact that trade (under capitalist conditions) is not barter, and, that therefore the seller of a commodity is not necessarily at the same time the buyer of another. This whole subterfuge then rests on abstracting from money and from the fact that we are not concerned with the exchange of products, but with the circulation of commodities, an essential part of which is the separation of purchase and sale. (Marx, 1968, pp. 532–3)

In a barter economy, the two acts of selling and purchasing are simultaneous, and this is true for all goods brought to the market. In such a case Say's Law certainly holds. A generalized overproduction of goods is impossible. In so far as the exchange of commodities takes place through barter, 'no one can be a seller without being a buyer or a buyer without being a seller' (Marx, 1968, p. 509).[3] The very nature of barter prevents any seller from deferring their purchase, so it is impossible for aggregate demand to fall short of aggregate supply: supply creates its own demand. However, the same analytical results can be achieved even if the hypothesis of barter is removed and it is assumed that exchange of commodities takes place through money, provided that it is assumed that money is used and demanded only as a means of circulation, that it is never kept idle. This is Ricardo's world.

For Marx, by contrast, in a capitalist economy money may be kept idle. Money, in Marx's terminology, may also be hoarded. If it is admitted that money can be kept idle, there is no longer any reason why the act of purchasing should coincide with the act of selling. The seller might not buy commodities at all, or spend only a part of their money on commodities, and hold the remaining part idle. In particular, the possibility arises that in some circumstances the money holders prefer not to buy commodities at all but to keep money hoards. In such a case, aggregate demand necessarily falls short of aggregate supply and a general overproduction occurs if commodities cannot be sold and their prices fall.

Thus, the possibility to keep money idle turns out to be of crucial importance for Marx's approach to the problem of effective demand. The next two sections are devoted to a more detailed exposition of Marx's notion of hoarding.

2.4 MARX'S CONCEPT OF MONEY HOARDS. THE CRITICISM OF THE QUANTITY THEORY OF MONEY

Marx initially introduced the notion of money hoards in criticizing Ricardo's theory of money prices. He then developed his analysis by considering the motives that may induce the capitalist class to increase its demand for money hoards.

Also for Marx (1954, p. 115) the quantity of money, M_T, which is demanded in order to make commodities circulate, is given by the equation

$$M_T = \frac{1}{V} \sum_{i=1}^{n} X_i p_i \qquad (2.2)$$

which is formally identical to Ricardo's equation (2.1). But for Marx this equation does not imply that changes in the supply of money, M_S, bring about corresponding changes in prices. He observed:

> given the sum of the values of commodities, and the average rapidity of their metamorphoses, the quantity of precious metal current as money depends on the value of that precious metal. The erroneous opinion that it is, on the contrary, prices that are determined by the quantity of the circulating medium and that the latter depends on the quantity of the precious metals in the country; this opinion was based by those who first held it, on the absurd hypothesis that commodities are without a

price, and money without a value, when they first enter into circulation, and that, once in the circulation, an aliquot part of the medley of commodities is exchanged for an aliquot part of the heap of precious metals.[4] (Marx, 1954, pp. 123–5)

Money prices, thus, are independent of M_S. This, however, raises a question. If the money prices of commodities are independent of M_S, there is no longer any guarantee that $M_T = M_S$. The equality between the demand for money as a means of circulation and the supply of money is no longer ensured. For Marx, however, money is demanded not only to effect exchanges but also to be kept idle, hoarded. More precisely, if the circulation of commodities itself is to take place smoothly, a certain share of M_S must be kept idle:

> along with the continual fluctuations in the extent and rapidity of the circulation of commodities and in their prices, the quantity of money current unceasingly ebbs and flows. This mass must therefore be capable of expansion and contraction. ... In order that the mass of money, actually current, may constantly saturate the absorbing power of the circulation, it is necessary that the quantity of gold ... in a country be greater than the quantity required to function as coin. This condition is fulfilled by money taking the form of hoards. These reserves serve as conduits for the supply or withdrawal of money to or from the circulation, which in this way never overflows its banks.[5] (Marx, 1954, p. 134)

Thus Marx introduced a wider and more general notion of demand for money. Money is not only demanded for the circulation of commodities, but it is also demanded as a liquid reserve (hoarded):

$$M_D = M_T + M_H \qquad (2.3)$$

where M_D is the total demand for money, M_T is the demand for money as a means of circulation, and M_H is the demand for money hoards.

Once the possibility of hoarding has been introduced, the direct relationship between the level of money prices and the supply of money, which was accepted by Ricardo, no longer holds. Given the quantities of commodities, their values and the velocity of circulation of money as a means of circulation, the equality between the supply of and the demand for money ($M_S = M_D = M_T + M_H$) needs no longer be established through changes in the level of money prices – it can be ensured by changes in the level of money hoards.

Marx, however, was not always completely consistent on this point; in fact, when dealing with paper money instead of gold, he seemed to accept the Ricardian quantity theory. He observed: 'If the paper money exceeds its proper limit, which is the amount in gold coins of the like denomination that can actually be current, it would ... represent only that quantity of gold which, in accordance with the laws of the circulation of commodities, is required, and is alone capable of being represented by paper' (Marx, 1954, p. 128). Such a point of view is consistent only if paper money is regarded as a mere means of circulation that cannot be hoarded.

However, if a nominal instrument is accepted as money, there is no reason why it should not be hoarded. In order for any nominal instrument to play the role of money, it has to have received social acceptance, which *per se* ensures that hoarded nominal money can be transformed into any other commodity at any future date.

Elsewhere, as we shall see in the next section, Marx himself explicitly admitted the possibility of hoarding nominal money. Therefore, from now on, Marx's viewpoint on paper money will be ignored. Money can be hoarded regardless of it being gold or a nominal instrument.

2.5   HOARDING AND THE REJECTION OF SAY'S LAW

The introduction of the concept of money hoards also makes it possible to deny the validity of Say's Law. Once it is recognized that money may be kept idle, it is no longer necessarily true that the entire money income of a country is always spent on commodities (directly or indirectly). However, dealing with this aspect requires that hoarding be considered from a different perspective.

So far we regarded changes in the demand for hoarded money only as a consequence of changes in the money supply. [6] But Marx also considered the possibility that M_H changes not because of changes in M_S, but because of variations in the economic system's 'propensity to hoard', that is to say an increase in the demand for money to be kept idle, M_H. An increase in M_H is central to Marx's explanation of general overproduction crises. When the demand for idle money rises, aggregate demand falls short of aggregate supply.

If the vector $\mathbf{X}$ represents the national output at a given time, $\mathbf{p}$ is the vector of the commodities' normal prices (say their prices of production expressed in money terms) and V is the velocity of circulation of money as a means of circulation (assumed constant), the quantity of money required to allow commodities to be exchanged at their prices is

$$M_T = (1/V)\mathbf{Xp}$$

Let us also suppose that $M_T < M_S$, that is that a certain quantity of money is already hoarded. The exchange of all commodities at their prices can take place only if the quantity of money which is actually advanced to buy them is equal to M_T, which means that the amount of hoarded money has to be

$$M_H = M_S - M_T$$

If the money holders decided to hoard a larger quantity, $M'_H > M_H$, it would be impossible for all the commodities produced to sell at their normal prices: actual prices would fall because aggregate demand has fallen short of aggregate supply.[7]

Therefore the possibility of an overproduction crisis comes from capitalists' decisions to increase their hoards instead of spending (directly or indirectly) on commodities. The reason why the capitalist class as a whole should increase its propensity to hoard has to be found in the essential characteristics of a capitalist economy, namely in the motives for production and accumulation that characterize the behaviour of capitalist entrepreneurs.

In a capitalist economy, entrepreneurs do not simply produce commodities in order to satisfy (directly or indirectly) their own wants. Rather they start production and investment processes in order to make a profit, indeed in order to maximize profits. Crises can be analyzed only by taking account of this fundamental characteristic of the capitalist mode of production:

> In reproduction, just as in the accumulation of capital, it is not only a question of replacing the same quantity of use-values of which capital consists, on the former scale or on enlarged scale (in the case of accumulation), but of replacing the value of the capital advanced along with the usual rate of profit. ... If, therefore, through any circumstance or combination of circumstances, the market prices of the commodities ... fall *far below* their cost-prices, the reproduction of capital is curtailed as far as possible. Accumulation, however, stagnates even more. Surplus-value amassed in the form of money (gold or notes)[8] could only be transformed into capital at a loss. It therefore lies idle as a hoard in the banks or in the form of credit money. ... Purchase and sale get bogged down and unemployed capital appears in the form of money. (Marx, 1968, p. 494; emphasis added)

In this passage Marx clearly refers to situations in which a significant part of the class of capitalist producers is induced to increase its demand for hoards. In fact, he focused his attention on such situations:

> the supply of all commodities can be greater than the demand for all commodities, since the demand for the general commodity, money, exchange-value, is greater than the demand for all particular commodities, in other words the motive to turn the commodity into money, to realise its exchange-value, prevails over the motive to transform the commodity again into use-value. (Marx, 1968, p. 505)

Marx's explanation of the way in which an increase in the propensity to hoard gives rise to overproduction crises raises some questions, which need further consideration. In particular, two questions are posed. The first is what Marx meant by prices falling 'far below' their cost-prices (prices of production). This question is crucial because Marx held that an increase in hoarding, with the consequent overproduction crisis, takes place only when market prices fall 'far below' their normal level. The second question is whether Marx was referring just to actual, or to both actual and expected prices and rates of profit.

To answer the first question requires a detailed analysis of Marx's explicit and implicit hypotheses and assumptions on the behaviour of capitalist firms. The next chapter deals with this problem. As to the second question, the answer is easier. Although Marx did not use the terms 'expected prices' or 'expectations' very often, it is clear that in the passages considered above he is implicitly saying that an actual fall in market prices induces capitalist entrepreneurs to expect future prices to be 'far below' their normal level. Only if expectations are introduced, in fact, does talk of hoarding make sense.

That a reduction in prices lowers profits and that this may lead to a reduction in the rate of accumulation is obvious. Lower profits imply that capitalists' funds are reduced, so less is left for investment. But in this case, hoarding need not take place. Investment may decline, but all the money capital is nonetheless spent. Only if capitalists expect too low a future rate of profit do they not invest but hoard money.

Furthermore, Marx's concepts of capitalist production and exchange are such that all capitalists' decisions must be based on expectations. They make decisions and produce commodities within a market framework which cannot be known with certainty. The division of labour itself prevents any individual firm from knowing with certainty what commodities and what quantities will actually be demanded.[9] Each firm has to make its decisions in an economic environment characterized by uncertainty. The following quotation from Marx clearly shows how firms try to defend themselves from uncertainty and how individual decisions, made in an uncertain setting, affect aggregate results.

> Since ... the autonomization of the world market (in which the activity of each individual is included), increases with the development of monetary relations ... and vice versa, since the general bond and all-round interdependence in production and consumption increase together with the interdependence and indifference of the consumers and producers to one another; since this contradiction leads to crises, etc., hence, ... efforts are made to overcome it: institutions emerge whereby each individual can acquire information about the activity of all others and attempt to adjust his own accordingly. ... This means that, although the total supply and demand are independent of the actions of each individual, everyone attempts to inform himself about them, and this knowledge then reacts back in practice on the total supply and demand. (Marx, 1973, pp. 160–1)

2.6   THE PROPENSITY TO HOARD AND THE CAPITALIST PROCESS OF REPRODUCTION

The crucial role played by the propensity to hoard can be illustrated also by referring to Marx's schemes of reproduction and his famous formula

$M - C - M'$ (with $M' > M$), which he used to depict essential features of the capitalist mode of production.[10]

The objective of capitalist entrepreneurs is to produce and sell goods in order to obtain more money than they advanced to buy means of production and hire workers. In other words, they produce in order to make money profits, the difference $(M' - M)$. The capitalist process of production and circulation starts with money, the capital advanced to produce and invest, and ends with an augmented quantity of money.

In order that the capitalist process takes place, the whole produced surplus must necessarily be sold in the market, so that there are no imbalances between supply and demand and profits are realized. In other words, the realization of profits requires that the sale of the produced aggregate output must yield an amount of money M' larger than the amount M that capitalist needed to start the production process.[11] In analyzing the process of reproduction, Marx asked the question where this additional quantity of money comes from and he answered that it is the capitalist class itself that must put into circulation the additional quantity of money necessary for the realization of profits.[12] This additional quantity of money $(M' - M)$ will flow back to the capitalists at the end of the process.

Let us start by considering a process of simple reproduction, in which the whole surplus accruing to the capitalist class is consumed. In such a case, the additional quantity of money, $(M' - M)$ is thrown into circulation to finance the consumption of the capitalist class: 'it is the capitalist class itself that throws the money into circulation which serves for the realisation of the surplus-value incorporated in the commodities. But, *nota bene*, it does not throw it into circulation as advanced money, hence not as capital. It spends it as a means of purchase for its individual consumption' (Marx, 1956, pp. 338–9). At the end of each period, the capitalist class gets back the total amount of money advanced and, hence, also the money advanced to buy the social surplus.

But where can capitalists initially find this additional money? Marx's answer is that the additional money is already in the hands of the capitalist class in the form of money hoards. Only an amount $M_T < M_S$ is used to buy means of production and hire the labour force; the quantity $(M_H = M_S - M_T)$ remains hoarded. But, in order for the whole social output to be sold, money has to be temporarily dis-hoarded and thrown into circulation.

Only if the surplus is sold can capitalists realise their full money profits. In a case of simple reproduction, the whole surplus must be consumed by capitalists; therefore its monetary value, that is the monetary value of aggregate profits, is determined by the additional amount of money that capitalists throw into circulation to finance their consumption. In other words, aggregate profits are determined by capitalists' consumption decisions which, in turn, imply a decision to reduce (temporarily) their levels of money hoards. The capitalist class decides on its consumption before the actual realization of profits; such decisions are based on expected values, namely on expected profits. The capitalist 'advances to himself … money in anticipation of surplus-value still to be snatched by him; but in doing so he also advances a circulating medium for the realisation of surplus value to be realised later'. How much is advanced depends on the 'customary or estimated revenue' (Marx, 1954, p. 424).

In a case of expanded reproduction, the analysis is similar. The produced surplus can be sold and money profits realized if capitalists throw additional money into circulation. But, in expanded reproduction, not all the surplus can be consumed; it must be at least partly used to expand the scale of production. Therefore, part of the additional money put into circulation, say $(M' - M)_I$, is now spent on investment goods by capitalists and another part, say $(M' - M)_C$, is spent on consumption goods.[13] The monetary value of aggregate profits is the same as in the case of simple reproduction but profits now depend on two sets of decisions by capitalists: their investment and consumption decisions. In general, therefore, aggregate profits depend on capitalists' expenditure decisions which, in turn, imply a decision to reduce the level of money hoards.

There is, however, another difference between simple and expanded reproduction. In so far as simple reproduction is considered, the required amount of additional money $(M' - M)$ does not change over time since the produced surplus is necessarily constant.[14] When expanded reproduction is considered, the surplus is growing over time and, consequently, a growing quantity of additional money is required to allow aggregate demand to keep pace with aggregate supply and aggregate monetary profits to grow. For Marx, the additional quantity of money may come from three different sources: i) an increase in the velocity of circulation (a greater economy in the use of circulating money); ii) a decrease in capitalists' liquidity preference, that is to say the decision to reduce permanently the amount of hoarded money M_H; iii) an increase in the supply of money (Marx, 1956, pp. 349–50).

To transform hoards into circulating money corresponds to a decrease in capitalists' liquidity preference, so capitalists as a whole must be willing to reduce their liquidity positions. However, this cannot represent a satisfactory solution in the case of expanded reproduction. If the quantity of money is given, dis-hoarding can represent only a temporary solution. If accumulation and growth proceed, the existing money hoards will be exhausted, and this would lead to the conclusion that accumulation and growth must stop because of scarcity of money, unless the velocity of circulation keeps on growing indefinitely. In order to avoid such a conclusion, it is necessary to allow for the possibility of increases in the total supply of money, the third case considered by Marx. If the capitalists' liquidity preference, the prices of commodities and the velocity of circulation of money as a medium of exchange do not change, the process of expanded reproduction can proceed if the supply of money grows at the same rate as the value of total production.

However, assuming that the money supply grows in step with total output does not imply that the capitalists' liquidity preference becomes less crucial. In fact, if the capitalists' liquidity preference were to rise, while V remains constant, the proportional increase in the money supply would not imply the full realization of the growing surplus produced. Both in the case of simple reproduction and in the case of expanded reproduction, if capitalists decide to advance an additional quantity of money $(M'' - M) < (M' - M)$, the level of aggregate profits would be negatively affected: aggregate monetary demand would fall short of aggregate supply and either stocks of commodities would pile up or the prices of commodities would decrease. Aggregate profits would decrease in either case.

2.7   CONCLUSION

In this chapter, we have outlined Marx's notion of a monetary economy, which represents a break with the Ricardian vision of the way markets work and the role that money plays. Marx's notion of money and the possibility that it is hoarded instead of being used only as a means of circulation are at the heart of his rejection of Say's Law. Differently from all those who, in one form or another, accepted the law, for Marx it is possible that the economy experiences disequilibria characterized by the aggregate supply exceeding the aggregate demand. The rejection of Say's Law implies that situations in which the level of aggregate demand is too low compared to aggregate supply are possible.

In particular, the rejection of the law has been associated with the possibility of general overproduction crises, that is situations in which the insufficient level of aggregate demand generates a generalized fall of prices together with the presence of unsold commodities in the market. However, it is important to emphasize that the criticism and rejection of Say's Law do not necessarily imply that the general overproduction crises envisaged by Marx will occur. An insufficient level of aggregate demand, generated by an increase in hoarding, could determine a lower level of aggregate profits but without the generalized fall of prices associated with the presence of unsold commodities in the market.

It could be that producers as a whole, who make their decisions on the grounds of their expectations, correctly forecast the level of effective demand and produce the correct amount of output, avoiding a general overproduction crisis. If the expected level of effective demand is below the level of output associated with the full use of the existing productive capacity, producers as a whole would produce below capacity. There would be a lower level of profits but no general overproduction.

Moreover, even if the producers' expectations are wrong and there is excess supply, this could lead to the piling up of stocks and a decrease in profits, again, without a generalized fall of prices. In turn, the increased amount of unplanned stocks would lead firms to reduce production in subsequent periods and the economy could adjust to a situation in which production is below capacity, profits are lower, employment of labour is lower and, nonetheless, prices are stable and aggregate demand and supply are equal.

But these possibilities were not really contemplated by Marx, who saw general overproduction crises as the 'natural' consequence of the non-validity of Say's Law. The next chapter looks at the analytical reasons why Marx related his rejection of Say's Law only to the possibility of general over-production crises.

NOTES

1. 'Every owner of a commodity wishes to part with it in exchange only for those commodities whose use-value satisfies some want of his. Looked at in this way, exchange is for him simply a private transaction. On the other hand, he desires to realise the value of his commodity, to convert it into any other suitable commodity of equal value, irrespective of whether his own commodity has or has not use-value for the owner of the other. From this point of view, exchange is for him a social transaction of a general character. But one and the same set of transactions cannot be simultaneously for all owners of commodities both exclusively private and exclusively social and general. ... His own commodity is the univer-sal equivalent for all the others. But since this applies to every owner, there is in fact, no commodity acting as universal equivalent, and the relative value of commodities possesses no general form under which they can be equated as values and have the magnitude of their values compared.' (Marx, 1954, pp. 89–90).

2. Relative prices p_i/p_j ($i, j = 1,2, \cdots n$), however, remain unchanged. It is the market price of gold, p_g that falls. The same reasoning applies if the role of money is played by a nominal instrument (such as paper money) instead of gold (Ricardo, 1951, pp. 164–5).

3. The supply would not create an equivalent demand only if the produced good has no use-value, or if there are no use-values to exchange against it. However, in such a case no exchange would take place, and no problem of supply and demand would arise (Marx, 1968, p. 508).

4. Here, Marx is assuming that commodities exchange according to their (labour) values, and that the role of money is played by gold.

5. Marx went further in his analysis, to consider the role of hoarding in an economy in which credit and banking exist. Credit makes hoarding still more necessary. People have to hold liquid reserves in order to be able to meet future payments at the due date: 'When the production of commodities has sufficiently extended itself, money begins to serve as the means of payment beyond the sphere of the circulation of commodities. It becomes the commodity that is the universal subject-matter of all contracts. Rents, taxes, and such like payments are transformed from payment in kind into money payments ... . The development of money into a medium of payment makes it necessary to accumulate money against the dates fixed for the payment of the sum owing. While hoarding, as a distinct mode of acquiring riches, vanishes with the progress of civil society, the forma-tion of reserves of the means of payment grows with that progress' (Marx, 1954, pp. 139–41).

6. In other words, M_H was a residual that adjusted to changes in the total quantity of money.

7. Of course, provided that the velocity of circulation of money, V, does not increase.

8. Notice that here Marx explicitly contemplates the possibility to hoard notes, that is paper money.
9. The capitalist market arises as a consequence of the social division of labour but 'division of labour is a system of production which has grown up spontaneously and continues to grow behind the backs of the producers' (Marx, 1954, p. 109).
10. A formalized exposition of Marx's schemes is presented in Appendix A.
11. M is the amount of money anticipated to buy means of production plus the amount of money to pay wages. This amount depends on the velocity of circulation of money.
12. That the money required for the realisation of capitalists' surplus has to be advanced by capitalists themselves is not paradoxical: 'For there are only two classes: the working class disposing only of its labour-power, and the capitalist class, which has a monopoly of the social means of production and money. It would rather be a paradox if the working class were to advance in the first instance from its own resources the money required for the realisation of the surplus-value contained in the commodities' (Marx, 1956, p. 425).
13. The capitalists' marginal propensity to consume must now be less than one.
14. It is assumed that there is no technical change.

3. General overproduction crises

3.1 INTRODUCTION

Marx's rejection of Say's Law allowed him to show that general overproduction crises are possible. This chapter is concerned with the exposition of Marx's explanation of how such crises actually occur and the reasons why, for him, the rejection of Say's Law does not imply different outcomes.

Marx like Ricardo and Malthus, always argued that the consequence of an insufficient level of aggregate demand is a general overproduction crisis.[1] This is because he held that there is a tendency for capitalist firms to produce and invest as much as possible, until a crisis takes place.

> Each particular capital operates on a scale which is not determined by individual demand (orders etc., private need), but by the endeavour to realise as much labour and therefore as much surplus-labour as possible and to produce the largest possible quantity of commodities with a given capital. (Marx, 1968, p. 484)

If this tendency exists, any fall in the level of aggregate demand (or even a rise smaller than the increase in aggregate supply) would lead to overproduction: up to that point firms have been producing to capacity and the insufficiency of effective demand must cause part of the commodities already produced to remain unsold, or to be sold at less than their normal price. This line of reasoning raises two questions: i) what makes capitalist firms produce to capacity and invest at the highest possible rate? ii) how does a general overproduction crisis come about?

To answer the second question is easier; in fact, Marx provided an analysis which is convincing enough and which is carried out in quite explicit terms. By contrast, Marx dealt with the first issue in a rather undeveloped fashion and most of his hypotheses and assumptions are left implicit. Yet an account of capitalist firms' tendency to produce and invest at the highest possible rates is in fact fundamental to a satisfactory explanation of general overproduction crises, so this issue needs careful treatment.

The following sections deal with Marx's original analysis of the actual occurrence of overproduction crises. Section 3.2 deals with the problem of the capitalist firms' tendency to produce and invest to the maximum possible extent. Section 3.3 looks at Marx's explanation of how partial (sectoral) overproduction generates a general overproduction crisis. Section 3.4 is concerned with Marx's individuation of the factor that is the fundamental cause of over-production crises, namely the capitalist constraint on the growth of the work-ers' wage rate and, therefore, on the growth of the demand for consumption goods. Section 3.5 looks at the possibility to find, in Marx, the existence of constraints on the expansion of the demand for capital goods as well (invest-ment). Section 3.6 considers the effects of crises. Section 3.7 deals with the analytical problems raised by Marx's analysis, by paying particular attention to the possibility of having unemployment and underutilization of capacity without a general overproduction crisis. Section 3.8 concludes with a summary of Marx's analysis carried out in this and the previous chapter.

3.2   THE CAPITALIST TENDENCY TO PRODUCE AND INVEST AS MUCH AS POSSIBLE: MARXIAN MICROFOUNDATIONS

The inherent feature of the capitalist mode of production is its tendency to push production, accumulation and growth to the highest possible levels. It is the capitalist drive to maximize profits that explains this tendency. The origin of profits is the surplus that the economy is able to produce. Profits, and the rate of profits, are determined by the produced surplus and by its distribution among industrial capitalists, workers and financial capitalists. Therefore, the capitalist process of production and growth is essentially constrained by the dynamics of income distribution and, in particular, by the dynamics of the wage rate and the profit rate. The growth of the wage rate, although possible, must be such as not to jeopardize the profit rate. Marx regarded this as the 'general law of capitalist accumulation': 'Either the price of labour keeps on rising, because its rise does not interfere with the progress of accumulation. ... Or, on the other hand, accumulation slackens in consequence of the rise in the price of labour, because the stimulus of gain is blunted' (Marx, 1954, p. 580).

However, this line of argument faces an obvious objection. The highest possible level of production ensures the highest potential rate of profit, but there is no reason why this necessarily corresponds to a high actual rate of profit. The commodities which have been produced might remain unsold or be sold at such market prices that the actual rate of profit is far less than the poten-tial. Moreover, in a capitalist economy characterized by a highly developed division of labour and a wage rate constrained by the tendency to maximize profits, each individual firm might be led to expect an actual rate of profit lower than the potential rate associated with the maximum feasible level of output. Division of labour prevents any single firm from knowing with certainty what the demand for its commodities and their future market prices will be. The limits to the increase in the wage rate, on the other hand, tell firms that the demand for consumption goods (and, indirectly, for means of production) is necessarily constrained. Firms, therefore, could tend to limit production and growth because of fear of producing a volume of commodities that will not be sold in the market at prices ensuring a rate of profit that is 'high enough'. The capitalist economy appears to be such that expectations should tend to be 'pessimistic' rather than 'optimistic'.

But Marx took care to point out that the tendency to maximise production and growth prevails. Only when prices and profits fall 'far below' their usual levels does the tendency to reduce production and investment gain the upper hand. Marx gave no explicit, fully detailed justification of such behaviour by capitalist firms. Below, we attempt to provide Marx's point of view with more rigorous analytical foundations.

3.2.1   Firms' Maximizing Behaviour in Competitive Markets

Let us first examine why firms are induced to produce to capacity.[2] This can be justified if we make the following two assumptions:

1.   The prevailing market form is free competition.
2.   Firms in the short period produce at constant unit variable costs and, hence, at decreasing average total costs. More precisely, unit variable costs are constant up to capacity; after that they start increasing steeply. In other words, the unit variable cost curve has the shape of a reversed L.

As to the first assumption, though Marx foresaw the transformation of competitive markets into monopolistic or oligopolistic markets, he mainly carried out his analysis under the assumption that capitalist markets were competitive; that is, that there are many relatively small firms unable to influence the price at which their commodities are sold and there are no barriers to the entry of new firms in any industry.[3] Within such a market, each single firm's expectations of demand for its commodity are necessarily formulated in terms of an expected price and, consequently, an expected rate of profit.[4] But for each single firm the expected price is independent of its supply. This applies both in the short period and in the long period, when the firm's productive capacity varies.

Let us now turn to the second assumption, the behaviour of costs of production. Marx did not carry out his analysis of this in a clear and explicit way; however, he generally regarded unit variable costs as independent of the quantity produced, and constant in the short period. Hence, the unit fixed cost is a decreasing function of the level of production, the average total cost is a decreasing function of production and reaches its minimum when production reaches its maximum (full use of the firm's productive capacity).[5] Several examples show that Marx assumed this kind of behaviour of costs in the short period (see, for example, Marx, 1959, pp. 77–8).

If, for the individual firm, the price at which its commodities are sold is given, and the unit variable cost is constant, the firm maximizes its rate of profit if it produces at the maximum level. Let K be the value of the firm's capital, which is given,[6] F be the fixed cost, v be the unit variable cost and p the price of the commodity, X_M be the level of production associated with the full use of the firm's productive capacity, and X be the actual level of production. The rate of profit is given by:

$$[(p - v) X - F]/K \tag{3.1}$$

If $p > v$, the rate of profit reaches its maximum, r_M, when $X = X_M$:

$$r = r_M \text{ when } X = X_M \text{ for } \forall p \geq v$$

The firm maximizes its rate of profit when it produces to capacity, provided that the price is not below the unit variable cost.[7] This point is illustrated graphically in Figure 3.1. The curve *ATC* depicts the total average cost, which tends asymptotically to v, the unit variable cost; X_M is the maximum output that the firm can produce; *OP* is the price; and the rectangle *APCB* is the firm's total profit, which is maximized at X_M. Since the firm's capital, K, is given, at X_M the rate of profit is also maximized.

The reasoning does not change if we introduce price expectations. Let p^e and r^e be the expected price and the expected rate of profit respectively, then

$$[(p^e - v) X - F]/K \tag{3.2}$$

and

$$r^e = r^e_M \text{ when } X = X_M \text{ for } \forall p^e \geq v$$

If the price expected by the firm is higher than, or equal to, its unit variable cost, its maximizing behaviour implies that it will produce as much as possible with its fixed capacity K. Only if $p^e < v$, will the firm reduce its production as much as possible and reduce, consequently, its demand for labour.

The expectations on which the firm bases its production decisions may be called 'short-term expectations' as they concern the level of use of the existing productive capacity. Thus, for each firm there is a crucial level, $p_m = v$, below which the expected price for its commodities cannot fall without implying the largest possible contraction of its production (and employment). Formally,

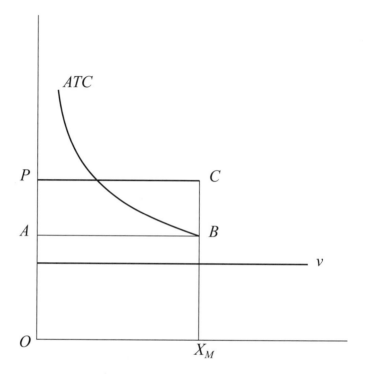

Figure 3.1   Profit maximization in the short period

$$X = X_M \text{ for } \forall p^e \geq v \tag{3.3}$$

$$X = X_m \text{ for } \forall p^e < v$$

where X_m is the minimum level of production that the firm can realize at a given time.[8]

Let us now consider capitalist firms' tendency to grow at the highest possible rate. Again, this tendency is explained by the tendency to maximize profits and the rate of profit. In the short period, each individual firm will push production to its maximum level even if the rate of profit is zero or negative: provided that $p > v$, it recovers the greatest possible share of its fixed costs by producing to capacity.[9] In the long period, however, a firm will presumably expand its productive capacity only if it expects a price that will generate at least a certain minimum rate of profit. Let us denote this minimum by r^*.[10]

For any expected price that ensures a rate of profit $r^e \geq r^*$, the firm will invest as much as possible in order to maximize its profits. Now, we are clearly referring to the firm's 'long-term expectations', as they concern investment and the expansion of its capacity. If, moreover, we grant Marx's assumption that the growth of the firm through investment is associated with increases in productivity and hence with decreasing average production costs (see, for example, Marx, 1954, pp. 582–9), the tendency to expand productive capacity is even more evident. Therefore, by denoting the increase in the firm's productive capacity with ΔK, we can write

$$\Delta K = \text{max for } \forall r^e \geq r^* \tag{3.4}$$

Thus in the long period, too, a firm maximizes profits and the rate of profit by maximum expansion. No firm will start an investment project if it expects that for (a relatively) long period of time the market price of its product will be such that not even the minimum rate of profit can be earned. In other words, for each firm there is a price p^* (associated with the rate of profit r^*) below which the expected price cannot fall without the firm stopping investment. Formally,

$$\Delta K \leq 0 \text{ for } \forall r^e < r^* \tag{3.5}$$

A last question has to be answered: how is the minimum rate of profit, r^*, determined? Marx offered no clear explanation of the factors that determine the rate below which the process of accumulation is brought to a halt. However, it is legitimate to hold that for him, r^* is essentially determined by the rate of interest.

Interest is a portion of gross industrial profit. Therefore, for each individual firm there is an inverse relationship between interest and profit and – given the firm's stock of capital and the expected price for its commodity – an inverse relationship between the rate of interest and the rate of profit.[11]

When firms make their decisions, the rate of profit is an expected value, while the rate of interest is known. In such a situation, if industrial capitalists expect a rate of profit lower than the rate of interest, they will not invest.[12] The expected rate of gross profit cannot fall below the given rate of interest. In this sense, the crucial minimum value of the rate of profit relevant to investment decisions is determined by the rate of interest.

3.2.2 The Rate of Interest

How is the rate of interest itself determined? If the rate of interest were dependent on the rate of profit itself, the reasoning above would be circular. For Marx, however, the rate of interest does not depend on the rate of profit but only on the demand for and the supply of money loans.[13] He distinguished between the 'market rate of interest' and the 'average rate of interest':

As concerns the perpetually fluctuating market rate of interest, however, it exists at any moment as a fixed magnitude, just as the market price of commodities, because in the money-market all loanable capital continually faces functioning capital as an aggregate mass, so that the relation between the supply of loanable capital on one side and the demand for it on the other, decides the market level of interest at any given time. (Marx, 1959, p. 366)

The average rate of interest is not determined by any 'natural' law but is merely the result of the continuous fluctuations of the market rate over a certain period of time: 'The average rate of interest prevailing in a certain country – as distinct from the continually fluctuating market rates – cannot be determined by any law. In this sphere there is no such thing as a natural rate of interest in the sense in which economists speak of a natural rate of profit and a natural rate of wages' (Marx, 1959, p. 362). The relationship between the rate of interest and the rate of profit is not such that a natural rate of interest can be determined. The rate of profit, according to Marx, only determines the maximum limit to the rate of interest.[14]

3.3   FROM PARTIAL TO GENERAL OVERPRODUCTION

Having considered the analytical reasons why firms are induced to produce and invest to the maximum extent, we can now look at the way in which general overproduction crises actually take place, bringing production and investment to a halt.

Marx's explanation of the way in which a general overproduction crisis is generated is best understood by referring to his schemes of reproduction, which analyze the interdependencies among the productive sectors of the economy. Marx starts by considering a case in which overproduction occurs in a single industry (cotton cloth) and studies the effects on other industries (Marx, 1968, p. 520). Part of the cotton cloth produced remains unsold or can only be sold 'well below' its normal price. In this situation the cotton entrepreneurs hoard their money instead of giving rise to reproduction and investment. As a result, employment in the industry decreases.[15]

In view of the interdependence between industries in the economy, it is obvious that other industries will be affected. Overproduction, and the consequent reduction in the level of activity in the cotton industry, causes a decrease in the demand for means of production by this industry. This in turn causes overproduction and unemployment in the industries that produce those means of production. The increase in unemployment there gives rise to a further decrease in the demand for cotton and other consumption goods, and so on.

[A] large number of other producers are hit by this interruption in the reproductive process of cotton: spinners, cotton-growers, engineers (producers of spindles, looms etc.), iron and coal producers and so on. ... All these industries have this in common, that their revenue (wages and profit, in so far as the latter is consumed as revenue and not accumulated) is not consumed by them in their own product but in the product of other spheres, which produce articles of consumption, calico among others. Thus the consumption of and the demand for calico fall just because there is too much of it on the market. But this also applies to all other commodities on which, as articles of consumption, the revenue of these indirect producers of cotton is spent. Their means of buying calico and other articles of consumption shrink, contract, because there is too much calico on the market. This also affects other commodities (articles of consumption). (Marx, 1968, p. 523)

If the reduction in the demand for inputs in the cotton industry has caused additional unemployment in the industries that produce them, this necessarily means that in those industries too a process of hoarding has taken place. Some of the employed workers are now unemployed and, *a fortiori*, new investment is not made. Moreover, the slowdown in activity in the industries producing inputs for the cotton industry also causes a reduction in their demand for means of production, so that other capital goods industries will be affected.

Thus, Marx implicitly made a significant assumption, namely that the overproduction of commodities is such as to determine a fall in market prices that induces capitalist entrepreneurs in most industries to expect future prices 'far below' their usual level, that is to say below the unit variable cost. Only on this assumption does hoarding take place, and investment and production are reduced.

Once the chain of events that follows an initial overproduction in one industry has been explained, it is easy to see that a general overproduction crisis will take place if the initial glut affects not only the cotton industry but also other industries producing 'leading articles' (Marx, 1968, p. 523). In this case, firms in all industries experiencing overproduction hoard money instead of producing and investing. This will affect other firms in many other industries, which hoard money in their turn. The demand for idle money increases dramatically, while that for money as a means of circulation falls; the eventual result is a general overproduction crisis with underutilization of capacity and unemployment of labour.

It is important to stress at this point that the fall in production and employment in all industries cannot be offset by a rise in output and employment in the industry which produces gold, even if it is assumed that only gold-money is used in the system.[16] In fact, the increased demand for hoards is offset by a decrease in the demand for 'active balances' (money as a means of circulation), so that the gold industry is not induced to produce and invest more by any significant increase in the demand for gold (money) at the aggregate level.

3.4   LIMITS TO THE DEMAND FOR WAGE-GOODS

So far, however, a general overproduction crisis has not really been explained.[17] We need to explain the initial overproduction in the consumption goods industries.

It is no accident that, explaining how a general overproduction crisis comes about, Marx elected to assume an initial overproduction in the consumption goods industries. He was convinced that these were the industries most likely to experience an initial overproduction. In fact, the bulk of the demand for consumption goods comes from the working class, whose purchasing power in a capitalist economy is constrained.

> Overproduction is specifically conditioned by the general law of the production of capital: to produce to the limit set by the productive forces, that is to say, to exploit the maximum amount of labour with the given amount of capital, without any consideration for the actual limits of the market or the needs backed by the ability to pay; and this is carried out through continuous expansion of reproduction and accumulation, and therefore constant reconversion of revenue into capital, while on the other hand, the mass of producers remain tied to the average level of needs, and must remain tied to it according to the nature of capitalist production. (Marx, 1968, pp. 534–5)

Thus, 'the ultimate reason for all real crises always remains the poverty and restricted consumption of the masses as opposed to the drive of capitalist production to develop the productive forces as though only the absolute consuming power of society constituted their limit' (Marx, 1959, p. 484).

Like all industries, the consumption goods sectors are driven to push production and investment to the highest possible levels, while the purchasing power of the majority of consumers of those goods is constrained. Thus there is no reason why the purchasing power of the working class should, or could, grow at the same rate as the supply of wage goods. Balanced growth of the supply of consumption goods and of the demand for them by the working class would be foreign to the nature of the capitalist mode of production. In general, the capitalist process of growth is not a balanced or proportionate one.[18]

The capitalist class as a whole, and the whole economic system, faces a dilemma. From the point of view of demand, wages should grow at a rate that ensures that consumption goods can be sold at their normal prices; from the point of view of the profitability of the process of production, wages are constrained. Marx pointed out the contradiction between wages as incomes and wages as costs for capitalist employers:

> To each capitalist, the total mass of workers, appears not as workers but as consumers, possessors of exchange values (wages), money, which they exchange for his commodity. However, each capitalist knows this about his workers, that he

does not relate to him as producer to consumer, and [he therefore] wishes to restrict his consumption, i.e. his ability to exchange, his wage, as much as possible. Of course he would like the workers of other capitalists to be the greatest consumers possible of his own commodity. But the relation of every capitalist to his own workers is the relation as such of capital and labour, the essential relation. (Marx, 1973, pp. 419–20)

The wage rate can increase, and over the cycle it actually does so, but its rate of increase must not be such as to lower profits below a certain critical rate. Subject to this constraint, there is no reason why the rate of increase of wages should always ensure a sufficient level of effective demand. A rate of increase of the wage rate that would guarantee sufficient effective demand over time could imply a fall in the rate of profit below the critical level. If this were to happen, the capitalist class as a whole would stop accumulation. This, in turn, leads it to curtail production and reduce employment. This provokes a general overproduction crisis. Firms no longer invest and produce; money is hoarded.

3.5   THE DEMAND FOR CAPITAL GOODS

In the previous section we saw that, in Marx's analysis, the expansion of demand for wage goods is constrained and this is the fundamental cause of general overproduction crises. It is then quite natural to ask whether for Marx limits also exist to the expansion of the demand for capital goods (investment), which could play an analogous role as that played by the constraint on the demand for wage goods.

So far the analysis has been carried out under the hypothesis that firms invest as much as possible until the expected rate of profit, r^e is higher than the minimum rate r^* and that r^e is independent of the volume of investment. This ensures that, provided $r^e > r^*$, the economy will always generate a demand for investment goods, say I^*, that absorbs their supply. The picture would be different if it is assumed that r^e is a decreasing function of the volume of investment.

If, for whatever reason, at the level of aggregate investment $\bar{I} < I^*$ the expected rate of profit is below r^*, firms could generate a demand for capital goods lower than their supply. In this case, the economy would experience a general overproduction crisis caused by a constraint on the demand for investment. The question, however, is whether it is possible to find in Marx any suggestion that there actually exists an inverse relationship between the expected rate of profit and the volume of investment, or the rate of accumulation.

So far there is nothing in Marx's theory, as we have considered it, to justify such a relationship. If we abstract from technical progress, the expected rate of profit is not influenced by the level of investment; if we take technical progress into account, firms are able to introduce, through investment, more productive techniques, so that the expected rate of profit should be regarded as an increasing function of the volume of investment rather than the other way around.

One could argue, however, that there actually is an aspect of Marx's theory that establishes an inverse relationship between accumulation and the rate of profit. Notoriously, Marx held that in a capitalist economy there exists a tendency for the rate of profit to decline. As accumulation proceeds, the organic composition of capital (the ratio of fixed plus circulating capital to direct labour) increases because the new techniques are more mechanized, and the rate of profit has to fall (Marx, 1959, pp. 211–66).[19]

But this inverse relationship between the rate of accumulation and the rate of profit cannot be used to explain overproduction crises due to an insufficient level of demand. To this purpose, we need an inverse relationship between the volume of investment and the *expected* rate of profit. On the contrary, Marx's law asserts an inverse relationship between the volume of investment and the *actual* rate of profit. In fact, firms introduce more mechanized techniques, which ultimately lower the rate of profit, because they *expect* a higher rate of profit. It is only *ex post* that they realize that the actual rate is lower.

Mechanization allows an innovative firm in an industry to produce at a lower cost, so that it can earn extra profit by selling its commodity at the prevailing price (associated with the prevailing method of production used by the other firms). The new technology is introduced therefore in view of a higher expected rate of profit, and in so far as the firm can produce at lower cost and sell at the old price, it actually does earn a higher rate of profit. Sooner or later, however, the other firms in the industry adopt the new technology. This lowers the price and extra profits disappear. The new ruling price is linked to a lower normal rate of profit, because of the higher organic composition of capital.

> No capitalist ever voluntarily introduces a new method of production, no matter how much more productive it may be, and how much it may increase the rate of surplus-value, so long as it reduces the rate of profit. Yet every such new method of production cheapens the commodities. ... He [the innovative capitalist] pockets the difference between their cost of production and the market prices of the same commodities produced at higher costs of production. ... His method of production stands above the social average. But competition makes it general and subject to the general law. There follows a fall in the rate of profit – perhaps first in this sphere of production, and eventually it achieves a balance with the rest – which is, therefore, wholly independent of the will of the capitalist. (Marx, 1959, pp. 264–5)

Thus the law can manifest itself just because capitalist firms are induced to adopt techniques with a higher organic composition of capital by their expectations of a higher rate of profit. But if this is so, it cannot be argued that firms might invest less than is required to ensure equality between aggregate supply and demand. One could argue that firms can foresee the eventual fall in the rate of profit, so they do not invest because they have 'rational' expectations. But if firms can foresee the eventual fall in the rate of profit, this does not imply that they will not invest. They could keep on investing by simply enlarging their productive capacity without technical innovations; they would still maximize their profits (with a constant rate of profit).[20]

3.6 EFFECTIVE DEMAND, OVERPRODUCTION CRISES AND UNEMPLOYMENT

During a crisis, not only do firms stop the investment process, they also curtail reproduction as far as possible. In fact, as we have seen, workers are actually thrown out of work. During a crisis, firms reduce their level of activity and leave part of their productive capacity idle.[21] This is what Marx calls the destruction of real capital:

> In so far as the reproduction process is checked and the labour process is restricted or in some instances is completely stopped, real capital is destroyed. Labour which is not exploited is equivalent to lost production. Raw material which lies unused is no capital. Buildings (also newly built machinery) which are either unused or remain unfinished, commodities which rot in warehouses – all this is destruction of capital. All this means that the process of reproduction is checked and that the existing means of production are not really used as means of production, are not put into operation. (Marx, 1968, pp. 495–6)

Thus a crisis generates unemployment together with underutilization of existing productive capacity, as a consequence of a lack of effective demand.

With this, Marx introduced a new concept of unemployment of labour. In Ricardo's analysis, for instance, unemployment of labour can only be the result either of an insufficient rate of accumulation with respect to the rate of growth of population, or of the introduction of machinery (Ricardo, 1951, pp. 386–97). In either case, however, the existing productive capacity is fully used and the corresponding level of employment is therefore the highest possible level at any given time.

Marx, too, paid much attention to unemployment due to technical progress. He elaborated on Ricardo's ideas and introduced the concept of the industrial reserve army, which plays an important role in the determination of wage rates (Marx, 1954, pp. 412–21 and 586–606). In the framework of his analysis of crises, however, Marx introduced a different concept of unemployment, which is more closely related to that of Keynes.

Sometimes, the unemployment of labour due to an insufficiency of capital equipment is called 'Marxian unemployment', and unemployment due to insufficient effective demand is called 'Keynesian unemployment' (see, for example, Morishima, 1984, pp. 199–203). The foregoing, however, shows that it would be more correct to denote the first type of unemployment as 'Ricardian', while unemployment due to lack of effective demand could be denoted as 'Marxian–Keynesian'.

3.7   A GENERALIZATION OF MARX'S ANALYTICAL FRAMEWORK

In the previous sections, Marx's description of general overproduction crises has been given a more precise and rigorous formulation. The crucial factors are, on the one hand, the capitalist tendency to push production and investment to the highest possible levels and, on the other hand, the constrained purchasing power of the working class.

In this analytical context, an initial overproduction of consumption goods drives their market prices down, which engenders capitalists' expectations of future prices so low that they stop investment and contract production. In other words, 'long-term expectations' in the consumption goods sectors are for a price lower than what was called p^*, while their 'short-term expectations' are for a price lower than p_m. Expected prices $p^e < p_m < p^*$ in the consumption sector, in turn, affect the demand for the output of the capital goods industries, so that here, too, market prices fall, giving rise to expectations that justify hoarding. This further depresses demand for consumption goods, and so on; a chain process starts, which generates a situation in which unemployment of labour and underutilization of capacity coexist. But the determination of this type of situations, which we can call 'underemployment levels of activity', raises two problems.

On the one hand, on the grounds of the analysis developed so far, we must arrive at the conclusion that the economy experiences underemployment levels of activity generated by a general overproduction crisis only under quite exceptional conditions. Marx held that crises are inevitable, because they are a manifestation of the fundamental contradiction between the capitalist tendency to produce and grow as much as possible, and the necessarily constrained purchasing power of the largest part of population (the working class). If general overproduction crises turn out to be exceptional phenomena, Marx's position is somewhat weakened.

On the other hand, Marx's analytical results appear to be quite different from those of Keynes. Not only did Keynes hold that underemployment levels of activity are not exceptional phenomena in a capitalist economy, he also held that such levels of activity may well represent equilibrium positions – in other words there is no force at work pushing the economy towards the highest possible employment of capacity and labour.

Keynes's analysis and its relationship to Marx's theory will be the subject of the next chapters. Here, we will be concerned with the exceptionality of 'underemployment levels of activity'. We show that, in a Marxian context, it is possible to have underemployment levels of activity under less restrictive conditions than those set out above. However, such underemployment levels of activity do not represent stable (equilibrium) positions for the economy.

3.7.1 Underemployment Levels of Activity without 'General Gluts'

We can show that underemployment levels of activity can also occur under less exceptional conditions if we can demonstrate that the economy can experience underutilization of capacity and unemployment without a general overproduction crisis of the type envisaged by Marx.

This result can be achieved if – at least in most industries – there are some firms that produce at costs allowing them to earn just the minimum rate of profit at current prices, while others earn a higher rate of profit because their costs are lower. In this case, a fall in current and expected prices could well lead the less efficient firms to stop investment and production, while the other firms keep on producing and investing at the highest possible rates.

The idea that all, or most, industries have a group of firms producing at costs that just barely allow them to earn a minimum rate of profit, derives from Marx himself. He pointed out several times that in any industry there are firms producing at different costs. For example, he considered industries composed of three different groups of firms: i) a group of firms (the majority in the industry) producing at a certain unit total cost and earning the 'usual rate of profit'; ii) a group producing at a higher unit total cost and earning a minimum rate of profit; iii) a group producing at lower unit total cost and earning a rate of profit higher than the usual (Marx, 1959, pp. 173–9). We call these three classes of firms 'average', 'marginal' and 'superior' respectively.

Under these hypotheses, and postulating that the good supplied by each industry is homogeneous and sold at a uniform price, the critical price levels p^* and p_m will obviously vary from group to group, and it is possible to envisage an example of underemployment levels of activity without a general glut. Let us suppose an initial overproduction in the consumption goods industries such that the decrease in the market prices of consumption goods induces only the marginal firms in those industries to expect a rate of profit below r^*, so that they cease to invest even if they keep on using their full productive capacity.

In the meantime, all the other firms in the consumption goods industries continue to produce and invest at the highest possible rates.

The reduction in the demand for capital goods by the marginal firms in the consumption goods industries affects the market prices of capital goods; they will fall. Let us suppose that the decrease is such as to induce the marginal firms in the capital goods industries to expect a rate of profit below r^*. In this case their investment stops and this in turn will further diminish the demand for consumption goods. As a consequence, the market prices of consumption goods will decline further. If this additional decrease in prices is such as to drive price expectations below p_m for the marginal firms in the consumption goods industries, they will also contract current production (and employment) as much as possible. This, again, affects the demand for means of production and we can suppose that the marginal firms in the capital goods industries also contract production and employment. A chain of events has started; when the marginal firms in the capital goods industries reduce their levels of activity, this will affect the demand for consumption goods once more, and so on.

This chain of events, of course, may well lead to a general overproduction crisis: as the demand for consumption goods and capital goods continues to fall, also average and superior firms may be led to expect such low prices that they cut investment and production. But there is no inevitability to this outcome. The decreases in prices could perfectly well induce only marginal firms in all (or most) industries to cut output and employment and hold productive capacity idle, while average firms and, *a fortiori*, superior firms keep on producing and investing as much as possible.

To get this result, in fact, we need only to assume that in every industry equality of demand and supply can be achieved under the following conditions:

1. for every industry, there exist prices that ensure equality between supply and demand, and which are above the p^* and p_m that apply to average firms (and, *a fortiori*, to superior firms in all industries);
2. in every industry, the equality between supply and demand can be realized at a level of production that corresponds to the level of production associated with the full use of the existing capacity of all average and superior firms.

Some elementary formalization may be helpful. Let us consider a simple two-industries, two-goods economy. Industry 1 produces capital goods, industry 2 produces consumption goods, which are demanded and consumed by the working class only.[22] For simplicity's sake we do not consider superior firms, so that in each industry, there are only marginal firms and average firms (the latter are the majority in both industries).

Let us suppose that, in a certain period, the total output of industry i ($i = 1, 2$) is

$$X_i = (1 - \alpha_i)X_i + \alpha_i X_i \qquad (3.6)$$

$$(1 - \alpha_i) < \alpha_i < 1 \ (i = 1, 2)$$

where $(1 - \alpha_i)X_i$ is the share of total production supplied by marginal firms, and $\alpha_i X_i$ is the share supplied by average firms.

Let us denote by $p^a_{m,i}$ and $p^m_{m,i}$ the minimum prices for average and marginal firms respectively, below which they stop producing, and by $p^*_{a,i}$ and $p^*_{m,i}$ the prices below which average and marginal firms respectively do not invest ($i = 1, 2$). Let us now suppose that, at a certain time, the expected price in the i–th industry, p^e_i, is such that marginal firms are induced not to invest and produce, while average firms produce and invest to the maximum extent. In symbols, it is

$$p^m_{a,i} < p^*_{a,i} < p^e_i < p^m_{m,i} < p^*_{m,i}$$

$$(i = 1, 2)$$

In this case, the demand for both capital goods and consumption goods falls and actual market prices fall as well. This will affect all firms in both industries and a cumulative chain process starts. Such a process, however, need not necessarily lead to a general overproduction crisis.

In order that a general overproduction is avoided, it is sufficient to assume that there exists a pair of prices $(\bar{p}_1, \bar{p}_2)$ such that the average firms in both industries are still induced to produce and invest as much as possible, and such that the equality between supply and demand in both industries is ensured. Such prices, however, are not high enough to induce marginal firms to produce and invest. In symbols, it must be:

$$p^*_{m,i} > p^m_{m,i} > p^e_i(\bar{p}_i) > p^*_{a,i} > p^m_{a,i} \qquad (3.7)$$

$$\alpha_i X_i \bar{p}_i = D_i(\bar{p}_i) \qquad (3.8)$$

$$(i = 1, 2)$$

where $D_i(\bar{p}_i)$ is the demand for the i–th good by average firms in both industries and $p^e_i(\bar{p}_i)$ is the expected price in the industry i, expressed as a function of the actual price $\bar{p}_i$. In other words, the economy ends up in a situation in which it does not experience a general overproduction of goods and, at the same time, there is unused capacity and higher unemployment because marginal firms do not produce.[23]

Of course, the one described above is only one of several conceivable cases. It makes no claim to generality; it is considered only to show that, with some modifications of Marx's original framework, it is possible to have a situation where the economy experiences unemployment and the simultaneous underutilization of capacity without a general overproduction crisis. Once the assumption that in every industry all firms produce at the same costs and earn the same rate of profit is abandoned, underemployment levels of activity are clearly a less exceptional phenomenon than in Marx's original context.[24]

3.7.2 Underemployment Equilibria in the Marxian Framework

Let us now turn to the second issue mentioned above. Can underemployment levels of activity constitute stable positions for the economy in a Marxian context? In other words, can underemployment levels of activity be underemployment equilibria? In order to answer this question as precisely as possible, we had better distinguish between Marx's original analytical framework and the framework which has been suggested in this section.

Within Marx's original analytical setting, in order to argue that an underemployment level of activity can represent a stable position, it must be maintained that crises are permanent phenomena, in the sense that once a crisis has taken place, there is no automatic mechanism to ensure recovery. But Marx himself pointed out that crises are not permanent. Once a general overproduction crisis has taken place, there are forces that push the economy to resume the process of growth and impel it towards full use of existing productive capacity. One main factor, in particular, propels the economy away from its underemployment level of activity: the fall in the general level of prices.

In order for the economy to remain at an underemployment level of activity, it is required that, over time and throughout the system,

$$p^e < v \qquad\qquad (3.9)$$

$$r^e < r^*$$

But the fulfilment of those conditions is not ensured. In fact, as a consequence of the fall in market prices, v falls as well and this will affect both conditions. If v falls, expected prices can become higher than unit costs, so that firms start to produce to capacity again. On the other hand, a fall in market prices also affects the expected rate of profit, $r^e = [(p^e - v)X - F]/K$. When prices fall, v, F and K fall as well and, of course, the expected rate of profit is positively affected. If r^* is given and constant, it is not necessarily ensured that $r^e < r^*$ holds over time.[25]

It was Marx himself who pointed out that the recovery is brought about by the fall in current prices. Because of a crisis, 'a large part of the nominal capital of the society, i.e. of the exchange-value of the existing capital, is once and for all destroyed, although this very destruction, since it does not affect the use-value, may very much expedite the new reproduction' (Marx, 1968, p. 496). In other words, when the economy is experiencing underemployment levels of activity there are forces at work that prevent such situations from becoming a permanent phenomenon. The tendency to produce and invest at the highest possible rate prevails again, and the economy is pushed towards the full use of its capacity and the corresponding level of employment. There is one case, not considered by Marx, in which an underemployment level of activity can become a rest state, though very special. If we suppose that, as market prices fall, expected prices keep on decreasing at a faster rate, the condition (3.9) above is fulfilled over time.[26] But such an economy would inevitably reach its rest state when output and employment are zero.

Let us now turn to the modified framework suggested in this section. Within the modified framework, we have that marginal firms do not produce and invest because expected prices have fallen below their p_m (and, *a fortiori*, below their p^*), while average firms still go on to produce and invest at the highest possible rates. If this is the case, the demand for both capital goods and consumption goods by average firms keeps on increasing. The increase in demand by average firms does not produce a rise of prices because it can be met by average firms themselves, which can increase supply because, through investment, their productive capacity grows. Therefore, prices would not change in such a way as to generate price expectations that induce marginal firms to start production and investment again.

Thus, it would seem that the economy can stabilize in a situation in which there is unused capacity and unemployment. This, however, is only an apparent solution. A situation in which equation (3.8) above is fulfilled cannot be regarded as stable. In fact, within a certain time span, marginal firms will leave the market and the economy will then again realize an equilibrium with the full use of its capacity. Moreover, as this process causes the disappearance of marginal firms, future crises due to an insufficient level of effective demand would generate general overproduction crises of the sort depicted by Marx (homogeneous firms). In conclusion, therefore, the hypothesis of heterogeneous firms does not change the analytical picture significantly with respect to Marx's original analytical framework. The economy cannot experience underemployment equilibria.

3.8   MARX'S ANALYSIS: SUMMARY AND CONCLUSION

Before turning to consider Keynes in the following chapters, it is useful to present here a summary of the main points that result from considering Marx's approach to effective demand and crises.

1. By introducing the possibility of keeping money idle (hoarding), Marx introduced the possibility that the level of effective demand falls short of the level of aggregate supply.
2. For Marx, an increase in the demand for idle money, at the aggregate level, takes place when the capitalist class as a whole is induced to regard investment and production as not profitable. In this way, Marx linked the analysis of effective demand to the analysis of the fundamental factors underlying capitalist production and growth.
3. Through his analysis of money, effective demand and general over-production crises, Marx showed that a capitalist economy may well experience unemployment of labour along with underutilization of productive capacity – what we have called underemployment levels of activity.
4. Marx could show only that underemployment levels of activity occur during, and as a consequence of general overproduction crises (that is wide and deep market perturbations). These results are achieved within a microframework characterized by firms producing at short-period decreasing average total costs and at decreasing (or constant) average total costs in the long period in a competitive economy (free competition).
5. It can be shown, following suggestions from Marx himself, that under-employment levels of activity can occur even if a general glut does not take place. We need only allow for the possible existence of firms which produce at different costs. Within such a context, however, it is still impossible to demonstrate that the economy as a whole can tend towards underemployment equilibria.

Thus, in conclusion, if we refer to Marx's original analysis, we have trade cycles, with an overproduction crisis in every trough and full-capacity use at every peak. After the crisis there is a period of stagnation, followed by recovery, and a boom up to a new crisis.[27] Employment follows the same pattern: it is at its lowest levels during the stagnation, and it reaches its maximum possible levels during prosperity.

If, on the other hand, we refer to the modified analytical setting which has been presented in the present chapter, we still have trade cycles but no longer necessarily a general overproduction crisis at the trough. We can have tempo-rary underemployment levels of activity followed by recovery implying the full use of capacity and the corresponding (highest possible) level of employment. In fact, underemployment levels of activity – characterized by the existence of marginal firms that do not produce – are only temporary states.

Thus, in either case, though subject to cyclical fluctuations, the economy tends to the full use of its productive capacity (which, however, does not imply full employment of labour) as capitalist firms as a whole, after the crisis, are impelled once again to produce and invest as much as possible.

NOTES

1. Ricardo and Malthus, when they dealt with the issue of effective demand, always took for granted that if demand fell short of supply at the aggregate level a 'general glut' would occur. Neither considered the possibility that a low level of effective demand could give rise to underemployment equilibria, that is situations in which firms are induced to produce below their capacity, yet the economy attains equilibrium in the goods market (the Keynesian case).
2. To produce to capacity should not be necessarily interpreted as meaning that firms push production to its physical (technical) limit. A notion of 'normal capacity' can be easily introduced, so that 'producing to capacity' means that production is at the level associated with the normal use of the existing capacity.
3. For some examples of Marx's concept of free competition, see Marx (1954, pp. 585–90, 706–7 and 714–5).
4. On this see Marx (1973, pp. 160–1), already quoted above in Chapter 2.
5. Or the normal use of the firm's productive capacity. From now on, for brevity, this qualification will no longer be made.
6. The firm's physical productive capacity is given, and so are the prices of its capital goods.
7. If $p < v$, at $X = X_M$ the firm would maximize its losses.
8. If the firm's losses are to be minimized, it must be $X_m = 0$.
9. (3.1) and (3.2) above do not ensure that r and r^e will be positive even when $X = X_M$. In order to have a positive rate of profit it is required that $p > [(F/X) + v]$.
10. We shall return to the determination of such a minimum rate of profit later on in this section.
11. 'Interest ... appears originally, is originally, and remains in fact merely a portion of the profit ... which the functioning capitalist, industrialist or merchant has to pay to the owner and lender of money-capital whenever he uses loaned capital instead of his own' (Marx, 1959, p. 370). Marx calls the share of gross profits that accrues to industrial firms 'profit of enterprise'.
12. 'The borrower borrows money as capital, as a value producing more value. But at the moment when it is advanced it is still only potential capital, like any other capital at its starting-point, the moment it is advanced. It is only through its employment that it expands its value and realises itself as capital. However, it has to be returned by the borrower as *realised* capital, hence as value plus surplus-value (interest). And the latter can only be a portion of the realised profit. Only a portion, not all of it. For the use-value of the loaned capital to the borrower consists in producing profit for him' (Marx, 1959, p. 353).
13. For further discussion of Marx's theory of the interest rate and his interpretation of money loans, see chapter 4 below. See also Fan-Hung (1939) and Panico (1980).
14. 'Since interest is merely a part of profit paid ... by the industrial capitalist to the money capitalist, the maximum limit of interest is the profit itself, in which case the portion pocketed by the productive capitalist would = 0. ... The minimum limit of interest is altogether indeterminable. It may fall to any low' (Marx, 1959, p. 358). Also in this respect, Marx's and Ricardo's views differ. For Ricardo, in fact, the interest rate is directly determined by 'real' factors, that is by the profit rate in the industrial sector (Ricardo, 1951, pp. 353–4).
15. 'The stagnation in the market, which is glutted with cotton cloth, hampers the reproduction

process of the weaver. This disturbance first affects his workers. Thus they are now to a smaller extent, or not at all, consumers of his commodity – cotton cloth – and of the other commodities which entered into their consumption. ... They now form a part of the temporary surplus population, of the surplus production of workers, in this case of cotton producers, because there is a surplus production of cotton fabrics on the market.' (Marx, 1968, p. 522).

16. Obviously, this problem does not arise if money is a nominal instrument.

17. Marx himself was well aware of this: 'If it is easily understood how overproduction of some leading articles of consumption must bring in its wake the phenomenon of a more or less general overproduction, it is by no means clear how overproduction of these articles can arise. For the phenomenon of general overproduction is derived from the interdependence not only of the workers directly employed in these industries, but of all branches of industries which produce the elements of their products, the various stages of their constant capital. In the latter branches of industry, overproduction is an effect. But whence does it come in the former? For the latter (branches of industry) continue to produce so long as the former go on producing, and along with this continued production, a general growth in revenue, and therefore in their own consumption, seems assured' (Marx, 1968, pp. 523–4).

18. 'All the objections which Ricardo and others raise against overproduction etc. rest on the fact that they regard bourgeois production either as a mode of production in which no distinction exists between purchase and sale – direct barter – or as social production, implying that society, as if according to a plan, distributes its means of production and productive forces in the degree and measure which is required for the fulfilment of the various social needs, so that each sphere of production receives the quota of social capital required to satisfy the corresponding need' (Marx, 1968, p. 529). On Marx's concept of growth and its relationship to balanced growth see also Sardoni (1981).

19. For Marx, the rate of profit (in value terms) is $r = S/(C + V) = (S/V)/[(C/V) + 1]$ where S/V is the rate of exploitation (S is the aggregate surplus value), C/V is the organic composition of capital(C is constant capital and V is variable capital). Increases in the organic composition of capital raise S/V, so that the tendency of r to fall may be offset (Marx, 1959, pp. 232–40), but eventually the tendency to fall must prevail. Marx (1959, p. 260) held that the productivity of labour (on which S/V depends) cannot increase indefinitely, because of natural limits.

20. Marx's law of the falling rate of profit has been regarded as correct and theoretically acceptable, even though it cannot be used to explain underemployment rest states. However, the law is unacceptable on more general grounds and has to be rejected. Marx's law is formulated in value terms; when the rate of profit is expressed correctly in price terms the law no longer holds, as many authors have shown. The introduction of more productive techniques can never cause the rate of profit (in price terms) to fall. Okishio (1961) showed that every innovation must engender a higher rate of profit (in price terms). Later on, others have generalized Okishio's theorem by extending it to the case of an economy which uses fixed capital too (Roemer, 1979, pp. 385–93). Schefold (1976) has demonstrated that, under the assumption that innovations take a particular form, the maximum rate of profit (the rate prevailing when $w = 0$) in a (price) system with fixed capital actually falls. But this does not imply that the actual rate of profit also falls when innovations are introduced. For further developments of the debate on Marx's law, see also Shaikh (1978, 1980); Steedman (1980); Nakatani (1980); Armstrong and Glyn (1980); Bleaney (1980).

21. 'The capital already invested is then, indeed, idle in large quantities because the reproduction process is stagnant. Factories are closed, raw materials accumulated, finished products flood the markets as commodities' (Marx, 1959, p. 483).

22. The workers' propensity to consume is 1; the capitalists' propensity to consume is 0.

23. In the example above, no particular assumption on the behaviour of the wage rate when employment decreases is made. In fact, no particular behaviour of the wage rate need be assumed. Whether the wage rate is assumed to fall or not when employment decreases, it is always possible to make the hypothesis that two prices, $\bar{p}_1$ and $\bar{p}_2$, which fulfil (3.8) above, exist.

24. Analogous results could be obtained if, instead of postulating firms producing at different

costs, we assume firms having plants producing at different costs. In this case, instead of underemployment levels of activity characterized by average firms producing to capacity that co-exist with idle marginal firms, we have underemployment levels of activity, in which all or most firms produce below capacity as expected prices are below the unit costs of the less efficient plants. We shall return to this case only when considering Keynes's micro-foundations because Marx did not contemplate it.

25. Here we abstract from the fact that firms could adopt new technologies that lower their costs. This would represent a further factor which brings about the recovery.

26. This means, from a formal point of view, that $dv/dt > dp^e/dt$ and $dr*/dt > dr^e/dt$ (all derivatives are negative).

27. 'The life of modern industry becomes a series of periods of moderate activity, prosperity, overproduction, crisis and stagnation' (Marx, 1954, p. 427).

4. Keynes's critique of Say's Law

4.1 INTRODUCTION

This chapter is mainly devoted to present Keynes's critique of Say's Law and to point out the significant similarities to Marx's own critique. However, before turning to consider these issues, a number of qualifications and clarifications are necessary.

First of all, it is necessary to understand what Marx and Keynes meant by the term Say's Law. Marx dealt with the law as expressed by Ricardo; Keynes, especially in *The General Theory*, criticized the law expressed in terms that appear quite foreign to the Ricardian formulation. Keynes's criticism is addressed to what can be defined as the neoclassical version of Say's Law. There are significant differences between the two versions of the law. It is then important to point out these differences. Section 4.2 is devoted to this topic and to Keynes's criticism of Say's Law as presented in *The General Theory*.

Despite the differences in the definition of Say's Law in classical and neoclassical economics, it is still true that there also exist important similarities and, for this, it is possible to find similarities between Marx's and Keynes's criticisms of the law. These similarities are easier to detect in writings of Keynes other than the final version of *The General Theory*. They are most evident in some earlier drafts of the book, where Keynes went as far as to use Marx's formula ($M - C - M'$) to argue against the validity of Say's Law. Section 4.3 deals with Keynes's earlier drafts of *The General Theory*.

In his drafts of *The General Theory*, Keynes did not give the interest rate a primary role to play. We know, however, that the interest rate and Keynes's monetary theory of it, play a crucial role in his theory of effective demand as formulated in the final version of *The General Theory*. It is then important to compare Keynes's theory of the interest rate with Marx's, especially in view of the fact that several interpreters tend to stress the differences rather than the similarities between them. Again, the similarities between Marx and Keynes emerge more clearly if one looks at Keynes's writings other than *The General Theory*, in particular after its publication. Section 4.4 is concerned with this topic.

The fact that the most significant similarities between Marx and Keynes can be found in Keynes's works either before or after *The General Theory* requires some explanation. Although not in a thorough way, section 4.5 tries to explain the reasons why such similarities are hardest to perceive in *The General Theory*. Section 4.6 concludes and summarizes Marx's and Keynes's positions by using a uniform terminology.

4.2 SAY'S LAW IN CLASSICAL AND NEOCLASSICAL ECONOMICS AND KEYNES'S CRITIQUE IN *THE GENERAL THEORY*

The issue in dispute between Ricardo and Malthus was the possibility of having general overproduction crises.[1] To admit that they were possible meant conceding that the process of accumulation and growth could be interrupted by phenomena which implied a fall in the general level of market prices and profits, a wastage of capital, and an increase in the level of unemployment. Denying the possibility of general gluts implied considering capitalistic accumulation and growth as a fundamentally smooth process that could be interrupted or slackened only by a permanent increase in wages, due to decreasing returns to land.

What was never discussed by Ricardo and Malthus was the neoclassical idea that the validity of Say's Law must imply the full employment of labour. For Ricardo, the validity of the law implied that, in a country, any amount of capital could have been used without facing any obstacle on the demand side.[2] This means that the economy necessarily experiences the full utilization of its productive capacity. If profits are high enough (the motives for accumulation are strong enough) and whatever amount of commodities can be sold, the capitalists' tendency to maximize profits implies that they produce, and invest, as much as possible.

However, the full utilization of capacity and the tendency to invest at the highest possible rate do not imply, within Ricardo's framework, that there must be full employment of labour. For Ricardo there is no necessary reason why, at any given time, the full use of existing capital should allow the employment of all the available workforce. Nor does the highest possible rate of accumulation imply that full employment of labour will eventually be achieved: the rate of growth of population may well exceed the rate of growth of capital.[3] But perhaps the most telling evidence that Ricardo did not associate Say's Law with full employment is his analysis of machinery and its effects on employment. In the famous Chapter 31 of the third edition of the *Principles* (1951, pp. 386–97), Ricardo undoubtedly assumed the validity of the law and, in spite of it, pointed out that the process of accumulation could cause unemployment of labour to rise.

It is hard to find a neoclassical economist who expressed Say's Law in the same terms as Ricardo. None the less, neoclassical economics did not challenge the law.[4] Some basic aspects were accepted: money was still regarded essentially as a mere device to make exchanges efficient, and it was held that saving is necessarily transformed into investment. However, there were also significant differences between the classical and neoclassical versions of the law. First of all, classical economists simply assumed that saving *is* investment, so that any discrepancy between the two variables is impossible; neoclassical economists, instead, admitted the possibility that saving and investment diverge. Such a divergence, however, would be eliminated by an equilibrating mechanism.

For Ricardo and the other classical economists, the transformation of saving into investment was essentially a direct process, in the sense that savers themselves were those who invested. For the neoclassicals, the process was essentially indirect: saving and investment decisions are not necessarily made simultaneously and by the same people. For this reason saving and investment may diverge, but market mechanisms take care of this by ensuring that the equality is restored. The variable that plays this equilibrating role is the rate of interest. Abstaining from present consumption (that is saving, – the supply of capital) is a direct function of the interest rate, and investment (the demand for capital) is an inverse function, so that any divergence between the two variables is eliminated by variations in the interest rate.

Secondly, the validity of the law for neoclassical economics also implied the full employment of labour. Also in this case, unemployment of labour would be eliminated by an equilibrating mechanism. For the classics, the possible existence of unemployment did not give rise to any adjusting mechanism that would bring the economy to the full employment of labour; for neoclassical economists, variations of the (real) wage rate bring the economy to full employment. If there is an excess supply of labour, a decrease in the real wage rate would induce firms to increase their demand for labour and eliminate unemployment.

The analytical differences between classical and neoclassical economics with respect to Say's Law can also be pointed out by expressing the law in two different ways: as an *identity* and as *equality*. Classical economists, by assuming that saving is investment, accepted the law as an identity (the equality between aggregate supply and demand is always true); neoclassical economists, by concentrating on equilibrating mechanisms, accepted the law as an equality, which is true only in equilibrium (Sowell, 1972, pp. 34–8).

Keynes criticized the law in its neoclassical version; therefore, he had to consider those specific aspects on which neoclassical economists concentrated. In particular, he had to reject the idea that there is an equilibrating mechanism that brings aggregate supply and demand to equality by ensuring the equality between saving and investment. For Keynes, saving is not necessarily transformed into investment.

The act of saving does not imply the supply of a corresponding amount of funds to those who wish to invest. Once the amount of saving has been decided, the individual has to decide whether to keep it in the form of money or to part with it for a certain time, in other words to lend it. Such a decision depends on the individual's liquidity preference. This vision of saving decisions implies that the interest rate is not a return to saving on waiting as such. In fact, 'if a man hoards his saving in cash, he earns no interest though he saves as much as before'. The interest rate, instead, is 'the reward for parting with liquidity' (Keynes, 1936, p. 167). Therefore, the rate of interest cannot play the equilibrating role that is given to it in neoclassical analysis. There can be situations in which liquidity preference is so high that the interest rate is at too high a level to allow investment to reach its full-employment level, that is the level that ensures the level of aggregate demand needed for the full employment of labour and capacity. In other words, it is not true that any level of supply generates an equal level of demand.[5]

Since it was difficult to find the law clearly expressed by a specific neoclassical economist,[6] in *The General Theory* Keynes reformulated it in his own terms without realizing that this version of Say's Law did not reflect the Ricardian version and its analytical conclusions.[7] Keynes defined Say's Law in the following terms:

> The classical theory assumes ... that the aggregate demand price (or proceeds) always accommodates itself to the aggregate supply price; so that, whatever the volume of N may be, the proceeds D assume a value equal to the aggregate supply price Z which corresponds to N. That is to say, effective demand, instead of having a unique equilibrium value, is an infinite range of values all equally admissible; and the amount of employment is indeterminate except in so far as the marginal disutility of labour sets an upper limit. (Keynes, 1936, p. 26)

In this context, competition would lead to an expansion of production and employment up to the level at which the supply of output is perfectly rigid, that is to say the full-employment level of production.

But for Keynes only one level of employment can be consistent with equilibrium, 'since any other level will lead to inequality between the aggregate supply price of output as a whole and its aggregate demand price. This level cannot be greater than full employment, that is, the real wage cannot be less than the marginal disutility of labour. But there is no reason, in general, for expecting it to be equal to full employment' (Keynes, 1936, p. 28).[8]

Put in this form, Say's Law and its criticism by Keynes hardly resemble Ricardo's formulation and Marx's criticism. However, in earlier writings Keynes carried out the critique of Say's Law and its implications in a rather different way. There, the similarities with Marx appear much clearer and more obvious.

4.3   KEYNES'S CRITIQUE OF SAY'S LAW IN THE 1933 DRAFT OF *THE GENERAL THEORY*

In his 1933 article, 'A monetary theory of production' (Keynes, 1973c, pp. 408–11), Keynes dealt with the traditional approach in economics in a way that appears much closer to the Marxian criticism of Ricardo. Keynes argued that economics was unable to explain crises because of its unsatisfactory approach to money: 'In my opinion the main reason why the problem of crises is unsolved, or at any rate why this theory is so unsatisfactory, is to be found in the lack of what might be termed a monetary theory of production' (Keynes, 1973c, p. 408).

Economists have distinguished a barter economy from a monetary economy, holding that the latter is characterized by the use of money to exchange commodities. Money, in this view, is only a useful instrument, making exchange easier and more rapid and with neutral effects upon the economy as a whole. Keynes calls such an economy a 'real-exchange economy', which is very different from his conception of a monetary economy. In the latter, money influences motives and decisions and affects the rate of interest as well as the relationship between total output and expenditure.[9]

In Keynes's opinion, most economists, Marshall and Pigou in particular, were aware of the fact that the real economy is a monetary economy. None the less, most treatises on economics and money were written under the assumption that a capitalist economy behaves as if it were a 'real-exchange economy'. However, in order that money be neutral, so that a monetary economy functions like a 'real-exchange economy', some conditions have to be met:

> the conditions required for the 'neutrality' of money, in the sense in which this is assumed in – again to take this book as a leading example – Marshall's *Principles of Economics*, are, I suspect, precisely the same as those which will insure that crises *do not occur*. If this is true, the real-exchange economics ... is a singularly blunt weapon for dealing with the problem of booms and depressions. For it has assumed away the very matter under investigation. (Keynes, 1973c, pp. 410–1)

The essence of Keynes's criticism of Marshall and Pigou coincides with Marx's essential criticism of Ricardo. Like Ricardo, Marshall and Pigou were able to hold that Say's Law applies to the extent that they assumed, explicitly or implicitly, that money is neutral, that is a mere medium of exchange that does not affect the fundamental laws of the economy. But Keynes's 1933 article does not go on to provide either a more complete criticism of the concept of 'real-exchange economy' or an analysis of a monetary economy in the Keynesian sense.[10]

Most of Keynes's points were developed more fully in a 1933 draft of several chapters of *The General Theory*,[11] even though there Keynes was no longer dealing directly with the problem of crises.[12] He also partly changed the terminology adopted in the article, now calling a 'real-exchange economy' a 'co-operative economy', while a monetary economy is called an 'entrepreneur economy'. Moreover, Keynes introduced a further notion, what he called a 'neutral entrepreneur economy', or 'neutral economy'.

A co-operative economy, though money is used to effect exchanges, is essentially a barter economy, which is characterized by the fact that the factors of production are rewarded by a share of the real output.

> I define a *barter economy* as one in which the factors of production are rewarded by dividing up in agreed proportions the actual output of their cooperative efforts. It is not necessary that they should receive their share of the output *in specie*; the position is the same if they share the sale-proceeds of the output in agreed proportions. Since this economy does not exclude the use of money for purposes of transitory convenience, it might perhaps be better to call it a *real-wage economy*, or a *co-operative economy* as distinct from an *entrepreneur economy*. In a barter economy (or co-operative) only miscalculation or stupid obstinacy can stand in the way of production, if the value of the expected real product exceeds the real costs. (Keynes, 1979, pp. 66–7)

If the rewards to factors of production are established in agreed proportions, money can be used only as a 'transitory convenience', to buy the predetermined share of real output. In such an economy, full employment of all factors is ensured: both the demand for and the supply of each factor depend on the expected amount of the rewards in terms of output, and as long as the expected output exceeds its cost, production will be carried on. At the point at which the expected value of the output does not exceed its cost, full employment is reached.[13]

But the same analytical results can still be achieved assuming a more realistic economic system. In fact, even if some factors do not use all their reward to buy a share of the current output but divert part of it to purchase a share of pre-existing wealth, full employment is still attained, provided that the sellers of the pre-existing wealth in turn use the proceeds to buy current output. In this context, again, money is a transitory convenience.[14] This is an economy in which income may be spent on commodities (and/or services) or saved by each individual factor, but nevertheless what is saved is spent.

At this stage it is possible to conceive of an economy in which the same conditions apply, even if there exists a class of entrepreneurs who start productive processes in order to sell the produced commodities for money. Keynes calls such an economy a 'neutral entrepreneur economy'. It is an economy in which the starting up of productive processes largely depends on a class of entrepreneurs who hire the factors of production for money and look to their recoupment from selling the output for money, provided that the whole of the current incomes of the factors of production are necessarily spent, directly or indirectly on purchasing their own current output from entrepreneurs. (Keynes, 1979, p. 77)

In this system 'there is a mechanism of some kind to ensure that the exchange value of the money incomes of the factors is always equal in the aggregate to the proportion of current output which would have been the factor's share in a co-operative economy' (Keynes 1979, pp. 78).

Therefore, a capitalist economy behaves like a co-operative economy, ensuring the same results in terms of effective demand and full employment, only under these restrictive conditions. The whole tradition of economic thought has implicitly assumed that in the real capitalist economy those conditions actually are fulfilled:

> The classical theory ..., as exemplified in the tradition from Ricardo to Marshall and Professor Pigou, appears to me to presume that the conditions for a Neutral Economy are substantially fulfilled in general; – though it has been a source of great confusion that its assumptions have been *tacit*, so that you will search in vain for any express statement of the simplifications which have been introduced or for the relationship of conclusions demonstrated for a Neutral Economy to the facts of the real world. (Keynes, 1979, p. 79)

Keynes's definitions of co-operative and neutral economy correspond to concepts that are characteristic of neoclassical economics. Concepts such as factors of production, full employment, 'a mechanism which ensures the equality between saving and investment', and so on, were not used by Ricardo and the other classical economists. But, if two important qualifications are made, Keynes's criticisms apply to Ricardo as well. These two qualifications are: i) the validity of Say's Law does not imply that there is necessarily full employment of labour; ii) the equality between saving and investment is not ensured by any particular mechanism but is simply assumed. With these provisos, it can be argued that Ricardo also carried out his analysis within the context of a neutral entrepreneur economy.

Thus, Keynes, like Marx, regarded a mistaken notion of money as the essential factor enabling Say's Law to hold. It is possible to show that Say's Law applies to a capitalist economy only by postulating characteristics that are not its actual ones:

> It is easy to show that the conditions for a Neutral Economy are not satisfied in practice, with the result that there is a difference of the most fundamental importance between a co-operative economy and the type of entrepreneur economy in which we actually live. For in an entrepreneur economy, ... the volume of employment, the

marginal disutility of which is equal to the utility of its marginal product, may be 'unprofitable' in terms of money. (Keynes, 1979, p. 79)

Keynes moved still closer to Marx's approach when he described the essential features of an 'entrepreneur economy'. He even used the Marxian terminology:[15]

> The distinction between a co-operative economy and an entrepreneur economy bears some relation to a pregnant observation made by Karl Marx – though the subsequent use to which he put this observation was highly illogical. He pointed out that the nature of production in the actual world is not, as economists seem often to suppose, a case of $C - M - C$; i.e., of exchanging commodity (or effort). That may be the standpoint of the private consumer. But it is not the attitude of *business*, which is the case of $M - C - M'$; i.e., of parting with money for commodity (or effort) in order to obtain more money. (Keynes, 1979, p. 81 and pp. 81–2n)

Capitalist entrepreneurs start productive processes not simply in order to produce more commodities, but in order to earn a profit from their production; a profit which is necessarily in monetary form.

Economists, for Keynes, assume that the entrepreneurs' willingness to give rise to productive processes depends on the expected amount of real output which will accrue to them, so that the larger the share of real output, the higher the level of employment. But, 'in an entrepreneur economy this is a wrong analysis of the nature of business calculation. An entrepreneur is interested, not in the amount of product, but in the amount of money which will fall to his share. He will increase his output if by so doing he expects to increase his money profit, even though this profit represents a smaller quantity of product than before' (Keynes, 1979, p. 82).

As soon as the factors of production are rewarded in money and, therefore, starting a productive process implies the disbursement of money and not of products in kind, entrepreneurs are interested in money profits rather than the volume of output. Entrepreneurs will direct money to those activities which they regard as most profitable (in terms of money). In particular, there are two alternative destinations for money: spending it to start productive process (and employ labour) and keeping it idle:

> It is of the essence of an entrepreneur economy that the thing (or things) in terms of which the factors of production are rewarded can be spent on something which is not current output, to the production of which current output cannot be diverted (except on a limited scale), and the exchange value of which is fixed in terms of an article of current output to which production can be diverted without limit. (Keynes, 1979, p. 85)

If the demand for money increases while the demand for current output declines, the result is a decrease in employment.[16] Capitalist entrepreneurs prefer to keep (demand) money when they do not expect profitable productive processes because money is the best store of value.

> Money in terms of which the factors of production are remunerated will 'keep' more readily than output which they are being remunerated to produce, so that the need of entrepreneurs to sell, if they are to avoid a running loss, is more pressing than the need of recipients of income to spend. This is the case because it is a characteristic of finished goods, which are neither consumed nor used but carried in stock, that they incur substantial carrying charges for storage, risk and deterioration, so that they are yielding a negative return for so long as they are held; whereas such expenses are reduced to a minimum approaching zero in the case of money. (Keynes, 1979, p. 86).

This makes it more likely that effective demand will fall short of aggregate supply than increase in excess of it.

4.4   MARX AND KEYNES ON THE RATE OF INTEREST

In the previous section we showed that Marx's and Keynes's criticisms of Say's Law have some significant similarities, despite the fact that they were addressed to different versions of the law. These similarities appear more evident when looking at Keynes's 1933 drafts, because there he did not pay much attention to the role of the rate of interest in his theory of effective demand. The role of the interest rate, instead, is central in *The General Theory*.

In *The General Theory*, there is no longer a direct relation between the capitalist drive to accumulate wealth for the sake of profit and the propensity to hoard. Both the decisions to invest and to demand idle money depend on the rate of interest. The demand for idle money due to the 'speculative motive' can keep the interest rate at a level that is too high to ensure a full-employment level of investment.

In these terms, Keynes's approach appears quite distant from Marx's. However, a more careful reading of Marx's works shows that important similarities between the two economists remain even when the rate of interest is brought into play. This section aims at emphasizing these similarities, a task that can be more easily accomplished by looking at Keynes's writings after *The General Theory* (Keynes, 1937a, b, c), when he expressed his theory of the rate of interest in terms more easily comparable to Marx's approach.

4.4.1   Keynes on the Interest Rate after *The General Theory*

The rate of interest is determined by the demand for and the supply of money (liquidity). Two types of demand may be distinguished: active demand, which depends on the scale of activity in the economy, and inactive demand, which depends on the state of confidence among the holders of claims and assets (Keynes, 1937a, pp. 667–8). The rate of interest represents the premium that is required to induce people to part with money – that is, not to hold it as a store of value.

> The rate of interest obviously measures – just as the books on arithmetic say it does – the premium which has to be offered to induce people to hold their wealth in some form other than hoarded money. The quantity of money and the amount of it required in the active circulation for the transaction of current business (mainly depending on the level of money income) determine how much is available for inactive balances, i.e. for hoards. The rate of interest is the factor which adjusts at the margin the demand for hoards to the supply of hoards. (Keynes, 1937c, pp. 216–7)

If the supply of money is given, changes in the level of hoards can take place only if changes in the level of money income occur; otherwise, the rate of interest is affected. Changes in the rate of interest will affect the prices of capital assets, and as a consequence the demand for them (investment) will change. But the prices of capital assets are influenced by other factors too; in particular, by the expectations as to the return on them.[17]

> Thus if the level of the rate of interest taken in conjunction with opinions about their prospective yield raise the prices of capital assets, the volume of current investment ... will be increased; while if, on the other hand, these influences reduce the prices of capital assets, the volume of current investment will be diminished. ... Nor is there any reason to suppose that the fluctuations in one of these factors will tend to offset the fluctuation in the other. When a more pessimistic view is taken about future yields, there is no reason why there should be a diminished propensity to hoard. Indeed the conditions which aggravate one factor tend, as a rule, to aggravate the other. For the same circumstances which lead to pessimistic views about future yields are apt to increase the propensity to hoard. (Keynes, 1937c, pp. 217–8).

The demand for money as a store of value is related to the accumulation of wealth in an uncertain context. Wealth is accumulated in order to produce results at a distant date. The fact that knowledge of the future is 'fluctuating, vague and uncertain' compels those who must make decisions concerning the accumulation of wealth to rely on a variety of techniques which are based on 'flimsy foundations'. Therefore, such decisions are subject to 'sudden and violent changes' (Keynes, 1937c, pp. 213–4). The demand for money represents the way to cope with a rising uncertainty about the future results of the accumulation of wealth:

> to hold money as a store of wealth is a barometer of the degree of our distrust of our own calculations and conventions concerning the future. ... [T]his feeling about

money … takes charge at the moments when the higher, more precarious conventions have weakened. The possession of actual money lulls our disquietude; and the premium which we require to make us part with money is the measure of the degree of our disquietude. (Keynes, 1937c, p. 216)

The fundamental way in which wealth is accumulated in a capitalist economy is through investment decided by entrepreneurs. In this perspective, Keynes's 1937 observations can be translated into his 1933 terminology: the alternative to the accumulation of wealth through investment is holding idle money. The demand for idle money increases when investing now is not expected to produce 'satisfactory' results (profits) in the future.

The reasoning so far has been conducted under the hypothesis of a constant given supply of money. However, such a hypothesis has to be removed to make the analysis more general and to emphasize the crucial role that banks can play in the determination of the rate of interest. In *The General Theory*, Keynes retained the assumption of a given supply of money, but earlier, in the *Treatise on Money*, and later, in his 1937 articles, he removed it and considered the role of banks.[18]

In the *Treatise*, individuals face the alternative of holding savings deposits with banks (which is equivalent to hoarding) or holding securities (equivalent to investing) (Keynes, 1971b, p. 127).[19] If the propensity of the public to hoard increases (the demand for savings deposits increases), the price of securities decreases (the price of capital assets decreases). This result, however, can be affected by the behaviour of banks: if they act counter to the actions of the public, buying the securities the public does not want and creating against them the additional saving deposits the public does want, the price of securities does not have to fall. Therefore, the price of securities – and hence the rate of interest – depends on 'the sentiment of the public and the behaviour of the banking system' (Keynes, 1971b, p. 128).

The same line of reasoning is followed in 1937. An increase in the public's propensity to hoard makes the rate of interest rise if banks do not operate in such a way as to offset the increased demand for idle money by the public: 'If the banks stand firm, an increased propensity to hoard raises the rate of interest, and thereby lowers the prices of capital assets other than cash, until people give up the idea of selling them or of refraining from buying them in order to increase their hoards' (Keynes, 1937a, p. 251).[20]

4.4.2   Marx on the Interest Rate

Although Marx paid a good deal of attention to credit, banks and the determination of the rate of interest (Marx, 1959, pp. 338–613), he never managed to develop a satisfactory organic study of these issues.[21] Here, we consider only those aspects of Marx's theory that relate more directly to Keynes's analysis. A superficial examination of Marx's analysis of the determination of the rate of interest might lead to the conclusion that it differs significantly from that of Keynes. In fact, most differences are essentially terminological rather than substantive.

As we saw in Chapter 3, for Marx the rate of interest is determined by the demand for and the supply of money loans. On the demand side, he distinguished three different forms of borrowing:

> *First case.* – A receives from the bank amounts loaned on his own personal credit, without giving any security for them. In this case he does not merely receive means of payment, but also unquestionably a new capital until the maturity date. *Second case.* – A has given to the bank securities, national bonds, or stocks as collateral, and received for them, say, up to two-thirds of their monetary value as a cash loan.... *Third case.* – A had the bank discount a bill of exchange and received its value in cash after the deduction of discount. In this case he sold a non-convertible money capital to the bank for the amount in convertible form. He sold his still running bill for cash money. The bill is now the property of the bank.[22] (Marx, 1959, p. 455)

On the supply side, Marx's analysis is influenced by the specific historical period he studied,[23] but if we abstract from its peculiarities we can say that in general the supply of money loans is determined by the policy of the central bank and the private banks' propensity to lend.[24] The amount of deposits which banks lend depends essentially on their discretionary decisions.[25] Banks' decisions whether or not to lend are similar to decisions to keep money idle or else to employ it in such a way that a prospective return can be earned. In other words, banks may have a higher or a lower 'liquidity preference' and this affects the rate of interest.

In so far as Marx regarded the rate of interest as contingent on the supply of and the demand for money loans, whereas Keynes explicitly held that it depends on the supply of and the demand for money, one may conclude that the two theories are different. Fan-Hung (1939), in fact, argued that Marx's theory of the rate of interest is closer to Robertson's theory of 'loanable funds' than to that of Keynes.[26] It is well known that Keynes firmly opposed any interpretation likening his theory to those based on the demand for and the supply of credit, such as those of Robertson (1936), Hicks (1936) and Ohlin (1937a, b). Keynes conceded only that the demand for credit to finance investment was one of the factors affecting the rate of interest.[27]

However, to liken Marx's theory of the rate of interest to Robertson's approach does not seem right, for Marx used the concept of demand for loans in a wider sense than Robertson. In Marx's terminology, people are taking loans from banks even when they sell securities and discount bills. But selling securities and discounting bills is to demand liquidity, not to borrow from a bank in order to expand productive capacity. Borrowing to finance investment is only the first of the three forms of borrowing considered by Marx (1959, p. 425). In fact, Marx defines borrowing to expand production as a loan of money-capital, whereas the other two forms of loans are simply called advances of money (Marx, 1959, pp. 428–9). From this perspective, Marx's theory resembles that of Keynes more closely; that is, the demand for finance is only one factor and the demand for liquidity must also be taken into account.

Now that what Marx meant by demand for money loans has been clarified, the similarities between his and Keynes's analyses of the demand side of the determination of the rate of interest become more evident. When we look at the supply side of the process, too, the similarities are significant. In both analyses, banks play a crucial role. The role of the banks during a crisis, when the demand for liquidity is very high, is stressed by Marx in the following terms:

> As long as the social character of labour appears as the money-existence of commodities, and thus a thing external to actual production, money crises … are inevitable. On the other hand, it is clear that as long as the credit of a bank is not shaken, it will alleviate the panic in such cases by increasing credit-money and intensify it by contracting the latter. (Marx, 1959, pp. 516–7)

4.5   KEYNES AND MARX: FROM THE 1933 DRAFTS TO *THE GENERAL THEORY* AND BACK

It is peculiar that the resemblances of Keynes's theory to that of Marx emerge in a more clear and straightforward way in Keynes's writings either before or after *The General Theory*. It is in *The General Theory* itself that the similarities are hardest to perceive.

Keynes's critique of Say's Law, which in the 1933 draft was based on the distinction between a neutral economy and an entrepreneur economy, appeared in the final version in a different form. And the form in which his theory of the rate of interest was presented in *The General Theory* differs from the form he chose afterwards, in the 1937 articles.

It is outside the scope of this book to deal with the reasons why Keynes made those changes. In general, it is possible to argue that there were both tactical and analytical reasons behind Keynes's choice. As for the tactical reasons, it can be suggested that *The General Theory* was addressed to Keynes's fellow economists to 'bring to an issue the deep divergences of opinion … which have for the time being almost destroyed the practical influence of economic theory' (1936, p. vi). His fellow economists had to be convinced of the validity of Keynes's analysis and results. If this is so, it is not at all surprising that Keynes should have chosen to introduce the innovative aspects of his analysis into a framework deliberately kept as familiar and as acceptable as possible to the economists of the day. From this point of view, it was easier to convince economists of the weakness of Say's Law the way Keynes did in *The General Theory* than the way he did in the earlier drafts.

In other words, Keynes tried to translate his analysis of capitalism into the language that was most easily comprehensible to other economists, convinced as he was that what was required was first to win their acceptance in order to exert, later on, the widest possible influence on the practical plane. To achieve all this, Keynes was extremely flexible and amenable to suggestions aimed at making his fundamental results more palatable to his peers by framing them in a context not too far removed from the traditional one.[28]

However, when Keynes was engaged in developing his new ideas and was not much worried about their formal, final exposition, his line of reasoning was closer to that followed by Marx. On the other hand, when after the publication of the *The General Theory* he had to defend his own theory, clear up misunderstandings and refute wrong interpretations, he expounded his basic ideas more clearly and directly, so that the essential affinities with the original Marxian theory resurface and can be more easily perceived.

As for the analytical reasons, it is interesting to look at some aspects of the evolution of Keynes's exposition and arguments between 1933 and 1936. By mid-1934, Keynes had abandoned his previous approach to the critique of Say' Law. In April, he had written to Kahn: 'I have been making rather extensive changes in the early chapters of my book' (Keynes, 1973a, p. 422). In a table of contents, written before the first proofs of *The General Theory* (October 1934), the chapters on the distinction between a co-operative and an entrepreneur economy had disappeared (Keynes, 1973a, pp. 423–4). Now classical economists are no longer criticised for having assumed that a capitalist economy behaves like a co-operative economy, but for the assumption that aggregate demand is always equal to aggregate supply: 'The fundamental assumption of the classical theory, "supply creates its own demand", is that $OW = OP$ *whatever* the level of O, so that effective demand is incapable of setting a limit to employment which consequently depends on the relation between marginal product in wage-good industries and marginal disutility of employment' (1973a, p. 422).[29]

In *The General Theory*, Keynes followed the same line. Although he still observed that the classical assumption concerning the equality between aggregate supply and demand prices could be derived by assuming that a capitalist economy is essentially equivalent to a barter economy, the distinction between a co-operative economy and a capitalist economy ceased to play a central role. The fact that Keynes was criticizing the neoclassical version of Say's Law can explain his choices.

In 1933, Keynes, like Marx, had criticised his predecessors for having assumed that a capitalist economy behaves like a barter economy. But Marx had an advantage over Keynes – he could easily refer to Ricardo's explicit statements that a monetary capitalist economy is essentially the same as a barter economy and that all that is saved is always invested. Keynes, instead, found it much more difficult to point out passages from Marshall's or Pigou's works where equivalent statements were made as clearly and explicitly as those by Ricardo.[30] Moreover, if Say's Law is to imply full employment, it is necessary to assume that there exists a process of adjustment.

In *The General Theory* Keynes reached what he regarded as a satisfactory and thorough criticism of the neoclassical analysis of the mechanisms which ensure full employment: a decrease in money wage rates does not necessarily yield a higher level of employment; the rate of interest, determined by monetary factors, does not work as the equilibrating mechanism of saving and investment. Monetary factors can keep the rate of interest at too high a level to allow enough investment to ensure full employment. The critique of Say's Law is now based on the rejection of the traditional theory of the rate of interest. The rate of interest does not vary in such a way as to ensure $S = I$ at the full-employment level of income.

In referring to Pigou's theory of unemployment, the target *par excellence* of his critique, Keynes observed: 'it is assumed that the rate of interest always adjusts itself to the schedule of the marginal efficiency of capital in such a way as to preserve full employment. Without this assumption Professor Pigou's analysis breaks down and provides no means of determining what the volume of employment will be' (1936, pp. 274–5).

4.6   CONCLUSION

This chapter has pointed out some relevant similarities between Marx's and Keynes's analyses. Both held that Say's Law does not apply when money is introduced into the analytical framework and is not regarded as a mere means of circulation. Money, and its specific role within the economy, must be taken into account if we are to study and understand real economic systems. Marx's and Keynes's critiques are based upon their insistence on a theory whose abstractions, assumptions and hypotheses are more adequate to describe and understand the object of study, namely the capitalist economy.

When they looked at the essential characteristics of capitalist economies, they were not far apart. Both held that the decisions and actions of capitalist entrepreneurs, impelled as they are to maximize their profits, are the crucial factor. Investment and production are controlled by entrepreneurs and are regulated by their drive to obtain the highest possible reward. In so far as the entrepreneur class expects that investment and production will yield a 'satis-factory' reward, the economy proves to be able to meet the needs and wants of the society. But when investment and production are no longer advantageous from the point of view of the capitalist class, the ability of the economic and social system to meet the needs of the society through production is checked.

However, the comparison of Marx to Keynes poses other questions. The first and most important has to do with why Marx and Keynes – though they started from similar criticisms of their predecessors and had a fundamentally similar vision of the essential characteristics of a capitalist economic system – could arrive at different analytical results concerning underemployment equilibria. This issue is taken up in the next chapter. For now, let us summarize Marx's and Keynes's positions by using a uniform terminology.

If capitalists' expectations as to the profitability of their productive processes are 'pessimistic', the demand for idle money (hoarding) increases while the demand for commodities (along with the demand for labour) decreases. In this case it is money that is demanded and not any other commodity. Money is the best store of value.

An increase in the demand for money is essentially different from an increase in the demand for any other commodity. An increased demand for any given commodity, along with a decreased demand for other commodities, causes a shift in employment but not necessarily a decrease in its aggregate level. An increase in the demand for money causes a decrease in employment of labour in the production of commodities with no increase (or no significant increase) in the level of employment in the production of money. This holds for both Marx and Keynes, whether money is a commodity (gold) or a nominal instrument.

For both, Say's Law applies in an economy in which money is a 'transitory convenience' to effect exchanges. But actual capitalist economies imply the additional use of money as a store of value. Capitalist entrepreneurs may spend money to start productive processes, or they may keep it idle. The profitability of production and investment is the essential factor determining how money is used. We also find affinities between Marx and Keynes with respect to the theory of the rate of interest. In one fundamental respect, their theories resemble one another – namely, that for both of them the rate of interest is determined by monetary factors.

NOTES

1. Here Ricardo and Malthus are taken as the representatives of the contrasting positions on the validity of Say's Law. For a detailed examination of the debate on the law in classical economics, see Sowell (1972) and Baumol (1977).

2. 'There cannot ... lie accumulated in a country any amount of capital which cannot be

employed productively, until wages rise so high in consequence of the rise of necessaries, and so little consequently remains for the profits of stock, that the motive for accumulation ceases. While the profits of stock are high, men will have a motive to accumulate' (Ricardo, 1951, p. 290).

3. On the relationship between the full use of productive capacity and full employment of labour in Ricardo, see Garegnani (1978, pp. 338–41) and Milgate (1982, pp. 39–40).

4. For a history of Say's Law from classical to neoclassical economics, see Sowell (1972).

5. In Chapters 2 and 19 of *The General Theory* (1936, pp. 4–22 and 257–79), Keynes also criticized the neoclassical idea that variations of the real wage rate can ensure full employment. For more details on this aspect of Keynes's critique of neoclassical economics, see for example, Chick (1983, pp. 132–58), Davidson (1983), Sardoni (1997b). We shall return to this aspect of Keynes's theory in the next chapter, as it is not of particular relevance when considering his similarities with Marx.

6. Ackley (1961, pp. 105–67), who expounds the neoclassical version of Say's Law, points out that it can hardly be attributed to a specific neoclassical author.

7. Keynes did not hesitate to lump Ricardo together with Marshall, Pigou and the others as 'classical economists'. For him, 'classical economists' where all those who 'adopted and perfected' Ricardo's theory, including Marshall, Pigou, etc. (Keynes, 1936, p. 3n). On the other hand, Marshall – who exerted so deep an influence on Keynes's thinking – always regarded his own theory as a development of Ricardo's. On Marshall's interpretation of Ricardo and Ricardian economics, see Bharadwaj (1978).

8. For a discussion of Keynes's criticism of the law in *The General Theory*, see also Schumpeter (1954, pp. 622–5).

9. A monetary economy is one in which 'money plays a part of its own and affects motives and decisions and is, in short, one of the operative factors in the situation, so that the course of events cannot be predicted, either in the long period or in the short, without a knowledge of the behaviour of money between the first state and the last' (Keynes, 1973c, pp. 408–9).

10. The article was a 'research project', and Keynes, at the end, referred to his ongoing work for *The General Theory* (Keynes, 1973c, p. 411).

11. In 1933, Keynes worked out two draft tables of contents (Keynes, 1979, pp. 62–3) and drafted several chapters of the second one. In the drafts of the first, second and third chapter (1979, pp. 66–8, 76–87 and 87–111 respectively), he developed the issues which we are concerned with. The draft tables of contents of several chapters were only published in 1979. On this see the 'Editorial Note' to Volume 29 of Keynes's *Collected Writings* (1979, pp. xiii–iv) and also Robinson (1980a).

12. After his 1933 article, Keynes briefly returned to the problem of crises in the final edition of *The General Theory* (1936, pp. 314–6).

13. In other words, the 'second postulate' of 'classical economics' holds (Keynes, 1936, pp. 5–7).

14. 'Nor is it necessary that current output should comprise the whole of wealth; the position is still substantially the same if the factors of production swap their wage in respect of current output for other forms of wealth, provided that those with whom they swap intend to employ the whole sum forthwith to purchase some part of current output. … The essential point is that by whatever roundabout methods every factor of production ultimately accepts as its reward a predetermined share of the expected current output either in kind or in terms of something which has an exchange value equal to that of the predetermined share' (Keynes, 1979, p. 77).

15. Keynes (1979, p. 81n), however, regarded Marx's developments as illogical. His conclusion might derive from the fact that he did not directly refer to Marx's works but to McCracken's *Value Theory and Business Cycles* (1933). On McCracken's interpretation of Marx and the possible reason why it induced Keynes to regard Marx's analysis as illogical, see Sardoni (1997a, pp. 271–2).

16. This is true even if money is a commodity (such as gold), provided that there is some limit to the growth of its production: 'Nor is it necessary that the means of remuneration should be no part of current output, provided that there are strict limits to the extent to which output can be diverted to it. … If, indeed, it were easily practicable to divert output towards gold

on a sufficient scale for the value of the increased current output of gold to make good the deficiency in expenditure in other forms of current output, unemployment could not occur; except in the transitional period before the turn-over to increased gold-production could be completed' (Keynes, 1979, pp. 85–6). Clearly, Keynes is talking about what he later on called the 'essential properties of money' (Keynes, 1936, pp. 222–4).

17. 'This, then, is the first repercussion of the rate of interest, as fixed by the quantity of money and the propensity to hoard, namely, on the prices of capital assets. This does not mean, of course, that the rate of interest is the only fluctuating influence on these processes. Opinions as to their prospective yield are themselves subject to sharp fluctuations. ... It is these opinions taken in conjunction with the rate of interest which fix their prices' (Keynes, 1937c, p. 217).

18. On the supply of money in Keynes's analysis, see also Dow (1997).

19. Keynes's definition of investment here is different from that given in *The General Theory* (1936, p. 62) and also from a previous definition in the *Treatise* itself (1971b, p. 127n).

20. For Keynes's point of view on the power of banks in a capitalist economy, see also Keynes (1937b).

21. See Engels's observations in the preface to the third volume of *Capital* (1959, p. 4).

22. The three different forms of borrowing are associated with different lengths of time and different specific rates of interest. For simplicity, however, we refer to a single rate, taken to mean the existing complex of rates.

23. See especially *Capital Book III*, Ch. 34 ('The Currency Principle and the English Bank Legislation of 1844') (1959, pp. 546–64). See also Fan-Hung (1939, pp. 35–9).

24. Albeit in a rather rudimentary way, Marx used the concept of the bank credit multiplier; see e.g. Marx (1959, pp. 71–2).

25. 'The banker, who receives the money as a loan from one group of the reproductive capitalists, lends it to another group of reproductive capitalists, so that the banker appears in the role of a supreme benefactor; and at the same time, the control over this capital falls completely into the hands of the banker in his capacity as middleman' (Marx, 1959, p. 506).

26. For more details about the aspects of Robertson's theory more directly related to Marx, see Sardoni (1998).

27. 'Planned investment ..., may have to secure its "financial provision" *before* the investment takes place; that is to say, before the corresponding saving has taken place. ... There has to be, therefore, a technique to bridge this gap between the time when the *decision* to invest is taken and the time when the correlative investment and saving actually occur. ... [L]et us call this advance provision of cash the "finance" required by the current decision to invest.' And further: 'If by "credit" we mean "finance", I have no objection at all to admitting the demand for finance as one of the factors influencing the rate of interest. For "finance" constitutes ... an additional demand for liquid cash in exchange for a deferred claim. It is, in the literal sense, a demand for money. But finance is not the only source of demand for money' (Keynes, 1937a, pp. 246–8). On Keynes's analysis of the 'finance motive', see Davidson (1978, 1995); Coddington (1983, pp. 73–82); Kahn (1984, pp. 162–8); Graziani (1984); Asimakopulos (1985); Harcourt (1995); Bibow (1995).

28. From this point of view, Harrod exerted a great influence on Keynes. See, for example, his letter of 1 August 1935, and Keynes's answer of 9 August 1935 (Keynes, 1973a, pp. 533–4 and 537–9). See also Harrod (1975, p. 452): 'My main endeavour was to mitigate his attack on the "classical school".' For more details on Keynes's tactics, see Harcourt and Sardoni (1994).

29. W is marginal prime cost, O is output and P is the expected selling price. In Keynes's theory, '$OW \neq OP$ for *all* values of O, and entrepreneurs have to choose a value of O for which it *is* equal; – otherwise the equality of price and marginal prime cost is infringed. This is the real starting point of everything' (Keynes, 1973a, pp. 422–3).

30. After quoting a passage from Marshall's *Pure Theory of Domestic Values* (1930), where it is explicitly said that all is saved is necessarily invested, Keynes had to admit that it was difficult to find similar passages from Marshall's later work or in Pigou (Keynes, 1936, p. 19). See also Keynes (1973a, p. 410) and (1979, pp. 78–9).

5. Keynesian underemployment equilibria

5.1 INTRODUCTION

We saw in the previous chapter that, on some occasions, Keynes directly dealt with the problem of crises in a way that was not too dissimilar from Marx's approach.[1] However, Keynes's main concern was not the analysis of crises.[2] Keynes wanted to show that the economy may experience underemployment equilibria, that is to say situations in which the economy experiences unemployment of labour and underutilization of capacity, but where there is no significant market perturbation and no force at work pushing towards full employment of labour and capital.

This is a fundamental difference between Keynes and Marx. Not only did Marx concentrate on crises and take little interest in equilibrium but, as we saw in Chapter 3, his analysis cannot be developed to provide a satisfactory explanation of rest states (equilibria) characterized by a persistent situation of underemployment of labour and capital. This chapter is devoted to examining how Keynes arrived at the conclusion that underemployment equilibria can exist. This is done by considering the microeconomic foundations of Keynes's macroeconomics. The differences from Marx's microfoundations emerge clearly.

The chapter is organized as follows. Section 5.2 deals with Keynes's position concerning the prevailing market form in which firms operate. It is argued that Keynes essentially based his analysis on the hypothesis of (Marshallian) perfect competition. Section 5.3 looks at Keynes's microfoundations in the competitive context defined in the previous section. Section 5.4 takes into consideration the relation of the equilibrium conditions at the micro level to those at the macro level. In section 5.5, the main results of the analysis carried out in the previous sections are reformulated by developing a simple model. Section 5.6 concludes.

5.2 KEYNES ON PERFECT AND IMPERFECT COMPETITION

In *The General Theory*, Keynes paid little attention to the problem of the market form in which his macroeconomic analysis was set. In Chapter 18 of *The General Theory*, he stated that the degree of competition was one of the givens in his analysis. This suggests that he thought that any hypotheses on market forms would have left his results fundamentally unaffected.[3] He chose to concentrate on those aspects that he regarded as basic flaws of the prevailing doctrine, that is monetary theory and effective demand.

However, it is possible to argue that Keynes implicitly adopted a hypothesis of perfect competition. While he rejected the second postulate of classical economics (the utility of the real wage of a given amount of labour employed is equal to the marginal disutility of that amount of employment), he accepted the first postulate, that is to say, the real wage is equal to the marginal product of labour under the hypothesis of perfect competition (Keynes, 1936, p. 5). The postulate implies an inverse correlation between the level of output (and employment) and the real wage.[4]

Since the inverse correlation between the real wage and the level of employment holds throughout *The General Theory,* the conclusion that Keynes assumed perfect competition in *The General Theory* seems to be acceptable. Moreover, in 1939, Keynes explicitly recognized that in *The General Theory* he had accepted the then prevailing generalization that short-period increasing marginal costs substantially coincide with marginal wage costs and that prices are governed by marginal costs (Keynes, 1939, p. 400).

However, what is meant by perfect competition in *The General Theory* needs qualification. Keynes's interpretation of perfect competition is substantially different from other theoretical traditions. According to Joan Robinson, Keynes 'relied upon a rather vague concept of competition, with short-period diminishing returns' (Robinson, 1965a, p. 97). Keynes was largely influenced by Marshall and developed his theory by referring to Marshall's work and to the Marshallian tradition prevailing in Cambridge at that time. Marshall himself, who never used the term 'perfect competition' but preferred 'free competition', left the concept vaguely defined (Marshall, 1920, pp. 1–11).[5]

In Keynes's notion of perfect competition, there is no implication of perfect foresight, since uncertainty is a pervasive element in his analytical framework. His notion, therefore, is different from the concept adopted by Knight, for example, who stressed that perfect competition also implies perfect knowledge and, hence, absence of uncertainty (Knight, 1921, p. 77).[6]

Here, therefore, the term perfect competition is interpreted in the sense just outlined above, which, moreover, was adopted by economists very close to Keynes. In 1929, Kahn defined perfect competition as a situation in which there is a large number of separate firms; each firm is relatively small with respect to the whole market; there is no agreement among firms; and price differences for the same good do not persist for an appreciable period of time (Kahn, 1989, pp. 12–3). Also Joan Robinson's definition of perfect competition is compatible with Keynes's world: perfect competition is a situation in which every single firm is too small to affect the price of its output by changing its level of production.[7]

It was only in 1939 that Keynes partly changed his position concerning market forms. In 1938–39, Keynes's analysis of the behaviour of real wages was questioned. Dunlop (1938), Tarshis (1939) and Kalecki (1938) observed that real wages do not behave in the way predicted by Keynes. They provided alternative explanations of the distributive shares which were based on the hypothesis of short-period constant returns and the introduction of some form of imperfect competition. While remaining convinced that the hypothesis of short-term decreasing returns was reasonable, Keynes (1939) accepted the idea that it was sensible to incorporate some form of imperfect competition.

5.3   KEYNES'S MICROFOUNDATIONS

Let us now consider the behaviour of the individual firm and the shape of its cost curve in the short period. Marshall's influence is crucial in this case as well.[8] In Marshallian economics, in the short period the firm seeks to maximize its profit by pushing production up to the level at which the marginal cost equals the price; the marginal cost curve is increasing over the relevant range; and the price is independent of the volume of output of any single firm. What determines the firm's level of output is the expected price.[9]

These were also Keynes's microfoundations, which were clearly expressed in his draft of *The General Theory*:

> Each firm calculates the prospective selling price of its output and its variable cost in respect of output on various possible scales of production. Its variable cost per unit is not, as a rule, constant for volumes of output but increases as output increases. Output is then pushed to the point at which the prospective selling price no longer exceeds the marginal variable cost. In this way, the volume of output, and hence the volume of employment, is determined. (Keynes, 1979, p. 98)

The demand for labour by the firm, in turn, is increasing in the level of production and, therefore, it is an increasing function of the expected price:

$$L_i = f(p_i^e) \tag{5.1}$$

$$dL_i/dp_i^e > 0$$

(L_i is the level of employment in the *i–th* firm and p_i^e is its expected price).

Once it has been made clear how each single firm, in each production period, determines its level of output and employment, the same analytical reasoning may be applied to the aggregate macro level.[10] If we consider a two-industry economy, in which the first industry produces investment goods and the second consumer goods, and we assume, for simplicity, that each firm in each industry has an increasing supply curve with the same elasticity, we have

$$X_{i,1} = f(p^e_{i,1}) \text{ with } dX_{i,1}/dp^e_{i,1} > 0 \ (i = 1, 2, \dots n) \tag{5.2}$$

$$X_{j,2} = g(p^e_{j,2}) \text{ with } dX_{j,2}/dp^e_{j,2} > 0 \ (j = 1, 2, \dots m)$$

where $X_{i,1}$ is the output of investment goods in the *i–th* firm of the first industry; $X_{j,2}$ is the output of consumer goods in the *j–th* firm of the second industry; $p^e_{i,1}$ is the expected price by the *i–th* firm in the first industry; $p^e_{j,2}$ is the expected price by the *j–th* firm in the second industry. [11]

Given the state of expectations in each firm and each firm's supply curve, both the total output and the aggregate level of employment are determined.

$$L_{i,1} = \psi(X_{i,1}) \ (i = 1, 2, \dots n)$$

$$L_{j,2} = \gamma(X_{j,2}) \ (j = 1, 2, \dots m)$$

$L_{i,1}$ is the level of employment in the *i–th* firm in the first sector and $L_{j,2}$ is the level of employment in the *j–th* firm in the second sector, so that the aggregate level of employment is

$$L = \sum_{i=1}^{n} L_{i,1} + \sum_{j=1}^{m} L_{j,2} \tag{5.3}$$

The expectations of all firms together determine the aggregate levels of output and employment in each current period. Given the shape of individual short-period cost curves and the maximizing behaviour of firms, there is no reason why the economy as a whole should, in any current period, generate full employment. The levels of output and employment that result from firms' decisions may be anywhere, with full employment being the upper constraint.

So far, it has been assumed that firms' expectations turn out to be correct. They may, of course, be wrong, but allowing for this implies no substantial changes. First of all, the possible disappointment of firms' expectations cannot affect the levels of production and employment within any given current period. Equality between the marginal cost and the expected price maximizes the firm's *expected* profit. Its *actual* profit depends on the price actually fetched by the commodities produced when they face the demand for them in the market, which may well differ from the expected price. The actual results of the firm's decisions, therefore, may imply a lower than expected profit or even a loss. This possibility, however, cannot prevent entrepreneurs from making decisions on the basis of their expectations. Entrepreneurs make decisions in an environment characterized by uncertainty and by the fact that production takes time, so that the results of decisions made in the present will be known only in the future.

The disappointment of expectations cannot affect the level of production and employment *within* the current period. Once the commodities produced confront the actual demand for them, the firm has already produced them and has already given rise to the level of employment corresponding to that volume of production. If the expectations prove to have been mistaken, it is impossible to change decisions made in the past. The disappointment of expectations can only affect production and employment in subsequent periods.[12]

The actual market prices, different from the expected prices, will presumably induce entrepreneurs to change their expectations and make their decisions, in the next period(s), accordingly. Again, however, there is no reason why the new set of expectations need lead the economy to full employment. In general, some firms will have been too optimistic in their expectations and will make losses rather than profits; while others will earn even higher profits than they expected because they will have been too pessimistic. As a consequence, the former will tend to contract production and employment, the latter to increase them.[13]

The resulting new level of employment may rise or decline. Keynes, however, focused on cases in which the aggregate level of employment remains unchanged with respect to the previous period. This point is of interest, because Keynes based on it his criticism of the neoclassical argument for full employment. The success or failure of some firms will not affect the aggregate level of employment in the following periods, provided that the supply curves of all firms have the same degree of elasticity and, more important, that aggregate expenditure remains equal to aggregate costs:

> If over any period the aggregate expenditure is approximately equal to the costs which have been incurred on output which has been finished during that period ... [and] assuming the firms to be similar in their response to a given expectation of gain or loss ... there will be no tendency ... for the aggregate of employment to change. For when one firm is reducing employment because of its poor prospects, some other firm will be increasing employment to an equal extent because of its good prospects due to its success in attracting to itself the expenditure which the first firm is failing to attract. (Keynes, 1979, p. 90)

If, for whatever reason, the level of aggregate demand does not change from one period to the next, there is no possibility of change in the aggregate level of employment. Thus, full employment would not be achieved if aggregate demand and supply happen to coincide at a level of production and employment which is below full employment.

5.4 KEYNES'S CRITICISM OF NEOCLASSICAL ECONOMICS: UNDEREMPLOYMENT EQUILIBRIA

In the 1933 draft of *The General Theory*, Keynes illustrated the conditions that must obtain if aggregate demand and aggregate supply are to be equal (Keynes, 1979, pp. 92–4). He adopted the following definitions and symbols, all of which refer to the current unit of time:

- X'_1 is the increase in the cost of unfinished goods in the hands of firms as a whole;
- X_1 is the cost of firms' finished output;
- $X_1 + X'_1$ is the firms' current cost of production;
- X_2 is the sale-proceeds of output, whose cost is X_1.

An inequality between X_2 and X_1 may stem from either of two causes. First, X'_1 may not be zero. If $X'_1 \neq 0$ (that is firms' working capital is changing), total income is given by $X_1 + X'_1$, while the current supply of firms' finished output is X_2, so that we have an inequality even on the hypothesis that all current income is spent on current production. Second, all incomes may not be spent on current production, that is we allow for the possibility of lending and hoarding. Now the income can be used in the following ways:

- To buy finished goods, X_2.
- Hoarded in cash, H.
- Lent to firms to finance an increase in their working capital or to compensate their losses, Λ.
- To purchase an asset from a bank or pay off a debt to a bank; $-M_1$ is the net amount of purchases and payments of debts.

Therefore we have

$$X_1 + X'_1 = X_2 + H + \Lambda - M_1 \tag{5.4}$$

from which it follows, of course, that $X_1 = X_2$ if

$$H + \Lambda = X'_1 + M_1 \tag{5.5}$$

This condition is satisfied if any increase in hoarding is offset by an equivalent increase in banks' purchases of assets (that is $H = M_1$), and if the loans to firms are equal to the increase in firms' working capital $\Lambda = X_1'$). Any divergence between $(H + \Lambda)$ and $(X_1' + M_1)$ corresponds to a divergence between the level of effective demand, in the current period, and the level of aggregate supply. In so far as money keeps more readily than any other commodity, the tendency for demand to fall short of supply, $(H + \Lambda) > (X_1' + M_1)$, is stronger than the tendency for demand to equal or exceed supply.

If aggregate demand falls short of aggregate supply – that is, equation (5.5) above does not hold good – a general overproduction crisis could take place. The commodities produced cannot all be sold at those expected prices that induced firms to produce them. Developing the analysis along these lines would lead to an analysis of crises not very different from Marx's. This, however, was not Keynes's main concern. He aimed to demonstrate that even if (5.5) holds good, the economy may still experience an underemployment level of activity that represents a stable equilibrium position. In other words, he aimed to demonstrate that aggregate demand, though equal to aggregate supply, is not necessarily at a level that implies full employment.

The analytical framework that has been used so far is a 'pure' Marshallian setting, but it nevertheless does not ensure that full employment will be achieved. To get this result, Keynes argued, neoclassical economics had to introduce two special qualifications (or assumptions):

> if ... some mechanism is introduced into an entrepreneur economy so as to insure (1) that the aggregate expenditure and aggregate costs always keep step and change by equal amounts and (2) that chance causes operating to keep employment below full employment are counteracted, then our entrepreneur economy will behave in the same way as a co-operative economy, and will therefore satisfy the conditions laid down by our definition for a neutral economy. (Keynes, 1979, p. 91)

That aggregate expenditure and costs keep step, *per* se, does not ensure full employment. Equality between aggregate demand and aggregate supply may be found at any level of production and employment. To guarantee full employment, it is necessary to postulate the existence of an automatic mechanism that pushes the economy to its true equilibrium. Such a mechanism is the possibility for the wage rate to variate, namely to be a decreasing function of the unemployment rate. In so far as there is unemployment, the wage rate declines; firms are induced to employ more labour and to produce more. The additional production can be sold, because it is assumed that aggregate demand and aggregate supply keep step; the increase in production will stop when full employment is reached, just as in a co-operative economy.[14]

Keynes questioned the argumentation outlined above. In the 1933 draft, he expounded his criticism as follows. Suppose that firms as a whole – possibly after a process of trial and error – realize that aggregate demand cannot rise to the level that would ensure full employment, and that balance between demand and supply can be achieved only at a level lower than full employment. This necessarily affects the firms' willingness to employ additional factors of production.

> This possibility introduces a new cause affecting the volume of employment of which the classical theory has taken no account; and the situation is characterized by the following features.
> I. The firms, taken as a whole, cannot protect themselves from loss by the expedient of producing more of this and less of that, which is appropriate when effective demand is changing in direction but not in amount. It may, therefore, be to their advantage to reduce employment in the aggregate.
> II. The firms, taken as a whole, cannot protect themselves from loss by making revised (i.e. more favourable) money bargains with the factors of production. ... So long as their outgoings ... are not returning to the firms in full, there is no conceivable money bargaining between the firms and their factors of production which will protect them, taken as a whole, from loss. (Keynes, 1979, pp. 97–8)

Revised money bargains would help only if it were assumed that, in any case, the whole income of the factors of production is necessarily spent; that is, it returns to firms 'in full'. If this assumption is removed, no conceivable money bargaining can protect the firms from loss.

The crux of Keynes's argument is simple: full employment cannot be achieved thanks to changes in the wage rate if aggregate demand does not rise to the required extent. If, despite the decline in the wage rate, aggregate demand does not increase with respect to its initial underemployment level, there is no way to have full employment.

We can express this point by using the concepts and terminology of *The General Theory*. Let us consider the usual Keynesian model of a two-sector economy, where the rate of interest is determined by the demand for and the (exogenously given) supply of money.[15] Aggregate demand, in each current period, is

$$D = C + I$$

C, the demand for consumption goods, depends on the level of production and the propensity to consume. I, the demand for investment goods, depends on the marginal efficiency of capital, e, and the rate of interest, i.

The key variable is investment. Given the rate of interest, firms will expand their investment to the point at which the marginal efficiency of each type of capital is equal to the rate of interest. The marginal efficiency of each type of capital, in turn, is a decreasing function of the amount of it demanded,[16] so that the marginal efficiency at the aggregate level is also a decreasing function of the level of aggregate investment. In the economy as a whole, investment will be pushed to the point at which the marginal efficiency of capital is equal to the market rate of interest.

Therefore, given the rate of interest, the actual demand for investment goods is determined. On the other hand, the actual demand for consumption goods is determined by the short-term expectations of firms. Such expectations determine the level of income and, hence, the level of demand for consumption goods. The aggregate equilibrium condition is

$$Y = C(Y) + I(e, i) \tag{5.6}$$

If firms' short-term expectations are correct, the economy is in equilibrium. Aggregate supply equals aggregate demand.

There is no necessary reason, however, why such an equilibrium position should imply the full employment of capacity and labour. At the given rate of interest, and with the given investment demand schedule, the actual level of investment may well be less than is required for full employment and, for Keynes, there are no forces at work to push the economy towards full employment.

But expectations may be wrong. Any disappointment of firms' expectations will cause adjustment in the subsequent period(s). Firms will increase or decrease output (and employment) according to the direction in which expectations were disappointed. This, however, does not affect the equilibrium position in equation (5.6), provided that I does not change. The demand for consumption goods, given the propensity to consume, depends on the level of production and will therefore vary with Y. If changes in Y do not affect I (that is if changes in Y do not imply changes in the rate of interest and in long-term expectations), the aggregate equilibrium condition is unaffected, and the economy will converge to such a position through changes in the level of production (and employment). I being fixed, there is only one value of Y which fulfils equation (5.6).

On the other hand, even if one allows for the possibility that the disappointment of short-term expectations may affect I (the marginal efficiency of capital and/or the rate of interest), there is no reason why the new level of I should be that associated with full employment. If I changes, so does the equilibrium position for the economy; the economy will converge to this new position, but again, the position does not necessarily ensure full employment.

Thus, in the Keynesian framework, the fulfilment or the disappointment of the short-term expectations is basically irrelevant to the determination of the level of employment. Given the characteristics of the forces that determine the rate of interest and the tendency of the marginal efficiency of capital to fall as investment increases, there is no necessary reason why the equilibrium position to which the economy tends should imply the full employment of all factors of production and, in particular, of labour.[17]

The analysis above has been carried out by assuming that the money wage rate is fixed, a hypothesis that Keynes maintained for most of *The General Theory*; but in Chapter 21 he lifted the hypothesis and analyzed the effects on output and employment of a change in the wage rate. Keynes did not deny that changes in money wages can affect the aggregate level of employment; namely that a decrease in money wages can have a positive effect on employment, but his position was different from the classical one: 'A reduction in money-wages is quite capable in certain circumstances of affording a stimulus to output, as the classical theory supposes. My difference from this theory is primarily a difference of analysis' (Keynes, 1936, p. 257).

In Keynes's analytical approach, a change in wages is able to affect the level of employment if it affects either the community's propensity to consume, the marginal efficiency of capital, or the rate of interest. If these variables – which together determine aggregate output and employment – are left untouched by a change in wages, entrepreneurs would behave irrationally by increasing employment when the money wage rate decreases (Keynes, 1936, pp. 260–1).[18]

A reduction in the money wage rate, for Keynes, is likely to reduce the community's marginal propensity to consume and, hence, to have a negative effect on employment. He argued that the reduction in wages determines a redistribution of income in favour of the sections of society with a lower marginal propensity to consume (Keynes, 1936, p. 262). As to the effects of a wage reduction on the marginal efficiency of capital, Keynes distinguished between two cases: when the reduction in the money wage rate is expected to be a reduction with respect to future money wages; and when the current reduction in the money wage rate leads to expectations of further reductions in the future. In the first case, the decline in wages raises the marginal efficiency of capital and has a positive effect on investment; in the second case, the effect is negative (Keynes, 1936, p. 263). If wages are expected to rise again in the future, firms are more willing to invest now in order to benefit from the current lower costs; if wages are expected to decrease further, firms are induced to postpone investment in order to benefit from future lower costs.

5.5 A SIMPLE KEYNESIAN MODEL OF UNDEREMPLOYMENT EQUILIBRIUM

It is now possible to summarize the analysis carried out above by using a simple model, which allows us to present in a clear way some of Keynes's main results: the crucial role of investment decisions in the determination of the macroeconomic equilibrium and the inability for the economy to achieve full employment through wage variations.[19]

Let us assume a two-industry economy in which a consumer good, C, and an investment good, I, are produced by n and m firms respectively. Firms in both industries produce under decreasing returns and maximize expected profits by pushing production to the point at which marginal cost equals expected price, taken as independent of the output of each individual firm. The total demand for the investment good is obtained by aggregating the $(n + m)$ firms' demand for I, derived from Keynes's marginal efficiency of capital schedule; total demand for C is derived by aggregating the demands of individuals.

5.5.1   Industry Supply and Demand Functions

The firms' production decisions depend on costs and expected prices. Costs, in turn, depend on the (given) technology, the produced quantity, and wages. Price expectations (short-term expectations) are taken as exogenously given.[20] p_h^e is the price expected by the h–th firm producing the consumer good C. The money wage rate (w) is taken as given and independent of variations in the level of employment offered by the firm.

The firm's output is obtained by solving:

$$\max\ (\pi_h) = p_h^e C_h - q_h\ (C_h, w)$$

$$(h = 1, 2 \ ... \ n)$$

where $q_h(C_h, w)$ denotes the h–th firm's total cost function. Therefore, the h–th firm's supply curve can be written as

$$C_{Sh} = f_h(p_h^e, w) \tag{5.7}$$

$$(h = 1, 2, \ ... \ n)$$

If, for simplicity, it is assumed that firms have uniform price expectations, that is $p_1^e = p_2^e = \ ... \ = p_n^e = p^e$, and that the wage is uniform throughout the economy, the aggregate supply function of C can be written as

$$C_S = F(p^e, w) \tag{5.8}$$

$$\partial C_S / \partial p^e > 0,\ \partial C_S / \partial w < 0$$

The individual supply functions and the total supply function of the capital good I are obtained in the same way, so that

$$I_S = G(r^e, w) \tag{5.9}$$

$$\partial I_S / \partial r^e > 0, \; \partial I_S / \partial w < 0$$

where r^e is the expected price of the capital good.

As to the demand functions, the demand for the capital good by the j–th firm depends on the current price of the capital good (r), the real interest rate (i), taken as given and constant,[21] and the firm's long-term expectations (E_j):

$$I_{Dj} = h_j(r, i, E_j)$$

$$(j = 1, 2, \dots n + m)$$

If it is assumed that $E_1 = E_2 = \dots = E_{n+m} = E$ (firms have uniform long-term expectations), the total demand for the capital good can be written as

$$I_D = H(r, i, E) \tag{5.10}$$

$$\partial I_D / \partial r < 0, \; \partial I_D / \partial i < 0, \; \partial I_D / \partial E > 0$$

As to the demand function for C, here it is sufficient to hypothesize that income is not entirely spent on the consumer good, so that if c is the given overall marginal propensity to consume, and $rI_S + pC_S$ is total nominal income, the total demand function for C is

$$C_D = c[(rI_S/p) + C_S] = M(c, p, r, p^e, r^e, w) \tag{5.11}$$

where p is the current price of the consumer good.

Employment is an increasing function of output in both industries. Therefore,

$$L_C = L_C(C_S) \tag{5.12}$$

$$L_I = L_I(I_S)$$

with $\partial L_C/\partial C_S > 0$, $\partial^2 L_C/\partial C_S^2 > 0$ and $\partial L_I/\partial I_S > 0$, $\partial^2 L_I/\partial I_S^2 > 0$, since decreasing returns are assumed in both industries.

Total employment is

$$L = L(C_S, I_S) \tag{5.13}$$

5.5.2   The Equilibrium Conditions

For equilibrium to obtain, demand and supply must be equal in both industries:

$$C_S = C_D$$

$$I_S = I_D$$

In equilibrium $p^e = p$ and $r^e = r$. From (5.8), (5.9), (5.10) and (5.11) we thus obtain

$$F(p, w) = M(c, p, r, w) \tag{5.14}$$

$$G(r, w) = H(r, i, E) \tag{5.15}$$

(5.14) and (5.15) together yield the equilibrium prices for C and I.

From inspection of (5.14) and (5.15), it emerges that r, the price of the capital good is independent of p, the price of the consumer good; p, on the contrary, depends on r. Once r is determined, the equilibrium quantity of I is determined as well. The equilibrium price and output of the capital-goods industry are independent of the consumer-goods industry, whereas the reverse does not hold: both the equilibrium price and the quantity in the consumer-goods industry depend on r and I. More precisely, we have

$$r^* = \varphi\,(w, i, E) \tag{5.16}$$

$$p^* = \tau\,(r^*, w, i, E) \tag{5.17}$$

where r^* and p^* denote the equilibrium values of the price of the capital good and the consumer good respectively.

It is interesting to look at how p^* changes in response to changes in r^*. It is easy to demonstrate[22] that at $r = r^*$ and $p = p^*$ it is

$$\partial p/\partial r > 0 \tag{5.18}$$

An increase in the equilibrium price of the capital good is associated with an increase in the equilibrium price of the consumer good.

As to employment, from (5.12) and (5.13), and by denoting the equilibrium outputs in the two industries by C^* and I^*, we obtain

$$L^* = L(C^*, I^*) = L_C\,(C^*) + L_I\,(I^*) \tag{5.19}$$

where L^* is total employment in equilibrium, which is not necessarily equal to full employment.

5.5.3 Changes in Money Wages

The hypothesis of a fixed money wage rate is now removed in order to see how wage flexibility affects the equilibrium level of output and employment. The model does not establish a precise relationship between the money wage rate and the rate of unemployment. The money wage rate is made to change exogenously in order to inspect the effects on the equilibrium levels of output and employment.

As to the effects of a change in the money wage rate on the equilibrium prices of the capital good and the consumer good, it is easy to demonstrate[23] that, at $r = r^*$ and $p = p^*$, it is

$$\partial r/\partial w > 0 \qquad\qquad (5.20)$$

$$\partial p/\partial w > 0$$

A variation in the money wage rate determines a change in the same direction of both equilibrium prices.

In order to study the effects of a change in wages on output and employment, it is sufficient to look at the signs of the derivatives $\partial I/\partial w$, $\partial/\partial w\,(rI)$ and $\partial C/\partial w$ of the three functions at their equilibrium points, that is the derivatives with respect to w of the physical output of the capital good, the value of the output of the capital good, and the physical output of the consumer good respectively.[24] A positive effect of a decrease in the money wage rate on output, and hence on employment, is denoted by negative derivatives.

The sign of $\partial I/\partial w$ at the equilibrium point $r = r^*$, is determined from (5.15). It is

$$\partial G/\partial w = \partial H/\partial w$$

that is,

$$\partial G/\partial w + \partial G/\partial r\ \partial r/\partial w = \partial H/\partial r\ \partial r/\partial w$$

Since

$$\partial H/\partial r < 0 \text{ and } \partial r/\partial w > 0$$

it necessarily is

$$\partial G / \partial w < 0$$

But, at $r = r^*$,

$$G(r^*, w) = I^*$$

so that

$$\partial I^* / \partial w < 0 \qquad\qquad (5.21)$$

A decrease in money wages is unambiguously associated with an increase in the equilibrium output of the capital good.

However, the effect of the same decrease in money wages on the *value* of the equilibrium output is ambiguous. For a decrease in the money wage rate to have a positive effect on the equilibrium value of the capital-good output, it must be

$$\partial / \partial w \ (rI) = (\partial r / \partial w)I + r(\partial I / \partial w) < 0$$

After rearrangement, we obtain that the condition above is fulfilled if (at $r = r^*$ and $I = I^*$) it is

$$\varepsilon_{I,w} > \varepsilon_{r,w} \qquad\qquad (5.22)$$

where $\varepsilon_{I,w}$ and $\varepsilon_{r,w}$ respectively denote the elasticity of the capital-good output and the elasticity of the capital-good price to the money wage rate.

A decrease in the money wage rate and, hence, in costs causes a fall in the equilibrium price of the capital good; in order to have an increase in the equilibrium value of the output, it is necessary that the physical production grows more than proportionally to the fall in price.

As to the consumer-goods industry, we can see from (5.11) above that the equilibrium output of the consumer good is positively affected by a decrease in w if, at $p = p^*$, it is

$$p[(\partial r / \partial w)I + (\partial I / \partial w)r] - rI \ (\partial p / \partial w) < 0$$

After rearrangement, it can be shown that the condition above is satisfied if

$$\varepsilon_{I,w} > \varepsilon_{r,w} - \varepsilon_{p,w} \qquad\qquad (5.23)$$

$\varepsilon_{I,w}$ and $\varepsilon_{r,w}$ are the same as in (5.22) and $\varepsilon_{p,w}$ denotes the elasticity of the consumer-good price to w.

Condition (5.23) can be contrasted with condition (5.22): the condition for a positive increase in the equilibrium output of the consumer good is less restrictive than the one for the capital good. In fact, it is sufficient to have an elasticity of I to w whose absolute value is larger than $(\varepsilon_{r,w} - \varepsilon_{p,w}) < \varepsilon_{r,w}$. A lower elasticity of I to w is required because a decrease in wages also causes a decrease in p and this can compensate for a possible negative effect on rI.

Suppose, for example, that $\varepsilon_{I,w} < \varepsilon_{r,w}$ so that when wages fall the value of the equilibrium output of the capital-goods industry decreases and the monetary value of its demand for the consumer-good, $c(r^*I^*)$, decreases as well. This, however, is not sufficient to cause a fall in the demand for the consumer-goods in *real* terms. In fact, the decrease in the equilibrium price of the consumer-good can be such as to determine an increase in the *real* purchasing power of the industry I. In other words, the decrease in wages has both an *income* and a *price effect* on the demand for the consumer-good by the capital-goods industry. The *price effect* can be strong enough to compensate for a possible negative *income effect*.

On the other hand, it may well be that $\varepsilon_{I,w} < \varepsilon_{r,w} - \varepsilon_{p,w}$ and, in such a case, there would be a decrease in output and employment of the consumer-good industry. The decrease in employment in the consumer-good industry can be larger than the increase in the capital-good industry, so that a decline in the aggregate level of employment occurs as a consequence of a reduction in the money wage rate.

In general, in order that a reduction in the money wage rate gives rise to an increase in aggregate employment, it must be

$$\partial/\partial w \; [L_C(C) + L_I(I)] < 0$$

which is fulfilled if

$$L_C \varepsilon_{L_C,C} \, \varepsilon_{C,w} + L_I \varepsilon_{L_I,I} \, \varepsilon_{I,w} < 0 \tag{5.24}$$

($\varepsilon_{L_C,C}$ is the elasticity of employment with respect to output in the consumer-good industry; $\varepsilon_{L_I,I}$ is the elasticity of employment with respect to output in the capital-good industry). The direction of the change in aggregate employment depends on the elasticity of labour to changes in output (caused by a change in wages) in the two industries and on the distribution of labour between the two industries.

The results achieved so far show that a change in wages can affect employment through its effect on investment. If there were no changes in I^* or r^*I^* there would be no changes in the aggregate levels of output and employment. In the model, Keynes's view that changes in the money wage rate can produce effects on aggregate employment to the extent that the three crucial variables are affected (the overall propensity to consume, the marginal efficiency of capital and the rate of interest) is confirmed though in a specific form: changes in wages can only affect the marginal efficiency of capital through changes in the price of the capital-good because long-term expectations, the real rate of interest, and the marginal propensity to consume are all taken as exogenously given.

5.5.4   Long-term Expectations as a Function of Changes in Wages

Now we remove the hypothesis of exogenous long-term expectations, which become a function of changes in the money wage rate. Following Keynes, we consider both the case in which a decrease in wages positively affects expectations and the opposite case.

A reduction in wages positively affects long-term expectations
In this case it is

$$\partial E/\partial w < 0$$

and it is easy to see that there is no significant change with respect to the results of the previous section. Now the equality $\partial G/\partial w = \partial H/\partial w$ at $r = r^*$ becomes

$$(\partial G/\partial w) + (\partial G/\partial r)(\partial r/\partial w) = (\partial H/\partial r)(\partial r/\partial w) + (\partial H/\partial E)(\partial E/\partial w)$$

$\partial H/\partial r < 0$, $\partial r/\partial w > 0$, $\partial H/\partial E$ and, by hypothesis, $\partial E/\partial w < 0$, so that it necessarily is

$$\partial G/\partial w < 0$$

that is

$$\partial I^*/\partial w < 0$$

The signs of the two other derivatives depend on the same conditions as in (5.22) and (5.23).

A reduction in wages negatively affects long term-expectations
Now it is

$$\partial E/\partial w > 0$$

a decrease in wages gives rise to more pessimistic long-term expectations.

In order that $\partial I^*/\partial w < 0$ it must be

$$(\partial H/\partial r)(\partial r/\partial w) + (\partial H/\partial E)(\partial E/\partial w) < 0$$

but now $\partial E/\partial w > 0$. After rearrangement, it can be shown that the inequality above is fulfilled if

$$\varepsilon_{H,E}\,\varepsilon_{E,w} < \varepsilon_{H,r}\varepsilon_{r,w} \tag{5.25}$$

where the left-hand side of the inequality denotes the elasticity of the demand for the capital good to a change in expectations due to a change in w, while the right-hand side denotes the elasticity of the demand for the capital good to a change in its price due to a change in w.

In order that a fall in money wages produce an increase in the output of the capital good, the positive effect of a decrease in wages and prices on the demand for the capital good must be stronger than the negative effect due to the worsening of expectations.

As to the effect of the decrease in wages on the value of the output of the capital good, if (5.25) is fulfilled then the same results of the previous section hold. If (5.25) is not fulfilled, it is evident that the value of the output necessarily decreases: both the physical production and the price of the capital good decrease as a consequence of the decrease in wages.

Finally, looking at the effect of a decrease in money wages on the output of the consumer good, we have to consider two different cases. First, if (5.25) above is fulfilled, the output of the consumer good increases with a fall in wages if the same condition (5.23) above is satisfied. If, instead, (5.25) is not fulfilled, the condition (5.23) turns to

$$\varepsilon_{p,w} > \varepsilon_{r,w} + \varepsilon_{I,w} \tag{5.26}$$

because $\partial I^*/\partial w > 0$.

In order that the consumer-good output increases, the decrease in the equilibrium price of the consumer good must be such as to more than offset the decrease in the value of the output of the capital good due to the decrease in r^* and I^*. In such a way the real purchasing power of the capital-goods industry increases.

5.5.5 Changes in the Rate of Interest

Throughout the model, the real interest rate, i, has been taken as given. This is of course a simplification, however, it does not affect our results significantly. Below, an intuitive explanation of this is given.

When, as a consequence of a reduction of the wage rate, prices in both sectors decline, the real interest rate increases and this produces a negative effect on the demand for investment goods. On the other hand, the decline in prices, if associated with a decline in the value of total output, brings about a decrease in the nominal interest rate as the demand for money decreases. Consequently, the real rate of interest could increase less, remain unchanged or even decrease with obviously different effects on the demand for investment goods.

If the real interest rate remains constant, the results of the model would be, of course, totally unaffected. If the real interest rate increases, the conditions for an increase in employment following a decrease in the wage rate would become more restrictive than those determined above. These conditions would be less restrictive, however, if the real interest rate decreases as a result of the decrease in the nominal interest rate. Thus, in conclusion, to assume a given and constant real interest rate to make the model simpler seems a fair hypothesis.

5.6 CONCLUSION

It is now quite clear how much Marx's and Keynes's analytical results differ, and why. In a Marxian analytical framework firms produce and invest at the highest possible rates, unless expected prices fall below certain crucial values. This behaviour by capitalist firms follows from Marx's assumptions concerning the market form (competition), short-period cost curves (flat to capacity) and investment (the expected rate of profit is either independent, or an increasing function of the level of investment). Within Marx's original framework, the economy can experience only temporary 'underemployment levels of activity' during, and as a consequence of, a general overproduction crisis.

Keynes, on the other hand, could achieve his results because he based his analysis on different microfoundations. In so far as firms (producing in a competitive market) have increasing short-period cost curves, and the expected returns to investment are a decreasing function of its level, there is no reason why the economy as a whole should experience full employment of labour and full use of its existing capacity, even though no market perturbations occur. A level of aggregate demand below the full-employment level, within this context, does not necessarily imply general overproduction and may well represent a stable equilibrium position for the economy as a whole. The model of section 5.5 determines an aggregate equilibrium in which all firms maximize profits and the level of employment does not necessarily coincide with full employment. Even though unemployment might cause the money wage rate to fall, the resulting new equilibrium would imply a higher level of employment only under special conditions.

NOTES

1. In *The General Theory* (Keynes, 1936, p. 314–6), crises are essentially explained by a collapse in the inducement to invest rather than by an increase in the interest rate: 'I suggest that a more typical, and often the predominant, explanation of the crisis is, not primarily a rise in the rate of interest, but a sudden collapse in the marginal efficiency of capital. ... Moreover, the dismay and uncertainty as to the future which accompanies a collapse in the marginal efficiency of capital naturally precipitates a sharp increase in liquidity-preference – and hence a rise in the rate of interest.'

2. Or, more generally, of the trade cycle. Keynes (1936, p. 313) held that he was able to explain the cycle, in that he had given a general explanation of the factors and forces which determine employment at any time: 'since we claim to have shown ... what determines the volume of employment at any time, it follows, if we are right, that our theory must be capable of explaining the phenomena of the Trade Cycle.'

3. On this, see, for example, Kregel (1976, p. 218n) and Harcourt (1992). By taking the degree of competition as given, Keynes also revealed an unwillingness to enter the debate on market forms that was going on at the time. We shall return to some aspects of this debate later on.

4. ' ... with a given organisation, equipment and technique, real wages and the volume of output (and hence of employment) are uniquely correlated, so that, in general, an increase in employment can only occur to the accompaniment of a decline in the rate of real wages. ... Thus, *if* employment increases, then, in the short period, the reward per unit of labour in terms of wage-goods must, in general, decline and profits increase. This is simply the obverse of the familiar proposition that industry is normally working subject to decreasing returns in the short period during which equipment etc. is assumed to be constant; so that the marginal product in the wage-good industries ... necessarily diminishes as employment is increased' (Keynes, 1936, pp. 17–8). See also Marris (1997), who lists a number of cases in which Keynes implicitly assumes perfect competition.

5. On Marshall's notion of competition, see also Schumpeter (1954, pp. 974–5).

6. The two notions of competition are so different that, by following Chamberlin's suggestion, the kind of market form envisaged by Keynes should be called, more correctly, 'pure competition', a term which denotes only the absence of monopolistic elements in the markets (Chamberlin, 1962, p. 6). Also Schumpeter, who thought that the analysis in *The General Theory* presupposes competition, did not use the term 'perfect competition', but 'pure' or 'free' competition (Schumpeter, 1954, p. 1175).

7. 'By perfect competition I propose to mean a state of affairs in which the demand for the output of an individual seller is perfectly elastic' (Robinson, 1934, p. 1). Chick (1992), however, holds that Keynes's notion of competition does not even imply the assumption of small firms being price-takers. Sylos Labini (1988) has argued that Keynes's price theory in Chapter 21 of *The General Theory* is compatible with the full cost principle.

8. On the Marshallian derivation of Keynes's microfoundations, see Asimakopulos (1982, 1984) and Chick (1983, pp. 82–101).

9. 'As the expectations of price improve, an increased part of the production will yield a considerable surplus above prime costs, and the margin of production will be pushed outwards. ... In every case the price is that the expectation of which is sufficient and only just sufficient to make it worth while for people to set themselves to produce that aggregate amount; in every case the cost of production is marginal, that is, it is the cost of production of those goods which are on the margin of not being produced at all, and which would not be produced if the price to be got for them were expected to be lower.' (Marshall, 1920, pp. 373–4). For more details, and the distinction between the short period and long period, see Marshall (1920, pp. 363–80).

10. 'The *aggregate* volume of employment is determined in a similar way, provided that we allow for the fact that the decisions of each firm are influenced by the expected results of the decisions of other firms, so that a set of simultaneous equations has to be satisfied. If aggregate expenditure is kept constant relatively to aggregate variable cost, aggregate employment will

also be constant, except in so far as expenditure is shifted from firms having one type of supply function to firms subject to more or less elastic conditions of supply' (Keynes, 1979, pp. 98–9).

11. $p_{i,1}^e$ is determined by the expectations of the *i–th* firm in the first industry about the demand for investment goods by entrepreneurs in both industries, while $p_{j,2}^e$ is determined by the expectations of the *j–th* firm in the second industry about the demand for consumer goods by workers and entrepreneurs in both industries.

12. Real historical time, in which production actually takes place, is as it were a 'one-way road'. Keynes's analysis referred to historical, not to logical, time. On the distinction between the two concepts of time, see for example Robinson (1979) and Chick (1978).

13. '[The] entrepreneur firm is pitting its wits against the others' to make good bargains with the capitalists and the workers and to anticipate correctly the strength of demand for different classes of finished goods. The classical theory of the individual firm is concerned with the analysis of its behaviour under these influences. By good fortune or good management some firms will be more successful than others and will make profits over and above the rents and variable costs which they have incurred; whilst others will make losses. The former will tend to expand its capital equipment, the latter to contract. By this means there will be a tendency for the survival of the most efficient' (Keynes, 1979, p. 99). Here Keynes assumes that the disappointment of short-term expectations causes a change in long-term expectations, in that he considers firms increasing or contracting their capital equipment. It is not necessary, however, to assume that the long-term expectations are affected.

14. Firms' expectations are assumed to be correct, as they produce just as much as is demanded in any current period; but, from one period to the other, they are induced to change their expectations by changes in the wage rate. The possibility that expectations may be wrong, however, does not affect the result. In this case, too, the adjustment in firms' expectations occurs and the process which brings the economy to full employment begins.

15. The aggregate values are measured in wage-units.

16. The marginal efficiency of a capital good decreases, 'partly because the prospective yield will fall as the supply of that type of capital is increased, and partly because, as a rule, pressure on the facilities for producing that type of capital will cause its supply price to increase; the second of these factors being usually the more important in producing equilibrium in the short run, but the longer the period in view, the more does the first factor take its place. Thus for each type of capital we can build up a schedule, showing by how much investment in it will have to increase within the period, in order that its marginal efficiency should fall to any given figure' (Keynes, 1936, p. 136). We return to Keynes's marginal efficiency of capital in the next chapter.

17. In his 1937 lectures, Keynes made this point very clearly: 'I now feel that if I were writing the book again [*The General Theory*] I should begin by setting forth my theory on the assumption that short-period expectations were always fulfilled; and then have a subsequent chapter showing what difference it makes when short-period expectations are disappointed. … Entrepreneurs have to endeavour to forecast demand. They do not, as a rule, make wildly wrong forecasts of the equilibrium position. But, as the matter is very complex, they do not get it just right; and they endeavour to approximate to the true position by a method of trial and error. Contracting where they find that they are overshooting their market, expanding where the opposite occurs. It corresponds precisely to the higgling of the market by means of which buyers and sellers endeavour to discover the true equilibrium position of supply and demand. … The main point is to distinguish the forces determining the position of equilibrium from the technique of trial and error by means of which the entrepreneur discovers where the position is' (Keynes, 1973b, pp. 181–2). See also Kregel (1976) and Harcourt (1981).

18. Keynes's analysis was carried out under the hypothesis of a marginal propensity to consume less than one. If the marginal propensity to consume were equal to one, a decrease in wages would give rise to an increase in employment (Keynes, 1936, p. 261).

19. The model is based on microfoundations similar to those of Casarosa (1981). See also Asimakopulos (1991) and Parrinello (1980).

20. Short-term and long-term expectations are defined as in Keynes (1936, pp. 46–7).

21. For a justification of this assumption see section 5.5 below.
22. For the demonstration see Proposition 1 in Appendix B.
23. See Proposition 2 in Appendix B.
24. The sign of the derivative $\partial/\partial w$ (pC), that is the effect of a change in wages on the *value* of the output of the consumer-goods industry, is not interesting in that, under the hypothesis of $c < 1$, it does not have any implications for real output and employment.

6. A critique of Keynes's microfoundations

6.1 INTRODUCTION

Keynes's microfoundations are relevant to his macroeconomic results. In so far as firms produce at increasing marginal costs and push current production to the level at which the expected price equals the marginal cost, there is no reason why, in any current period, the economy should experience full employment and full use of capacity. In so far as the marginal efficiency of capital is a decreasing function of the level of investment, and the rate of interest depends on the liquidity preference and the supply of money, there is no necessary reason why the economy should find its equilibrium at full employment.

But Keynes's microfoundations are subject to criticisms, both about the hypothesis of short-period decreasing returns and the theory of investment. Once Keynes's assumptions both on short-period returns and the marginal efficiency of capital are changed to incorporate these criticisms, significant analytical difficulties arise. Keynes's macroeconomic results – the existence of underemployment equilibria in particular – are no longer ensured.

This chapter deals with these issues. Section 6.2 looks at Keynes's approach to the problem of short-period returns in a more detailed way than in the previous chapter. Section 6.3 criticizes the hypothesis of short-period decreasing returns. Section 6.4 looks at Keynes's theory of investment, which is criticized in section 6.5. The concluding section 6.6 examines the macroeconomic analytical implications of the criticism of Keynes's microfoundations.

6.2 KEYNES ON SHORT-PERIOD RETURNS

Keynes was always convinced that short-period returns are decreasing and, hence, that the short-period marginal cost curve is U-shaped. In 1939, he wrote:

> Even if one concedes that the course of the short-period marginal cost curve is downwards in its early reaches, Mr Kahn's assumption that it eventually turns

upwards is, on general common-sense grounds, surely beyond reasonable question; and that this happens, moreover, on a part of the curve which is highly relevant for practical purposes. Certainly it would require more convincing evidence than yet exists to persuade me to give up this presumption. (Keynes, 1939, p. 47)

Keynes's statement above is part of his response to some criticisms made by Dunlop (1938) who, on the grounds of empirical evidence, had questioned Keynes's view of the inverse relationship between the money wage rate and the real wage rate, which derives from the hypothesis of short-period decreasing returns. We return to Dunlop's criticism in the next section; we first look at Kahn's views on the problem of returns in the short period, as his analysis was invoked by Keynes to support his own position.[1]

Kahn's analysis of short-period returns was not based on the conventional treatment of the issue. It is therefore legitimate to infer that Keynes's position is also different from the conventional hypothesis of short-period decreasing returns, which is based on the idea that the productivity of the variable factor(s) applied to the given fixed factor(s) is decreasing.

In 1928–29 Kahn wrote a dissertation (for a fellowship at King's College, Cambridge) on the economics of the short period where he questioned the usual assumption of U-shaped cost curves (Kahn, 1989, pp. 45–63). He carried out a detailed analysis of how output is varied by firms in the short period and pointed out that two methods are chosen most often: (i) altering the amount of machinery in use; (ii) altering the number of working days per week or month.

With the first method, and if machines are of uniform efficiency, the unit prime cost curve is continuously decreasing up to full capacity; if machines are of different efficiency, the curve initially decreases, reaches a minimum before full capacity and then starts rising because of the cost increases from using less efficient machines.[2] With the second method, whether firms use uniform or different machines, the unit prime cost curve is flat up to capacity and then becomes vertical. The prime cost curve takes on a reversed-L shape.

Since in both cases the unit prime cost is the same at full-capacity, the first method is the most convenient only when the firm's machinery is not of uniform efficiency and increases in output are realized by using more and more inefficient machines. Kahn, however, held that in many industries firms are characterized by a fairly complete uniformity of machinery, so that the reversed L-shaped cost curve is the most adequate description of the behaviour of their prime costs. The average prime cost is, in general, independent of the level of output and the marginal prime cost is constant and coincident with the average prime cost. When full capacity is reached the cost curve becomes perfectly inelastic.[3]

In both cases, firms vary their output not by changing the number of workers who work on the given equipment but by changing both the number of workers and the amount of equipment in use. If equipment is homogeneous, the degree of its utilization is better varied by changing the length of time during which it is used over the week or month, in other words the optimal combination between factors is maintained by varying the degree of utilization of equipment. If equipment is heterogeneous, the degree of its utilization is better varied by choosing how much of it to use in any single unit of time; in this case, returns are decreasing because different parts of the equipment are of differing efficiency.

In 1929, Kahn did not deal with industry total supply functions, but his analysis leads to the conclusion that, for industries where firms have unit prime cost curves which are flat to capacity, the supply function has the same shape as individual cost curves. On the other hand, for those industries in which firms have U-shaped cost curves, the supply function is upward sloping. On these grounds, since there are industries of both types, the aggregate supply function of the industrial sector as a whole should be increasing as it is the combination of flat and increasing schedules.

It was in his 1931 article on home investment that Kahn turned to deal with the aggregate supply function of consumer goods by looking at the effects of an increase in public spending. In his analysis, for any increase in the demand for consumer goods, it is the shape of their supply curve that determines the extent of the increase in output and price levels. Kahn started by considering the case of a perfectly elastic supply function, which implies no price increase when demand rises; but he eventually assumed an upward sloping, though highly elastic, supply function (Kahn, 1931, p. 186). Since Kahn assumed constant money wages, it follows that an increase in demand brings about an increase in output and prices which is associated with a decrease in the real wage.[4]

Keynes's approach to these issues was significantly influenced by Kahn, as his justification of decreasing returns is based on the heterogeneity of the factors of production.[5] It is in Chapter 11 of *The General Theory* that Keynes expounded his notion of decreasing returns.[6] In his general analysis, Keynes considered a case of non-homogeneous factors of production, whose remunerations do not change all in the same proportion.[7] Moreover, he assumed that effective demand does not change in the same proportion as the quantity of money; the supply of some goods will become inelastic before full employment is reached at the aggregate level; and the wage-unit starts increasing before full employment.

The existence of factors of production of different efficiency does not imply, *per se*, decreasing returns. If factors are compensated proportionally to their efficiency, there will still be constant monetary returns. However, if the rate of remuneration is uniform regardless of the degree of efficiency of the marginal factors employed, costs will necessarily increase with increases in output and employment. Keynes also made this latter assumption and, therefore, that the 'supply price will increase as output from a given equipment is increased. Thus increasing output will be associated with rising prices, apart from any change in the wage-unit' (1936, pp. 299–300). Keynes generalized to the whole economy Kahn's analysis of the prices of consumer goods.

Furthermore, there is another aspect of Keynes's analysis that might seem to provide a justification for increasing cost curves regardless of the behaviour of returns. It is the notion of user cost, to which Keynes attached great importance (Keynes, 1936, pp. 66–73). The user cost, U, of output A is a measure of the total sacrifice involved in its production and it is defined as the difference between the maximum net value that the firm's capital would have if production were not carried out ($G' - B'$, with B' denoting the expenditure on the maintenance of the firm's capital) and the actual value of the firm's capital at the end of the production period (G) plus the amount spent to buy finished outputs from other firms (A_1):

$$U = (G' - B') - G + A_1$$

Keynes regarded user cost as a link between present and future, and also as a way to bring in uncertainty and expectations to the treatment of costs. User cost is determined by 'the expected sacrifice of future benefit involved in present use' and it is the marginal amount of such sacrifice that, along with the marginal factor cost, determines the scale of production. Therefore, user cost is an increasing function of entrepreneurs' expectations about prices at a future date when capital could be used instead of today. The higher these expected future prices are than expected prices in the current period, the higher is the user cost of current production. Marginal user cost is likely to be an increasing function of the level of output as increasing output affects entrepreneurs' expectations in a positive way (Keynes, 1936, p. 302). Thus, if the user cost can increase because of a change in entrepreneurs' expectations, marginal costs could be continuously increasing regardless of the behaviour of marginal factor costs which depends on returns.

6.3 CRITICISMS OF THE HYPOTHESIS OF DECREASING RETURNS IN THE SHORT PERIOD

Although they followed an unconventional path, both Kahn and Keynes arrived at conclusions about cost and supply curves that resemble conventional ones. In particular, they made an assumption of continuous upward sloping supply curves at firm and industry level, as well as at the aggregate level. But, in the 1930s, others had rejected such an assumption.

6.3.1   The Firm's Cost Curve

As we have already seen, Dunlop had criticized Keynes's assumptions on costs and supply curves on the grounds of empirical evidence.[8] He argued that the model adopted by Keynes to explain the relations between the money and real wage rates cannot account for the actual behaviour of wages, for a number of reasons (Dunlop, 1938, pp. 431–4). Specifically, he asserted that the assumption of increasing marginal costs had to be rejected and that in the short period the most realistic assumption is constant marginal cost up to the full utilization of productive capacity; beyond that point, cost and supply curves become steeply increasing.

Kalecki had also criticized the hypothesis of short-period decreasing returns.[9] In *Money and Real Wages*, he considered the case of a single firm with a given level of capital equipment:

> If, for instance, in a given establishment two shifts rather than one are worked, the cost of raw materials and labour will increase more or less proportionately. Only the third shift may involve some technical problems. It is therefore reasonable to assume that in an industrial enterprise the curve of marginal costs is horizontal over a rather long range of output and starts rising only when full capacity is approached. As experience shows, such full utilization is rather exceptional and therefore the assumption of increasing marginal costs must be dropped.[10] (Kalecki, 1991b, p. 31)

The best, most realistic short-period assumption is constant marginal costs, which thus coincide with the unit variable costs, while the individual supply curve is flat up to full capacity.[11]

More recently, Sylos Labini (1969, 1988) and Eichner (1976) have also developed the criticism of the hypothesis of short-period decreasing returns. Sylos Labini admits that firms' marginal costs can be increasing because of overtime work, machinery of different efficiency, and exceptional wear and tear when production is pushed beyond a certain level, but he rejects the possibility of adducing such elements in support of the traditional hypothesis of continuous marginal cost curves which are increasing over their relevant range. These elements imply 'not continuously rising marginal cost, but marginal cost rising stepwise, remaining constant on each tread' (Sylos Labini, 1969, p. 27).

The marginal cost curve, therefore, takes on the shape depicted in Figure 6.1. As long as the firm produces an output that is less than OX_1, it experiences a constant marginal cost OC_1; when the firm's output is larger than OX_1 but less than OX_2, its marginal cost jumps to OC_2 as this level of production requires the use of less efficient machines. If the output is larger than OX_2, the marginal cost rises to OC_3. When all the firm's capacity is used, the output reaches the level OX_{FC}; from this point on the marginal cost rises vertically. A

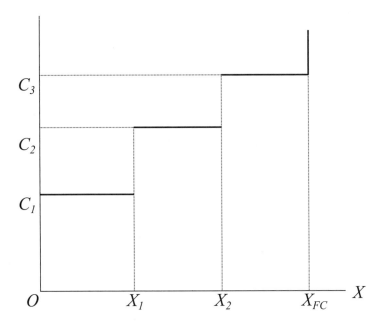

Figure 6.1   Marginal cost rising stepwise

similar curve is used by Harcourt and Kenyon (1976), who derived it from Salter (1966).

If the productivity differentials between contiguous types of machines are significantly large, an approximation of the stepwise curve by a continuous curve is not legitimate. A stepwise curve could be approximated by a continuous curve if it were assumed that the firm has a large number of types of machines and that the productivity differential between contiguous types of machines is small. But such a curve would be better depicted as a flat to capacity curve rather than as a traditional increasing cost curve; a point that is made by Eichner.

Eichner admits that the existence of plants of differing productivity implies that the firm's marginal cost curve has a stepwise shape, but he observes that these cost differentials are usually small and that, therefore, ignoring them does not have significant consequences. Small cost differentials can be assumed away and short-period marginal costs can be regarded as constant to capacity. In other words, short-period marginal cost curves can be assumed to have a reversed-L shape.

Thus, on the grounds of the considerations above, it seems safe to conclude that the traditional hypothesis of increasing short-period marginal costs has to be rejected. If marginal costs are increasing because of significantly heterogeneous factors of production, it is not legitimate to represent them with a continuously increasing curve; if marginal costs are constant or 'quasi-constant' up to full capacity, they can be represented by a curve that has a reversed-L shape; that is a flat curve with a point of discontinuity at full utilization of capacity.

However, the criticisms above seem to be insufficient to reject Keynes's hypothesis of increasing costs insofar as it is based on the notion of user cost. If the user cost can increase because of a change in entrepreneurs' expectations which are positively related to the level of output, marginal costs could be increasing continuously. But this conclusion is not correct. The key element in Keynes's reasoning is that an increase in output induces entrepreneurs to expect higher prices. A possible reason why entrepreneurs associate expected increases in output with rising prices is that they know that an expansion of output implies short-period decreasing returns. This explanation obviously is subject to the criticisms expounded above: even if firms have increasing costs due to differing equipment, an expansion of output does not necessarily bring about a generalized increase in prices.

A second reason for an increase in user costs has nothing to do with decreasing returns as such. Entrepreneurs could expect rising prices because the expansion in demand and output brings the economy as a whole, or at least some sectors, near to full capacity; in this case, prices rise because of excess demand rather than because of factors' productivity. However, if the latter is the rationale for increasing user costs, it is quite evident that it does not lend itself to be used for a general explanation of increasing cost curves. Costs and, hence, user costs would be increasing only near to full employment, not in situations of generalized underutilization of productive capacity and labour.

In conclusion, Keynes's notion of user cost is not able to provide a sounder justification for the hypothesis that firms experience short-period costs which are continuously increasing. In general, it is safer to assume that firms have either reversed-L or stepwise cost curves. It is on these grounds that the construction of industry supply functions and the aggregate supply function has to be re-examined.

6.3.2   The Industry and Aggregate Supply Functions

The fact that individual cost curves are either reversed-L shaped or stepwise does not necessarily exclude the possibility that industry supply functions, or the aggregate supply function, are continuously increasing. But to obtain such a result would imply accepting rather unrealistic results or the introduction of special *ad hoc* additional hypotheses.

Insofar as all firms in an industry are identical and have reversed-L shaped cost curves, the industry supply function takes on the same shape. But, if it is admitted that firms are of differing efficiency, it is possible to deduce a contin-

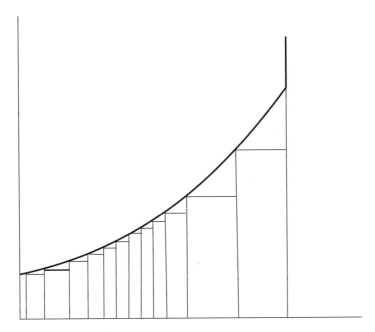

Figure 6.2   An increasing supply function by approximation

uously increasing supply function. If the number of firms is so large and the degree of their efficiency is so differentiated that all the discontinuities in the supply function are 'quasi-filled' by different firms, a continuously increasing supply curve is a good approximation of reality. Analogous observations can be made in the case of an industry in which firms have stepwise cost curves. If such firms are all equally efficient, the industry supply function will be step-wise as well; if firms are of differing efficiency, the discontinuities in the supply function might be filled by a sufficiently large number of different firms, so that the curve would appear as in Figure 6.2.

Continuously increasing supply functions obtained in this way, however, imply analytical consequences which seem to be too extreme and unrealistic. In an industry where all firms have reversed-L cost curves, any situation in which demand is below the level corresponding to the industry's full capacity implies that there must be some firms (the least efficient, marginal, firms) which do not produce at all, while all the others produce to full capacity.[12] This description of an industry in a slump was regarded as unrealistic both by Kahn (1989, p. 59) and Robinson (1969, pp. v–vi): in a situation of low demand all firms usually produce below full capacity.[13]

Assuming that firms have stepwise cost curves does not change the picture significantly. A low level of demand, that is below the level associated with the industry's full capacity, would still imply that the least efficient firms do not produce at all. The only difference from the previous case would be that now non-marginal firms can either produce to capacity or leave part of their equipment idle.

In order to obtain a continuously increasing supply function that does not imply that some firms necessarily shut down, it is necessary to introduce a further *ad hoc* hypothesis: all firms have some efficient machines that are in use for any price level, but less efficient firms also have less efficient machines that are more costly than the less efficient machines of more efficient firms.[14] The special *ad hoc* nature of this hypothesis is evident: if all firms have been able to adopt and introduce the best available technique, it is difficult to find a justification for the fact that some of them have been unable to get rid of the worst technique.[15] In conclusion, then, it seems that the simplest and most acceptable hypothesis is that, in general, industry supply functions are either flat up to capacity or increasing but discontinuous.

As to the shape and continuity of the aggregate supply function, the conclusions are analogous to those reached for industry supply functions. If industries' supply functions are reversed-L shaped, the aggregate supply function retains the same shape. Increases in effective demand do not give rise to increases in the general price level, unless the economy reaches full employment or one or more industries experience a bottle-neck.[16] Once the economy has reached full employment the aggregate supply function becomes vertical: further increases in demand give rise only to price increases since no expansion of output is possible. If one or more industries reach full capacity earlier than others, the aggregate supply function starts increasing before it becomes perfectly vertical.[17]

Similar conclusions hold if industries' supply functions are stepwise. As long as no industry 'jumps' to a higher level of costs, the aggregate supply function remains flat. When an industry can produce more output only by using less efficient factors of production, there is a jump in the aggregate function as well as in that particular industry supply function. The aggregate function, then, is discontinuous and stepwise like individual supply functions. This result holds even when some industries have stepwise supply functions and others have reversed-L shaped supply functions.

The last case to be considered is when industries' supply functions are continuous (all the gaps are filled). In this case, we obtain an aggregate supply function that is continuously increasing as well. This function, however, retains the same shortcoming as industries' supply functions: any level of effective demand below full employment implies that some firms, in some or all industries, do not produce at all. Similarly to the industry supply function, this difficulty can be overcome by making *ad hoc* assumptions on the distribution of differing capital equipment among firms.[18]

Thus it is safe to make the hypothesis that the aggregate supply curve is also flat to capacity or that it has a discontinuous stepwise shape. In both cases, increases in demand and output are not associated with a continuously increasing price level and, hence, with a continuously decreasing real wage rate.

6.4 KEYNES'S THEORY OF INVESTMENT

In Chapter 11 of *The General Theory*, Keynes formulated a demand schedule for investment. This demand schedule had to demonstrate why aggregate investment is not necessarily pushed to its full-employment level. The determination of the equilibrium level of investment is based on an investment demand schedule relating the rate of aggregate investment to the marginal efficiency of capital, the latter being defined as 'the relation between the prospective yield of a capital-asset and its supply price or replacement cost' (Keynes, 1936, p. 135). The rate of investment will be pushed to the point on this function where the marginal efficiency of capital (e) is equal to the rate of interest (i).

A stable equilibrium level of investment lower than its full-employment level can be found only if the investment demand schedule is downward sloping; that is, only if the marginal efficiency of capital is a decreasing function of investment itself. With a given rate of interest, a constant marginal efficiency of capital would imply either that aggregate investment is pushed to its full-employment level (when $e > i$) or that firms as a whole do not invest at all ($e < i$).

As is well known, Keynes held that the marginal efficiency of capital was in fact a decreasing function of the level of investment. He first dealt with individual investment demand functions and expounded the reasons why they are downward sloping:

> If there is an increased investment in any given type of capital during any period of time, the marginal efficiency of that type of capital will diminish as the investment is increased, partly because the prospective yield will fall as the supply of that type of capital is increased, and partly because, as a rule, pressure on the facilities for producing that type of capital will cause its supply price to increase; the second of these factors being usually the more important in producing equilibrium in the short run, but the longer the period in view the more does the first factor take its place. (Keynes, 1936, p. 136)

Individual functions are then aggregated to obtain the aggregate investment demand schedule. In symbols, if we denote the supply prices of investment goods by r, and the expected yields by E (long-term expectations), we have

$$e = f(r, E) \qquad\qquad (6.1)$$

$$\partial e/\partial r < 0, \ \partial e/\partial E > 0$$

with r and E, in turn, functions of the level of investment:

$$\partial r/\partial I > 0, \ \partial E/\partial I < 0$$

The supply price of investment goods will rise with the level of investment and expected yields will decrease as capital becomes less scarce thanks to investment. As investment increases, capital-goods supply prices increase because of the assumed short-period decreasing returns. On the other hand, as capital becomes more abundant in the long period, its returns decrease because returns to capital depend on its scarcity.[19]

Therefore, it is

$$I = g(e, i) \qquad\qquad (6.2)$$

$$\partial I/\partial e > 0, \ \partial I/\partial i < 0$$

The volume of investment so determined is associated with a certain level of aggregate output, which is not necessarily its full-employment level, and with a certain general price level. An increase in investment leads to an increase in output, an increase in prices and, with a given money wage rate, greater profits.

Keynes's analysis is based on the expected values for the variables, rather than on their current values. He repeatedly stressed that the marginal efficiency of capital had to be interpreted as a variable whose value depended on expected values.[20] In any current period entrepreneurs decide to carry out a certain volume of investment because they *expect* that more investment would have a lower rate of return than the current interest rate. Both the prices of capital goods and yields enter into the function of the marginal efficiency of capital as expected variables.

6.5   THE CRITIQUE OF KEYNES'S MARGINAL EFFICIENCY OF CAPITAL

Kahn's 1931 article exerted a strong influence on the development of *The General Theory*, in particular on the development of the concept of the multiplier. But Kahn's article also contains some interesting observations on investment that were ignored by Keynes. Because of Kahn's assumption of

moderately increasing short-period supply curves for consumer goods, a rise
in demand for consumer goods (due to an increase in employment caused by
greater public investment) brings about an increase in their price level along
with an increase in their output. The assumption of increasing supply prices
was accompanied by the assumption that money wages were constant (Kahn,
1931, p. 175), so greater demand also causes a decrease in the real wage rate
and an increase in profits.

Throughout most of his article Kahn ignored the effects that a rise in profits
has on private investment; only in the last two pages did he deal with this problem:

> An increase in output, and of the margin or profit that goes with it, cannot, taken by
> themselves, fail both to increase the attractiveness and to facilitate the process of
> investment at home ... . If there were no opposing forces in operation, it might
> easily happen that, in spite of the rise in the rate of interest, the ordinary processes
> of home investment would be promoted rather than retarded by a policy of public
> works. (Kahn, 1931, p. 197)

This holds under the assumption that government spending leaves the general
state of confidence unaltered. Changes in the state of confidence could affect
investment in either direction, but Kahn tended to believe that the state of
confidence would be positively affected.[21]

Kahn, differently from Keynes, did not examine the effects of an increase
in demand on the prices of capital goods, but his analysis can be generalized
and expressed in the following terms. An increase in public investment, or
more generally any increase in aggregate investment, leads to an expansion of
demand and output and to a rise in the general price level. If money wages do
not vary (or they increase less than prices), there is a decrease in real wages
and an increase in profits which will affect private investment decisions positively.

Kahn employed a sequential analytical approach: changes in investment,
output, prices, and their interactions are considered by looking at the economic
process over time as the system moves from one stage to another. Once investment changes, a cumulative process starts whereby past investment affects
current investment decisions through its effect on prices, profits and, possibly,
the state of confidence. This sequential approach differs from that of Keynes
in *The General Theory*, where the effects of investment over time are not dealt
with.[22] Keynes used some of Kahn's analytical blocks to elaborate his own
theory but, with respect to investment, he failed to take into account the positive effect that an increase in profits, determined by an increase in investment,
will have on entrepreneurs' expectations and investment decisions.

The overlooking of the effects of higher profits on expectations and investment is one of the core elements of Kalecki's criticism of Keynes.[23] Also

Kalecki, in criticizing Keynes, followed a sequential approach to the analysis of investment. In 1936, Kalecki wrote a review of *The General Theory* in which he held that Keynes's analysis 'does not say anything about the sphere of investment decisions of the entrepreneur, who makes his calculations in "disequilibrium" on the basis of existing market prices of investment goods. It shows only that if the expected profitability, calculated on the basis of this price level, is not equal to the rate of interest, a change in the level of investment will occur' (Kalecki, 1990c, p. 230).

The single firm makes its investment decisions on the basis of the current prices of capital goods and if, given the expectations of future returns, these prices are such that the expected rate of profit is higher than the rate of interest, the firm expands its investment as much as possible. Its demand for investment goods (for those investment goods which promise a rate of profit higher than the rate of interest) is perfectly elastic. In fact, no individual firm is able to foresee the effects on the prices of capital goods of the investment decisions of all firms taken together.[24]

Therefore, given a certain state of expectations, firms as a whole generate an expansion of investment, each firm trying to expand its productive capacity as much as possible. Robinson (1965a, p. 96), summarizing Kalecki's argument, has made this point still clearer:

> If there are schemes which promise a rate of profit greater than the rate of interest, would not each individual enterprise be willing and anxious to carry out an indefinitely large amount of investment? It was no use to reply that a faster rate of investment would raise the cost of capital goods and so reduce the prospective rate of profit; for the rise in costs would come about as a result of actual investment, *ex post*, while the marginal efficiency of capital concerns investment plans *ex ante*.

However, such a process must come to an end, thus establishing the aggregate level of investment. In the short period, on the assumption of increasing marginal costs,[25] a rise in the overall demand for investment goods by firms leads to an increase in their prices, so that the growth of investment will stop. At a certain stage the increase in the prices of investment goods makes further investment unprofitable, the rate of interest being given and fixed.

In this sense, Keynes's concept of decreasing marginal efficiency appears capable of explaining the *ex post* level of aggregate investment, though it does not offer a satisfactory or consistent explanation of investment decisions. Pointing to the process through which firms expand their investment, Kalecki observed: 'This will transform the existing situation into one in which expected profitability is equal to the rate of interest. Using the terminology of Swedish economists, one can say that Keynes' theory determines only the *ex post* level of investment but that it does not say anything about the *ex ante* investment' (Kalecki, 1990c, p. 230).

But Kalecki at once added that such a level of aggregate investment cannot be regarded as an equilibrium level. The level of aggregate investment so determined cannot produce an equilibrium position precisely because of the increase in prices. In fact, the rise in investment causes not only an increase in the prices of capital goods but an increase in the general price level. This means that the increase in investment makes profits rise while the real wage rate falls. This in turn affects expectations, which become more optimistic and improve the marginal efficiency of capital, making it diverge from the given rate of interest. Once again, investment starts to expand:

> the expectations will become more optimistic and a difference between the marginal efficiency of investment and the rate of interest will arise again. 'Equilibrium' then is not reached and the growth of investment will still persist (we are dealing here, as it can easily be seen, with a cumulative Wicksellian process). Therefore we see that the Keynesian concept, which tells us only how high investment should be in order that a certain 'disequilibrium' may become 'equilibrium' meets a serious difficulty along this way also. In fact the growth of investment does not result at all in a process leading the system toward the 'equilibrium'. (Kalecki, 1990c, p. 231)

Even though future prices were expected to rise less than current prices, long-term expectations would be affected and investment would change (increase). Thus, the initial equilibrium determined by the increase in current prices of capital goods is not stable.

Kalecki concluded his criticism of Keynes by holding that a satisfactory analysis of the investment process cannot fail to consider the sequential process by which current phenomena produced by past expectations affect current expectations of the future:

> Thus it is difficult to consider Keynes's solution of the investment problem to be satisfactory. The reason for this failure lies in an approach which is basically static to a matter which is by its nature dynamic. Keynes takes as given the state of the expectations of returns, and from this he derives a certain definite level of investment, overlooking the effects that investment will in turn have on expectations. It is here that one can glimpse the road one must follow in order to build a realistic theory of investment. (Kalecki, 1990c, p. 231)

Keynes did take account of the effect of a rise in prices upon the cost of investment, but he failed to consider the effect on expectations. He mixed *ex ante* and *ex post* factors together and in such a way as to obtain a downward-sloping curve (see also Asimakopulos, 1971, p. 384). The *ex ante* and *ex post* factors must be disentangled. It is not legitimate to assume that single entrepreneurs can foresee the effect of collective investment decisions on prices; the effect of the price rise will manifest itself only after time has elapsed, and only then will the investment process stop. Moreover, Keynes can be criticized for being 'selective': while he took into consideration the negative effect on expected yields of a lower degree of scarcity of capital, he ignored the positive effect on expectations produced by higher prices and profits.

Kalecki formulated the same criticism of Keynes's theory of investment in another article (Kalecki, 1937, pp. 83–4) that Keynes read and commented upon. In a letter to Kalecki, Keynes observed that this criticism would have been right only if all future prices were expected to rise in the same proportion as present prices. But Kalecki countered that his statement was independent of how much expected prices rise; in order that his reasoning holds good, it is sufficient that expectations of future prices improve to some extent.[26]

By taking these criticisms into account, it is easy to see that Keynes's explanation of investment cannot determine an underemployment equilibrium position. For any given rate of interest, investment will be pushed up to the point at which full employment is reached. The cumulative process will stop only at that stage.[27] Moreover, the analysis so far has been conducted under the hypothesis of increasing short-period marginal costs, for in this case Kalecki himself accepted it. The same conclusions apply, *a fortiori*, on the more realistic assumption of constant marginal costs. In that case, the initial process of expansion of investment stops only when all the capital goods produced have been purchased. Given the rate of interest and an expected rate of profits above it, firms invest as much as possible, the only constraint being the availability of investment goods.

Thus, Keynes's theory of investment does not seem to furnish a satisfactory justification of underemployment equilibria. However, one aspect of his analysis could provide that justification, even though the support it offers to the theoretical explanation of 'underemployment equilibria' is very feeble. So far, following Keynes, the money wage rate has been regarded as given and constant. The wage rate was to increase only when the economy reached full employment, and aggregate demand continued to rise. Keynes, however, also recognized that money wage rates may rise before full employment is reached.[28] An increase in wages implies a fall in profits, which means that the cumulative process might halt before reaching full employment. Keynes, however, observed that such an increase in wages would be 'not fully in proportion to the rise in the price of wage-goods' (Keynes, 1936, pp. 301–2). Moreover, he concluded, these wage increases 'do not lend themselves to theoretical generalizations'.

If money wages increase less than the prices of wage-goods, profits are still increasing, and this means that the cumulative process to full employment is not stopped, though it may be slowed.[29] On the other hand, an explanation of 'underemployment equilibria', based on the possibility that money wages might increase before full employment is reached, is not theoretically satisfactory, because it lacks generality.

Even though not provided by Keynes himself, an alternative justification for the downward-sloping investment demand function could be based on the hypothesis that investment projects exist with varying expected returns.[30] Entrepreneurs rank the projects in descending order with respect to their expected profitability. In this framework, entrepreneurs adopt only those projects whose expected profitability is larger than, or equal to, the current rate of interest. Therefore, the volume of investment is an inverse function of the rate of interest.

This line of reasoning is not subject to the type of criticisms levelled at Keynes by Kalecki, but neither does it offer a completely satisfactory explanation of investment decisions. In particular, the explication above does not explain why, at a given interest rate, firms should adopt less profitable investment projects in order to expand capacity. It would be more rational for them to adopt only the project with the highest expected profitability and expand by buying more units of that project.[31] Firms with projects whose expected profitability is higher than the given rate of interest would keep on investing. They would stop investing only when they realize, *ex post*, that the rise in the prices of capital goods has made the expected return from their projects lower than the rate of interest. Thus, this approach cannot provide a satisfactory justification either for decreasing individual investment demand functions.

This approach, however, could offer a justification for an *aggregate* investment function which, at any point in time, is a decreasing function of the rate of interest. But, again, such a result can be obtained only under a special assumption, that is to say that the most efficient projects available to different firms have a different expected profitability, which may depend on technological factors as well as on differing attitudes to uncertainty among firms. In this case, for any given rate of interest, there are a number of firms in all, or some, industries that decide to invest while others do not invest at all. The firms that invest are those whose most efficient available investment project has a higher expected profitability than the current rate of interest. As the rate of interest varies so does the number of firms that decide to realize their investment projects. Therefore the aggregate volume of investment is an inverse function of the rate of interest. Changes in the rate of interest give rise to changes in the volume of aggregate investment as well as to changes in the sectoral composition of the economy if projects of differing profitability are randomly distributed through industries. It is not difficult to perceive the special *ad hoc* nature of the hypotheses that are necessary to save the idea of a downward-sloping investment demand function.

6.6   THE MACROECONOMIC IMPLICATIONS OF THE CRITIQUE OF KEYNES'S MICROFOUNDATIONS

In the previous sections, we have seen that both Keynes's assumptions about short-period returns and his theory of investment are subject to criticism. In this concluding section we concentrate on the implications that these criticisms have for Keynes's macroeconomic analysis and, in particular, for his determination of underemployment equilibria.

Keynes's notion of short-period decreasing returns, although not based on traditional marginalist assumptions, is questionable. It is subject to two objections: one concerns the hypothesis that cost and supply functions can be satisfactorily represented by continuously increasing curves; the other concerns the hypothesis that individual short-period costs can be realistically assumed to be increasing though discontinuous. Continuously increasing supply functions can be obtained only if special assumptions on the distribution of different techniques among firms are made.

If such assumptions are not made we obtain that, when demand is below its full-employment level, some firms in all or in some industries do not produce at all rather than leave part of their equipment idle. In such a case, Keynes's underemployment equilibria would no longer be situations of low activity and employment for the whole productive system, but situations in which a portion of the system is completely idle. These situations are similar to those obtainable in the Marxian modified framework and are subject to similar criticisms. They can occur in reality but it is hard to regard them as equilibrium positions in a Keynesian sense.

Moreover, empirical evidence shows that, in many relevant cases, short-period marginal cost curves have a reversed-L shape. If this hypothesis is accepted there follow some significant implications. Keynes (1939) believed that assuming constant marginal costs would have reinforced his policy indications, because expansionary demand policies would not bring about price increases.[32] However, he failed to perceive that assuming constant marginal costs and flat supply curves has wider implications. In particular, assuming constant marginal costs requires the explicit abandonment of the hypothesis of perfect competition. As Kahn had realized in 1929 (1989, pp. 59–61), the adoption of the hypothesis of short-period constant returns leads to the collapse of perfect competition. If marginal costs are constant up to capacity, the competitive equilibrium condition of equality between marginal cost and price becomes meaningless: either a firm produces to capacity or it does not produce at all. A way out of this difficulty is to assume that individual firms face downward-sloping demand curves because they operate in imperfect markets.

The hypothesis of such reversed-L shaped cost curves, which imply a flat to capacity aggregate supply function, has another important implication for Keynes's analysis in *The General Theory*. If prices do not rise with output, then Keynes's idea that, at least in the short period, a decreasing marginal efficiency of capital is due to the fact that an increase in investment and (consequently) output brings about an increase in the prices of investment goods, loses its validity.

But Keynes's notion of the marginal efficiency of capital is also questionable for other reasons. A major weakness of Keynes's theory of investment is its inability to disentangle *ex ante* and *ex post* factors. Moreover, Keynes did not contemplate the possibility that entrepreneurs could incorporate into their expectations aggregate outcomes which would affect investment positively. Entrepreneurs are assumed to foresee the negative aggregate outcomes of their individual decisions, but they are assumed not to take account of the positive effect of an increase in investment – the rise in profits brought about by the rise in prices while the money wage rate remains constant. For Keynes, the rise in prices does not have positive effects on investment, whereas for Kahn and Kalecki rising prices induce entrepreneurs to invest.

Kahn and Kalecki developed their analyses of investment within a sequential approach. Such an approach is based on the distinction between expected and realized values of the relevant variables. In this context, *past actual* investment leads to an increase in *current* profits which, in turn, causes a positive change in *current expectations* about the future and, hence, in *current investment decisions*.

Keynes was reluctant to follow the *ex ante/ex post* approach because he thought it contained serious conceptual difficulties.[33] In fact, if the analytical concern is the determination of an equilibrium which can be characterized by the existence of unemployment, it is necessary to be able to compare aggregate results with aggregate expectations at a certain time. This is not possible in a sequential analysis unless strong simplifying assumptions on the length of periods are made.[34]

It is true, however, that the sequential approach has the merit of providing a clearer distinction between decisions and actual results, which is also important for Keynes's equilibrium approach. It is important to show that, given the level of investment, the economy can reach an underemployment equilibrium; but it is also important to provide a satisfactory explanation as to why the investment decisions made at a point in time might not give rise to full employment. Had Keynes drawn a sharper distinction between *ex ante* decisions and *ex post* outcomes, he might have avoided the flaws in his analysis of the marginal efficiency of capital.[35]

However, despite the fact that Keynes's analysis of investment is flawed, the need to find a justification for a downward-sloping investment demand function remains. The existence of a downward-sloping investment demand function is a necessary condition for the existence of an underemployment equilibrium. The justification for this function must be compatible with the fact that the analysis refers to entrepreneurs' *ex ante* decisions. If this cannot be accomplished, the only viable alternative is a sequential approach in which the investment process is halted before the economy reaches full employment by intervening *ex post* factors that entrepreneurs did not expect when they made their decisions.

Also in the case of investment, an answer to the difficulties met by Keynes can be found by abandoning the hypothesis of perfect or, for that matter, free competition. In the 1920s, Sraffa, who started the debate on imperfect competition, had argued that, in non-perfectly competitive markets, investment is limited by the fact that demand for goods is limited. If firms do not take account of these limits, they will be subject to decreasing profitability (Sraffa, 1926).[36]

Had Keynes given Sraffa's views more attention, and had he pointed out that demand is the crucial factor governing firms' investment decisions, he would have provided more solid foundations to his decreasing investment demand schedule. In considering how firms form their expectations of future returns to investment, Keynes took account of the role of expected demand, but his case would have been much stronger had he referred to firms operating outside a competitive framework. While it must be assumed that a purely competitive firm faces a perfectly elastic demand for its goods, it need not be so when we look at firms operating in the 'world in which we live', which is not a world of perfect or free competition. Firms in the actual economy know that the demand for their goods is limited, and they do not expand their productive capacity indefinitely.

It was Kalecki who took up this line of analysis. In fact, he did not content himself with merely criticizing Keynes's micro-framework. He also provided an alternative approach to the analysis of firms' behaviour and their investment decisions. His analysis is explicitly set in a non-perfectly competitive framework. This is the subject of the next chapter.

NOTES

1. For a more thorough analysis of this issue, see Sardoni (1994).
2. Kahn observed that, usually, prime costs include some inflexible elements that have an overhead nature. The inflexible component of prime costs has the same effect on them as that which fixed costs have on total costs. As a consequence, the initial portion of the unit prime cost curve is downward sloping.
3. Kahn, however, admitted that some firms with heterogeneous machinery use method (i) to vary their production. In such a case, the unit prime cost curve takes on a shape more similar to the traditional U-shape. Some industries may adopt method (i) also because workers are of different efficiency but paid the same wage rate (Kahn, 1989, pp. 49–51).

4. The rationale for Kahn's assumption of an increasing supply function could be that not all consumer-goods industries have flat to capacity supply schedules, but he never provided either this or a different justification for his hypothesis even though, on several occasions, he repeated that supply functions are upward sloping. For more details, see Sardoni (1994, pp. 71–2).

5. On this, see also Brown (1991).

6. The discussion was carried out in relation to the determination of the general price level. Keynes, in particular, analysed the effects of changes in effective demand brought about by changes in the quantity of money.

7. As a first step, Keynes assumed that: (i) the rates of remuneration of all factors of production change in the same proportion; (ii) all unemployed resources are homogeneous; (iii) the rates of remuneration of factors do not increase until there is no longer a surplus of them unemployed. Under these assumptions, he concluded that there are constant returns as long as there is unemployment. Therefore, changes in the quantity of money and, hence, in demand give rise to proportional changes in output and employment while prices do not vary. When full employment is reached, changes in the quantity of money give rise to proportional changes in prices while the real variables do not vary.

8. See also Tarshis (1939), for further empirical evidence of the relation between money and real wage rates.

9. Dunlop referred to Kalecki's ideas on the issue: 'The extent to which cost curves are rising, except at the very peak of the boom, has probably been over-emphasized in view of the presence of excess capacity in many industries. Mr. Kalecki has recently taken a similar position' (Dunlop, 1938, p. 432).

10. *Money and Real Wages* was published in Polish in 1939, but Kalecki had already argued that the hypothesis of constant marginal costs is the most realistic in an article published in English in 1938 in which he pointed out that firms in most sectors produce with marginal costs that are more or less constant up to the point of full use of the existing capacity (Kalecki, 1938, p. 101). On this see also Robinson (1977, pp. 10–12); Skouras (1981, pp. 200–8); Kriesler (1987, pp. 17–20).

11. For Kalecki, the sector in which increasing marginal costs prevail is agriculture (Kalecki, 1991b, p. 31).

12. Notice the similarity of this result with that we obtained within the Marxian modified framework in Chapter 3, section 3.7.

13. See also Robinson (1977).

14. If the latter condition were not fulfilled we would be back in a case of homogeneous firms and the industry supply curve would be discontinuous.

15. Unless we add another *ad hoc* hypothesis: firms with the less efficient machinery are in a transitory phase, that is they have not yet replaced their worst machines. However, when the transitory phase is over, we would be back to a case of homogeneous firms.

16. A possibility that Keynes took into consideration (Keynes, 1936, p. 296).

17. On the other hand, it is reasonable to think that reaching a bottleneck, which causes the prices of some goods to rise vertically, might give rise to changes in the composition of demand. In such a case, even if one or more industries reach full capacity earlier than others, the aggregate supply function could remain flat until full employment is reached: the increase in the prices of the goods in shortage could induce a shift of demand towards goods whose prices are still unchanged.

18. Here, for simplicity, we have considered only capital goods of different efficiency, but introducing the hypothesis that labour is also of different productivity would not affect the conclusions concerning both cost and supply functions: heterogeneous labour could imply more 'steps' in stepwise cost curves or the transformation of reversed-L curves into stepwise curves.

19. On Keynes's concept of capital, see Keynes (1936, pp. 210–21).

20. 'The most important confusion concerning the meaning and significance of the marginal efficiency of capital has ensued on the failure to see that it depends on the *prospective* yield of capital, and not merely on its current yield' (Keynes, 1936, p. 141).

21. 'There is strong justification for concluding on *a priori* grounds that the inauguration of an active economic policy would promote confidence rather than upset it' (Kahn, 1931, p. 197).

Kahn did not believe that entrepreneurs would react negatively to an expansionary policy. On the effects of government policy on the state of confidence, see also Kahn (1984, pp. 91–104).

22. Kahn himself noted that Keynes had no interest in the dynamic process by which the economy heads towards its equilibrium positions. Kahn referred, with approval, to those who criticized Keynes on this point. Kahn (1984, pp. 119–68) mentions Robertson's and Pigou's criticisms regarding this aspect of Keynes's theory. Quoting a passage from Pigou (1950), Kahn (1984, p. 125) held: 'Pigou devoted the final passage of his partial renunciation of his bitter and sarcastic review-article on the *General Theory* to an account – for the most part highly acceptable to Keynesians – of the same fundamental factors which I am identifying as determining the position of the economy'.

23. Kalecki's criticism has been further elaborated by Robinson (1965a, pp. 92–9) and Asimakopulos (1971). See also Harcourt (2006, pp. 55–65).

24. To assume that each firm is able to foresee the eventual increase in the price of capital goods, which will reduce the profitability of investment, implies some special and unrealistic assumptions: that each firm is aware of the fact that other firms, in its industry and in other industries, are also making similar investment decisions, and that each firm can accurately anticipate the effects on prices of these economy-wide investment decisions (Asimakopulos, 1971, pp. 383–4).

25. In his critique of Keynes's theory of investment, Kalecki maintained the hypothesis of increasing marginal costs.

26. Keynes wrote to Kalecki: 'It appears to me that it is only if future prices are expected to rise in the same proportion as present prices that you have established the result that "equilibrium is not reached and the investment continues to rise"'. Kalecki replied: 'my statement … is independent of how much expectations improve under the influence of the present rise of prices. I state … only that the increase of prices of investment goods which equates the marginal efficiency based on the initial state of expectations to the rate of interest, does not create an "equilibrium", for at the same time expectations improve to some extent and thus investment increases further' (in Keynes, 1983, pp. 791–6).

27. 'There is a limit to the amount of investment which can be carried out in a given short period. This limit is set by the availability of plant for producing investment goods or by the attainment of full employment when it is not possible to attract workers away from the consumer goods industries' (Asimakopulos, 1971, pp. 384–5).

28. 'Since each group of workers will gain, *cet. par.*, by a rise in its own wage there is naturally for all groups a pressure in this direction, which entrepreneurs will be more ready to meet when they are doing better business. For this reason a proportion of any increase in effective demand is likely to be absorbed in satisfying the upward tendency of the wage-unit' (Keynes, 1936, p. 301).

29. This is the same argument that Kalecki used in answering Keynes's comment on his 1937 article: what is important is not how much expectations improve but the very fact that they do improve to some extent.

30. See, for example, Pasinetti (1974, 1997) and Davidson (1994, pp. 56–62).

31. It is possible to hypothesize special cases in which a single firm cannot adopt the most profitable project more than once, but these special cases could hardly represent the basis for a general theory of investment.

32. Keynes (1939, p. 46) observed: 'it may be the case that the practical workings of the laws of imperfect competition in the modern quasi-competitive system are such that, when output increases and money wages rise, prices rise less than in proportion to the increase in marginal money cost.' Therefore, we have increasing real wages, a different hypothesis from that which is made in *The General Theory*.

33. In a 1937 letter to Ohlin, Keynes wrote: 'the *ex post* and *ex ante* device cannot be precisely stated without very cumbrous devices. I used to speak of the period between expectation and result as "funnels of process", but the fact that the funnels are all of different lengths and overlap one another meant that at any given time there was no aggregate realized result capable of being compared with some aggregate expectation at some earlier date.' (Keynes, 1973b, p. 185).

34. On the conceptual difficulties of period analysis, see Myrdal (1939, pp. 43–5).
35. To some extent, Keynes himself came to recognize that he should have paid more attention to the way in which *ex ante* decisions are made. In a 1937 lecture, he stated: '*Ex ante* decisions may be decided by trial and error or by judicious foresight, or (as in fact) by both. I should have distinguished more sharply between a theory based on ex ante effective demand, however arrived at, and a psychological chapter indicating how the business world reaches its ex ante decisions.' (Keynes, 1973b, p. 183).
36. We shall return to Sraffa's analysis in the next chapter.

7. Kaleckian macroeconomics: an outline

7.1 INTRODUCTION

Keynes's microfoundations have been criticized and his hypotheses of short-period increasing marginal costs and decreasing marginal efficiency of capital have been rejected. As a result of this, we obtain an analytical context that is not too different from Marx's framework: in a freely competitive context, firms would produce and invest at the highest possible rates. This process may come to an end if expected prices and expected rates of profit fall below some crucial minimum values. In this case a general overproduction crisis ensues.

This analytical picture may be made more realistic by assuming that firms produce at varying unit costs. Under this additional hypothesis, the economy may temporarily experience underutilization of capacity along with unemployment of labour even without 'general gluts'. But such an analytical framework does not make it possible to demonstrate that the economy can tend to underemployment equilibria.

We are, then, in a rather paradoxical situation. Realism of hypotheses and logical consistency combined take us, so to say, 'back' from Keynes to Marx and we lose an important analytical result, that is to say the possibility to show that the economy can experience prolonged states of underutilization of capacity and labour, even though it does not go through significant market perturbations.

The solution to this problem can be found by looking at Kalecki's contribution. In Kalecki's analytical framework, in fact, we can achieve the result of underemployment equilibria based on more solid microfoundations than Keynes's. The key factor that allows Kalecki to retain acceptable microfoundations and to show the possibility of underemployment equilibria is that he carried out his analysis by considering an economy in which the prevailing market form is not perfect, or free, competition.

This chapter looks at the basic features of Kalecki's macroeconomics, without any pretence of exhaustiveness. The main object of the chapter is to look at those aspects of Kalecki's contribution that relate more directly to the problems left unsolved by both Marx and Keynes, with which we have been dealing in the previous chapters.

The organization of the chapter is as follows. Section 7.2 looks at the problem of the firm's equilibrium in the short period. Section 7.3 is concerned with the growth of firms and Kalecki's theory of investment. Section 7.4 expounds the basic elements of Kalecki's macroeconomic model. Section 7.5 concludes with some considerations concerning Kalecki's approach in relation to Marx and Keynes.

7.2 THE EQUILIBRIUM OF THE FIRM IN THE SHORT PERIOD

Kalecki rejected the traditional hypothesis of increasing short-period supply curves, asserting that they are generally flat up to the full use of capacity, and only afterwards become steeply increasing. Under this hypothesis, the only way to establish an equilibrium level of production for the firm is to posit that it always produces to capacity unless the expected price falls below the unit prime cost; but this clashes with empirical reality, where firms do not always fully use their capacity even though the price is above the prime cost.[1]

The rationale of such behaviour has to be found in the type of markets in which firms operate:

> why does not the entrepreneur expand production even though he would in this case make additional profits? ... The question is not difficult to explain in the case of cartels ... . This, however, does not solve our problem fully. It is true that the cartelized sector in a modern capitalist economy is considerable, however, in a significant part of the economy competition of one type or another is still in existence ... . An ingenious but simple answer to this question has been given only recently. It appears that even non-cartelized firms compete with each other in a rather imperfect way.[2] (Kalecki, 1991b, p. 31)

If the firm does not operate in free competition, it faces a demand curve that is not perfectly elastic (both in the short and in the long period). In such a situation the level of production (and employment) at which the firm's profits are maximized is the one at which the (constant) marginal cost is equal to the (decreasing) marginal revenue. But this level does not necessarily imply the full use of the firm's capacity. The downward-sloping demand curve which the firm faces may prevent it from producing to capacity. Thus, the rejection of the assumption of free competition makes it possible to show that, in any current period, the level of employment is not necessarily the one that corresponds to the full use of existing capacity, even though prices are above unit variable costs.

However, the analytical framework considered so far cannot demonstrate that the economy could tend to underemployment equilibria. In a current period, firms may well produce below capacity and employ fewer workers than their plants would allow, but if aggregate demand is not constrained by any obstacle, the eventual result must still be, once again, the full use of capacity with its corresponding level of employment. This would be the 'true' equilibrium position. The demonstration of the possibility of under-employment equilibria is contingent on demonstrating that there exist constraints to an unlimited expansion of aggregate demand. Such constraints essentially derive from the existence of limits to firms' investment. Kalecki's approach to this issue, again, hinges on the rejection of the hypothesis of free competition.

7.3   THE LIMITS TO FIRMS' GROWTH AND THE THEORY OF INVESTMENT

Kalecki's explanation of why, in imperfect markets, firms do not necessarily grow at the highest possible rate, was also influenced by Sraffa's 1926 article. This is briefly summarized here, before we turn to consider Kalecki's own developments.[3]

7.3.1   Sraffa's Contribution

In his article Sraffa was concerned with the determination of the equilibrium position for a single firm in the long period, under the assumption of increasing returns, which were regarded as the most probable. In perfect competition this would imply that, in principle, the expansion of the firm should be infinite, which is tantamount to saying that, in each period, firms invest as much as possible. Sraffa's point, however, was that firms do not operate in perfect competition; they cannot grow (cannot invest) as much as increasing returns would induce them to do, because they meet obstacles on the demand side. Such obstacles imply that growing quantities can be sold either at a lower price or at increasing marketing expenses.

> Business men, who regard themselves as being subject to competitive conditions, would consider absurd the assertion that the limit to their production is to be found in the internal conditions of production in their firm, which do not permit the production of a greater quantity without an increase in cost. The chief obstacle against which they have to contend when they want gradually to increase their production does not lie in the cost of production – which, indeed, generally favours them in that direction – but in the difficulty of selling the larger quantity of goods without reducing the price, or without having to face increased marketing expenses. This ... is only an aspect of the usual descending demand curve, with the difference that instead of concerning the whole of a commodity ... it relates only to the goods produced by a particular firm. (Sraffa, 1926, p. 543)

Firms know that an increase in capacity would lower production costs, but they also know that there are constraints to the absorption of their output. If these constraints did not exist, each firm would expand its investment as much as possible, and the only limit to the process, in each current period, would be the capacity of the industries producing capital goods.[4]

In his analysis, Sraffa also brought in some aspects related to credit and banks. A firm that seeks to increase its productive capacity might encounter increasing difficulty in obtaining the required funds at a certain given rate of interest. A further expansion of investment might then be materially impossible or imply increasing costs. This, for Sraffa, is just a consequence of the particular conditions under which firms operate. The limited availability of credit to a firm 'is often a direct consequence of its being known that a given firm is unable to increase its sales outside its own particular market without incurring heavy marketing expenses' (Sraffa, 1926, p. 550).

Thus, even if the single firm wished to expand its productive capacity, banks can prevent the expansion of investment by withholding the required funds or making them available only at a higher rate of interest. Nor, moreover, are financial markets free competitive markets, so it cannot be assumed that industrial firms are perfectly indifferent as to the various sources of finance, and each bank can be in a privileged position with respect to a restricted group of firms. In such a case, even if a particular firm might be in a position to expand production without serious obstacles and to receive higher profits, the inducement to grow would be reduced by its bank exacting higher rates of interest.[5]

7.3.2 Kalecki's Developments

Turning to Kalecki's own analysis of the limits to the firm's growth, he too based his explanation on constraints on the demand side and in financial markets. Of the two factors usually cited as limiting a firm's size and growth rate (increasing costs caused by diseconomies of scale and demand limitations), Kalecki, like Sraffa, regarded only the second as relevant.

Kalecki, however, did not regard the demand constraint as a completely satisfactory explanation of the limits to the growth of firms. In fact, the demand constraint, *per se*, cannot account for the existence in an industry of firms of different sizes.[6] The decisive factor for a firm's growth is the amount of 'entrepreneurial capital' available to it. This is not only because the firm's own capital represents the main source of finance for new investment projects, but also because the amount of finance available to any firm in the market depends largely on its 'entrepreneurial capital'.

The access of a firm to the capital market … is determined to a large extent by the amount of its entrepreneurial capital. It would be impossible for a firm to borrow

capital above a certain level determined by the amount of its entrepreneurial capital. If, for instance, a firm should attempt to float a bond issue which was too large
in terms of its entrepreneurial capital, this issue would not be subscribed in full. ...
In addition, many firms will not use to the full the potentialities of the capital market
because of the 'increasing risk' involved in expansion. (Kalecki, 1965, pp. 91–2)[7]

Thus, if one combines Sraffa's observations with Kalecki's, an explanation of
the limits to the growth of the individual firm, even in the presence of increasing returns in the long period, emerges. Because of demand and financial
constraints, firms do not tend to establish an unlimited increase in their
productive capacity.

From these general conclusions, Kalecki derived a specific investment
function. In fact, he made many attempts at deriving a function that he
regarded as fully satisfactory.[8] A full treatment of Kalecki's theory of investment is beyond the scope of the present work. Here, we limit ourselves only
to look at some essential elements of his investment function by referring to
one of its latest versions (Kalecki, 1965, pp. 96–108).

In analyzing fixed investment, Kalecki drew a precise distinction between
investment decision and actual investment expenditures. Investment decisions
are followed by actual investment with a time lag, which mainly depends on
the construction period of capital goods. The investment decisions function at
time t can be written as:

$$D_t = aS_t + b(\Delta P_t/\Delta t) - c\,(\Delta K_t/\Delta t) + d \qquad (7.1)$$

S_t is total gross savings at t; $\Delta P_t/\Delta t$ is the rate of change in profits over the
current period; $\Delta K_t/\Delta t$ is the rate of change of productive capacity over the
same period and d is a constant (exogenously given) that reflects the influence
of long-run factors (such as technical progress).

Total gross savings affect investment decisions because they are related to the
firms' total gross savings (that is internal accumulation of capital) and we have
already seen that internal funds are crucial for firms' investment (Kalecki's
analysis of 'entrepreneurial capital');[9] the rate of change in profits influences
investment decisions because it is a proxy for expected profits; the rate of change
in productive capacity affects investment in that an increase in the capital equipment determines a fall in the rate of profit (if profits are constant).

The investment decisions made at time t will become actual investment
expenditures with a time lag of length, τ, so that

$$F_{t+\tau} = D_t$$

where $F_{t+\tau}$ is the level of fixed investment at $(t + \tau)$.

After a number of manipulations and after having added investment in inventories, Kalecki arrived at the function of total investment:

$$I_{t+\theta} = (a/(1 + c))S_t + b'\ (\Delta P_t/\Delta t) + e(\Delta O_t/\Delta t) + d' \qquad (7.2)$$

θ is the investment time lag; $\Delta O_t/\Delta t$ is the rate of change of output, which affects investment in inventories and $(1 + c)$ reflects the negative effect on investment of the existing stock of capital (Kalecki, 1965, pp. 107–8).

Our treatment of Kalecki's investment theory need not be further developed in the present context, but two final considerations are necessary.[10] The first concerns the interest rate and its role in the explanation of investment; the second concerns the great importance that Kalecki gave to social and political factors in the determination of investment and its dynamics.

In Kalecki's investment function the rate of interest does not explicitly appear as one of the independent variables. This is for two reasons: first, Kalecki observed, the influence that the rate of interest may exert on investment can be embodied in the coefficient of the rate of change in profits in the equation above (Kalecki, 1965, p. 99); second, and more important, the (long-term) rate of interest has a secondary role, because of its marked stability, so that it could be omitted from the investment equation (Kalecki, 1965, p. 88).[11]

This certainly represents a difference from Keynes's analysis, but it is not as significant as it might seem. In Keynes's theory, the rate of interest enters into the investment function to reflect the fundamental role of monetary factors in the determination of investment, as changes in the rate of interest reflect changes in liquidity preference. Changes in liquidity preference are as important for Kalecki as for Keynes, but they are not reflected in changes in the rate of interest. The crucial monetary and financial factor is the banks' propensity to lend (to finance investment); a lower propensity to lend (which amounts to a higher liquidity preference on the part of banks) implies the rationing of financial capital rather than increases in the cost of borrowing. In some cases, moreover, Kalecki took account of the relation between the interest rate and investment.[12] Thus, the two theories of investment retain important common characteristics.

Although Kalecki tried several different investment functions that can be tested econometrically, he never pretended that such functions could possibly explain investment in a complete and satisfactory fashion. For Kalecki, there are also social and political factors that can prevent the economy from achieving and maintaining the level of investment required to ensure full employment. Kalecki's ideas on the importance of 'non-economic' factors are perhaps most clearly set out in his 1943 article, 'Political Aspects of Full Employment' (Kalecki, 1990b), in which he pointed out that even if the economy as a whole could generate and maintain a level of investment corresponding to full employment, there are fundamental forces at work that prevent the system from doing so. These forces, in brief, consist in the opposition to full employment on the part of the capitalist class as a whole. In particular, the capitalists' opposition derives from 'their dislike of the social and political changes resulting from the maintenance of full employment'.[13] Conditions of full, or near full, employment imply stronger economic as well as political bargaining power for the working class, which can determine changes in income distribution.[14]

7.4　THE DETERMINATION OF AGGREGATE PROFITS AND OUTPUT

Most of the elements of Kalecki's theory considered so far can be embodied into a macroeconomic model for the determination of aggregate profits and the equilibrium level of the economy's output. This model also allows us to easily point out significant relationships between Marx's, Keynes's and Kalecki's analyses.

7.4.1　Investment and Profits

Let us consider a closed economy with no public sector that operates in conditions of non-perfect competition, so that prices are cost-determined.[15] From national accounting and the macroeconomic equilibrium condition, at time t it must be

$$P_t + W_t = I_t + C_{k,t} + C_{w,t} \tag{7.3}$$

(P denote gross profits, W wages, I gross investment, C_k capitalists' consumption and C_w workers' consumption).

If we also assume that the workers' average and marginal propensity to consume is 1, (7.3) reduces to

$$P_t = I_t + C_{k,t} \tag{7.4}$$

Aggregate gross profits equal gross investment plus the capitalists' consumption.

For Kalecki, (7.4) must be read 'from the right to the left', in the sense that total profits are determined by the capitalists' expenditure and not the other way around. In fact, capitalists as a class, in any period, can decide how much to invest and consume but they cannot decide how much to receive (Kalecki, 1965, pp. 46–7).[16]

Kalecki obtained the result above from his own version of Marx's schemes of reproduction (Kalecki, 1965, 1968). He considered an economy with three sectors: sector 1 that produces investment goods (I); sector 2 that produces consumption goods for capitalists (C_k); sector 3 that produces consumption goods for workers (C_w). In the first two sectors, gross profits are given by

$$P_1 = I - W_1$$

$$P_2 = C_k - W_2$$

respectively. The third sector, after having paid wages to its workers (W_3), is left with ($C_w - W_3$), which is bought by workers of the other two sectors. Equality between demand and supply of the consumption good for workers requires that

$$P_3 = C_w - W_3 = W_1 + W_2$$

Therefore, total profits are

$$P = P_1 + P_2 + P_3 = I + C_k$$

Were the capitalists to decide to spend less than ($I + C_k$), the economy as a whole would experience a lower level of profits as well as a lower level of production and employment. The similarity between Kalecki's determination of aggregate profits and Marx's approach is quite evident.

This line of analysis, however, raises a question,[17] which is essentially the same as the question asked by Marx in the schemes of reproduction (see section 2.6 of Chapter 2). If the economy has to grow from one period to the next, from where do capitalists get the funds to finance their increased investment and/or consumption? Kalecki's answer is similar to Marx's. Kalecki's answer is as follows.

In an economy that does not grow, past realized profits are used to finance capitalists' consumption and current gross investment (equal, of course, to replacement investment), that is

$$P_{t-1} = I_{t-1} + C_{k,t-1}$$

with

$$I_t = I_{t-1}$$

$$C_{k,t} = C_{k,t-1}$$

The capitalist class as a whole owns the required funds to finance its desired expenditure.

If we now assume that, from $(t-1)$ to t, investment and consumption grow at a certain rate $g > 0$, a problem of financing arises. The financing, for Kalecki, must be provided by the banking system. The increase in investment (and/or consumption) at the aggregate level is financed by banks, which become less liquid. At the end of the period, the loans are paid back and banks return to their initial liquidity position.[18]

If we combine the industrial capitalists and financial capitalists into a 'capitalist class', this class determines the level of its own income through its degree of liquidity preference and its decisions to invest and consume. In other words, it is the capitalist class itself that must throw into circulation the amount of money required to make it possible to realize the higher level of profits; the same conclusion as Marx.

In a world in which industrial and financial capitalists constitute two distinct groups, the latter play a crucial role in the process of growth of the economy. If banks have – for whatever reason – a high 'liquidity preference' and do not lend to industrial capitalists, or if they lend less than is needed to sustain expansion, the process of growth is stopped or slackened. Banks are capitalist firms as well; they may have a high 'liquidity preference' if they expect that lending is not profitable enough or too risky. It is not difficult to perceive the similarity between this line of reasoning and Keynes's considerations on the power of banks (Keynes, 1937a).

7.4.2   The Equilibrium Level of Output

Now we can move on the determination of the equilibrium level of output. Following Kalecki, the capitalists' consumption is assumed to depend on their profits with a time lag (λ):

$$C_{k,t} = qP_{t-\lambda} + A \qquad (7.5)$$

where $0 < q < 1$ is the capitalists' marginal propensity to consume and $A > 0$ is a constant denoting the autonomous component of consumption.

Since $P_t = I_t + C_{k,t}$, from (7.5) we obtain

$$P_t = I_t + qP_{t-\lambda} + A \qquad (7.6)$$

In turn, profits at $(t-\lambda)$ are determined by investment at $(t-\lambda)$ and by profits at $(t-2\lambda)$ and so on. Therefore,

$$P_t = \sum_{h=0}^{\infty} q^h I_{t-h\lambda} + A \sum_{h=0}^{\infty} q^h$$

which Kalecki approximates with

$$P_t = f(I_{t-\omega}) \qquad (7.7)$$

Profits at time t are a function of current and past investment, that is to say profits follow investment with a time lag (ω).

With a few manipulations (Kalecki, 1965, p. 54), we obtain that

$$f(I_t) = (I_t + A)/(1 - q)$$

so that (7.7) can be written as

$$P_t = (I_{t-\omega} + A)/(1 - q) \qquad (7.8)$$

The functional relation between profits, investment and aggregate output is obtained by considering the share of wages in gross income, α:[19]

$$W/Y = \alpha \ (0 < \alpha < 1)$$

Since $W = Y - P$,

$$Y_t = P_t/(1 - \alpha) \qquad (7.9)$$

Therefore, from (7.8), we have

$$Y_t = (I_{t-\omega} + A)/[(1 - q)(1 - \alpha)] \qquad (7.10)$$

which denotes the equilibrium level of output. $1/[(1 - q)(1 - \alpha)]$ is the Kaleckian version of the Keynesian multiplier.

As in Keynes's analysis, there is no reason why the level of output so determined should be associated with full employment. There is no reason why firms as a whole should invest to such an extent that the resulting level of aggregate demand corresponds to the full utilization of the existing productive capacity and to the highest possible level of employment. The actual level of investment may well imply underutilization of capacity and underemployment of labour.[20]

The similarity between Keynes's and Kalecki's equilibrium level of output is quite evident. For both, investment plays the crucial role and the economy's overall propensity to consume exerts a positive effect on the multiplier effect of investment. This latter relation, however, in Kalecki's analysis takes on a specific form: the multiplier is increasing in α, the wage share. This depends on the assumption that the workers' propensity to consume (equal to 1) is higher than the capitalists' ($q < 1$). Any increase in the wage share implies an increase in the economy's overall propensity to consume.

Kalecki's analysis does not terminate at this stage. By using the investment function illustrated in the previous section, he developed his theory of the business cycle and long-period growth (Kalecki, 1965, pp. 119–42 and 145–73 respectively). In this context, an increase in the wage share, which has a positive impact on the multiplier as expressed in (7.10), will produce lagged negative effects on profits and, hence, investment. Considering these other important aspects of Kalecki's economics is beyond the scope of this book.[21]

7.5   MARX, KEYNES AND KALECKI: CONCLUDING CONSIDERATIONS

The analysis above shows that Kalecki's theory represents a natural bridge between Marx and Keynes and between Marxian and Keynesian economists. Joan Robinson, the Keynesian economist who paid most attention to the relationships between Marx and Keynes, often pointed out that Kalecki was the natural *trait d'union* between the two.

Keynes, in writing *The General Theory*, was trying to escape from the 'habitual mode of thought and expression'. Kalecki did not have to struggle as hard as Keynes to get away from the traditional dominant theory; he was not very much influenced by it, as he had studied economics starting from Marx, Rosa Luxemburg and Tugan Baranowsky.[22]

Kalecki's theory of effective demand was inspired by Marx and this allowed him to reach some of Keynes's analytical results in a more direct and straightforward way. Joan Robinson observed:

> Keynes could never make head or tail of Marx ... . But starting from Marx would have saved him a lot of trouble. Kahn, at the 'circus' where we discussed the *Treatise* in 1931, explained the problem of saving and investment by imagining a cordon round the capital-good industries and then studying the trade between them and the consumption-good industries; he was struggling to rediscover Marx's scheme. Kalecki began at that point. (Robinson, 1965a, p. 96)[23]

This section concludes our study of the analytical relationships between Kalecki, Marx and Keynes by summarizing and stressing those aspects that are regarded as most relevant.

7.5.1 Kalecki and Marx

Kalecki carried out his analysis within a framework that departed from the hypothesis of free competition, assuming that imperfect competition and oligopoly are the prevailing market forms. Kalecki's notion of non-perfectly competitive markets was partly influenced by Marx's analysis of the capitalist tendency to concentration and centralization of capitals.[24] Marx's vision of the competitive process held that competition would be superseded by monopoly.

Marx regarded competition as a continuous struggle among firms for higher profits and larger market shares. In this struggle, technical progress and economies of scale play a central role. A firm which is able to adopt a new, more productive method of production than those generally in use obtains two advantages: (1) lower production costs and therefore a higher rate of profit than the average, and (2) a larger market share, should the innovative firm sell its commodities at a price which, though still high enough to yield extra-profits, undercuts the prevailing market price. Threatened with the progressive loss of their market, the other firms will be forced to adopt the new method of production. Eventually a new lower price will be established and no firm will receive an extraordinary rate of profit (Marx, 1954, pp. 301–2).

This process, however, can actually take place if it is assumed that there are no significant barriers or obstacles to firms in the industry adopting the new method. If, instead, such barriers are sufficiently strong, the innovative firm clearly enjoys a permanent monopolistic position. Marx allowed for this latter possibility. In the struggle to get a wider share of the market and higher profits, firms are induced to enlarge their scale of production to exploit economies of scale. The more successful firms grow faster than their competitors and keep the latter from growing fast enough to obtain analogous advantages.[25] Thus Marx envisaged a dynamic process starting from a competitive market and leading to one in which free competition is abolished.

In this sense, Kalecki's analysis can be regarded as a direct development of Marx's, even though such a conclusion must be qualified. Marx's analysis leads to the conclusion that the whole economy will eventually be characterized by the existence of few large monopolistic firms in every industry. But such a conclusion is just as unrealistic as the hypothesis of free competition ruling throughout the economy.[26] Kalecki's approach allows us to avoid this outcome. In Kalecki's analysis, there is a process of concentration that leads to the creation of large dominant firms, but it does not necessarily imply the disappearance of smaller firms. Many small firms coexist with a few large firms. 'Imperfections' and differentiations of markets make it possible for relatively small firms to remain in the market. In particular, as we saw, imperfections in the capital markets explain the existence of firms of different size.

7.5.2 Kalecki and Keynes

Kalecki carried out a thorough criticism of Keynes's theory of investment, which was crucial for the determination of underemployment equilibria. Kalecki then developed his own theory, which is set in a non-perfectly competitive framework where firms (operating at constant short-period returns) do not necessarily produce to capacity and their investment is constrained by demand and finance.

The so-called 'imperfect competition revolution' of the 1930s had also tried to provide a more realistic explanation of firms' behaviour than that deriving from the assumption of perfect competition.[27] But this attempt was not successful. The demonstration that, under the hypothesis of imperfect competition, firms could experience equilibria with excess capacity was based on hypotheses on the working of markets that, on the whole, remained unrealistic.[28]

Keynes was never very appreciative of the importance of imperfect competition. He was sceptical about the analytical results of the microeconomics of imperfect competition, and in *The General Theory* he maintained the competitive hypothesis. The reasons for Keynes's attitude and choices are many (see, for example, Harcourt and Sardoni, 1994); among them there probably is the conviction that a Marshallian 'vague' notion of competition was sufficiently solid to support the general theory of effective demand. Keynes, in fact, did not see any fundamental relationship between the issue of market forms and his principle of effective demand.[29]

Only in 1939 did Keynes explicitly concede that the actual economic system is characterized by the existence of 'quasi-competitive' markets. He, however, remained quite hostile to the economics of imperfect competition and failed to perceive the more general analytical implications of abandoning the hypotheses of perfect competition and upward-sloping short-period supply curves.[30] It was left to Kalecki to bring the theory of effective demand and the analysis of market forms together.[31]

NOTES

1. In 'Money and real wages', Kalecki observed: 'Then, however, a difficult problem arises. On the assumption of increasing marginal costs the production of an establishment was pushed up to a point where the price was equal to the marginal costs. Now the price is higher than the marginal costs when the degree of utilization of the establishment is not very high' (Kalecki, 1991b, p. 31).
2. The 'ingenious but simple answer' referred to, as a footnote makes it clear, was Sraffa's 1926 article on the laws of returns, which opened the debate on imperfect competition, even though the main intent of Sraffa's article – which followed a previous article in Italian (Sraffa, 1925) – was to criticize the Marshallian theory of value (see Bharadwaj, 1976;

Harcourt, 1982, 1983). On the 1930s debate on imperfect competition, see the admirable historical and critical reconstruction offered by Shackle (1983, pp. 13–70). See also Robinson (1969, pp. xiii–vi), on the influence that Sraffa exerted on her development of the concept of imperfect competition.

3. On the relationship between Sraffa and Kalecki, see also Sardoni (1984).

4. The reasoning above could be carried out using the concept of marginal revenue in the long period. Sraffa, however, did not employ this concept, which was explicitly used only later on, for instance by Harrod (1930). For the history of the introduction and adoption of the concept of marginal revenue, see Shackle (1983, pp. 22–42).

5. 'If a banker ... stands in a privileged position in respect to it [the firm], he can certainly exact from it a price higher than the current price for his supplies, but this possibility will still be a direct consequence of the fact that such a firm, being in its turn in a privileged position in regard to its particular market, also sells its products at prices above cost. What happens in such cases is that a portion of its monopoly profits are taken away from the firm, not that its cost of production is increased' (Sraffa, 1926, p. 550).

6. 'The limitation of the size of the firm by the market for its products is real enough but it leaves unexplained the existence of large and small firms in the same industry' (Kalecki, 1965, p. 91). Kalecki was concerned with all manufacturing industries and therefore he also had to account for those industries where firms of different sizes exist together. This was not Sraffa's concern, for his attention was focused on those industries whose characteristics closely resemble those of a competitive industry (a large number of relatively small independent firms) (Sraffa, 1926, p. 542).

7. 'Many economists assume, at least in their abstract theories, a state of business democracy where anybody endowed with entrepreneurial ability can obtain capital for starting a business venture. This picture of the activities of the "pure" entrepreneur is, to put it mildly, unrealistic. The most important prerequisite for becoming an entrepreneur is the ownership of capital' (Kalecki, 1965, pp. 94–5). The assumed 'business democracy' is, of course, the hypothesis of perfect competition.

8. His last attempt at formulating an investment function was in 1968 (Kalecki, 1991c), shortly before his death in 1970. In the introduction to *Selected Essays on the Dynamics of the Capitalist Economy, 1933–1970*, he wrote: 'It is interesting to notice that the theory of effective demand, already clearly formulated in the first papers, remains unchanged in all the relevant writing. ...However, there is a continuous search for new solutions in the theory of investment decisions, where even the last paper represents – for better or worse – a novel approach' (Kalecki, 1971, p. viii).

9. The firms' gross savings include depreciation plus undistributed profits; Kalecki (1965, p. 97) added to them also personal savings of the 'controlling groups invested in their companies through subscription to new share issues.'

10. For further developments of Kalecki's theory of investment, see Kalecki (1991c). See also Asimakopulos (1971, 1977); Steindl (1981); Sawyer (1985, pp. 43–69).

11. Kalecki's approach to the long-term interest rate resembles Kaldor's theory of the long-term interest rate, which in turn was significantly influenced by Hicks (1939). On this, see also Sardoni (2007).

12. In considering the role of the central bank in the determination of aggregate investment, he observed: 'The creation of the purchasing power for financing additional investment increases the output. ... It should be pointed out that the increase in output will result in an increased demand for money in circulation, and thus will call for a rise in credits of the Central Bank. Should the bank respond to it by raising the rate of interest ... no increase in investment would ensue and the economic situation would not improve. Therefore the precondition for the upswing is that the rate of interest should not increase too much in response to an increased demand for cash' (Kalecki, 1990a, p. 91).

13. Other reasons for their opposition are: '(i) the dislike of Government interference in the problem of employment as such; (ii) the dislike of the direction of Government spending (public investment and subsidising consumption)' (Kalecki, 1990b, pp. 349–50). In fact, for Kalecki, full employment could not be realized without state intervention, in particular fiscal policy. On Kalecki's article, see also Harcourt (2006, pp. 147–9).

14. On the analysis of the conflict over income distribution in conditions of non-perfect competition, see Kalecki (1991a).

15. With the exception of agriculture and the production of raw materials, where free competition prevails and prices are demand-determined. See Kalecki (1965, pp. 11–27) and Appendix C for more details.

16. If the model is generalized to include the public sector and the rest of the world, (7.3) becomes $P_t + W_t + T_t = I_t + (X_t - M_t) + G_t + C_{k,t} + C_{w,t}$, which reduces to $P_t = I_t + (X_t - M_t) + (G_t - T_t) + C_{k,t}$ under the assumption that workers consume all their wages.

17. See, for example, Kalecki (1935, p. 343).

18. In Kalecki's words, 'the circle will close itself'. Kalecki assumed that this occurs within a period, which amounts to assuming that the multiplier effect fully operates within the same period. But this assumption can be lifted.

19. Kalecki considers the share of wages plus salaries in gross income, which is $v/y = \alpha + B/Y$, B, positive and constant in the short period, denotes salaries, which fluctuate less than wages (Kalecki, 1965, pp. 39–40). For some more details on Kalecki's determination of the wage share, see Appendix C.

20. If firms' short-term expectations are correct, the economy finds itself in an underemployment equilibrium position. Firms are in equilibrium, as their current production is entirely absorbed by the market. If short-term expectations are wrong, adjustment processes are set in motion which lead the economy to its equilibrium position, provided that the aggregate level of investment does not change in the meantime.

21. See, however, Chapter 9 for some considerations about the relationship between Kalecki's interest in the trade cycle in relation to his determination of underemployment equilibria.

22. 'Kalecki had one great advantage over Keynes – he had never learned orthodox economics. ... The only economics he had studied was Marx' (Robinson, 1965a, pp. 95–6).

23. On Joan Robinson on Kalecki, see also Robinson (1973a, 1977).

24. Marx's notion of free competition, on the other hand, was closer to the classical view of competition rather than to the neoclassical notion of perfect competition. On this see McNulty (1968) and also Eatwell (1982).

25. 'The battle of competition is fought by cheapening of commodities. The cheapness of commodities depends, *ceteris paribus*, on the productiveness of labour, and this again on the scale of production. Therefore, the larger capitals beat the smaller. It will further be remembered that, with the development of the capitalist mode of production, there is an increase in the minimum amount of individual capital necessary to carry on a business under its normal conditions. The smaller capitals, therefore, crowd into spheres of production which Modern Industry has only sporadically or incompletely got hold of. Here competition rages in direct proportion to the number, and in inverse proportion to the magnitudes, of the antagonistic capitals' (Marx, 1954, pp. 586–7).

26. Moreover, Marx was analyzing a capitalist economy at its early stages of development, and according to his analysis, monopoly or oligopoly should have become the dominant, pervasive market form very early, if increasing returns have always characterized most industries since the beginning of capitalist development.

27. In the preface to the second edition of *The Economics of Imperfect Competition*, Robinson (1969, p. vi) provided a short reconstruction of the process that led to the development of the concept of equilibrium with excess capacity. Within the traditional context, firms always tend either to produce the level of output associated with their optimum size, or not to produce at all (when the price is lower than the average variable cost). Such a conclusion was evidently at odds with the reality of the 1920s and 1930s. The notion of imperfect competition and the associated type of equilibrium seemed to allow economists to offer a better explanation of the actual behaviour of firms.

28. For more details on the 1930s debate on imperfect competition and excess capacity, see Sardoni (1999). See also Steindl (1976, pp. 1–4).

29. See, for example, Keynes's observations on Ohlin's comments regarding Robinson's doctrine of imperfect competition in relation to *The General Theory* (Keynes, 1983, p. 190).

30. Indicative of his attitude is the correspondence with Robinson on an article that Kalecki, in 1941, had submitted for publication in *The Economic Journal*. Kalecki assumed that firms

always work below capacity, and Keynes observed: 'Is it not rather odd when dealing with "long run problems" to start with the assumption that all firms are always working below capacity?' (1983, p. 829). For Joan Robinson, it was not at all odd, because that was 'part of the usual bag of tricks of Imperfect Competition Theory' (cited in Keynes, 1983, p. 830). Keynes replied: 'If he [Kalecki] is extending the *General Theory* beyond the short period but not to the long period in the old sense, he really must tell us what the sense is. For I am still innocent enough to be bewildered by the idea that the assumption of all firms always working below capacity is consistent with a "long-run problem". To tell me that as for under-capacity working that is part of the usual pack of tricks of imperfect competition theory does not carry me any further. For publication in the *Journal* an article must pass beyond the stage of esoteric abracadabra' (Keynes, 1983, pp. 830–1).

31. With Kalecki, 'what began with Sraffa's objection to the lack of logic in orthodox economic theory and Professor Chamberlin's objection to its lack of realism opened up into a general indictment of the operation of the economic system itself' (Robinson, 1960a, p. 241).

8. The problem of market forms in modern macroeconomics

8.1 INTRODUCTION

Current mainstream macroeconomic models are very often based on an assumption of imperfect, or monopolistic competition, both in goods markets and in the labour market. In particular, New Keynesian macroeconomics is characterized by this assumption on market forms. From this point of view, therefore, modern macroeconomics can be put in relation to the Kaleckian approach expounded in the previous chapters. The present chapter briefly looks at the current mainstream in macroeconomics in order to better illustrate and understand this relationship.

The object of the present chapter is not to offer an exhaustive survey of the literature on macroeconomic models with monopolistic competition.[1] Here, we concentrate only on some aspects of these models. In particular, the chapter concentrates on those features of macroeconomic models with monopolistic competition that Solow (1998) regards as most interesting and with a 'Keynesian flavour'.

Solow regards macroeconomic models based on the hypothesis of monopolistic competition as an alternative to the New Classical Macroeconomics. Such models are able to provide different and more satisfactory analyses of the economy's behaviour at the micro and macro levels. First, non-perfectly competitive models can explain the existence of excess supply, or excess capacity. In fact, in imperfect competition firms would be generally ready to produce more at the existing current price if there were additional demand for their goods. As a consequence, in such a context, an increase in aggregate demand has a multiplier effect. Second, models based on monopolistic competition can explain price rigidity or stickiness, which allows changes in nominal variables to produce real effects.[2]

Another implication of non-perfectly competitive models is, for Solow, of particular importance from the macroeconomic point of view. Under imperfect competition, firms make their expectations in terms of quantities rather than prices.[3] This leads to strategic complementarity because the firm's expected demand depends on the expected behaviour of other firms and, more generally, on the expected aggregate demand. This aspect gives the models a 'Keynesian air': firms' expectations are necessarily influenced by 'animal spirits', that is optimism or pessimism about the future behaviour of demand affect the firms' current decisions about how much to produce and employ.

Finally, monopolistic competition makes it possible to assume the existence of increasing returns to scale, which again emphasize the relevance of Keynesian animal spirits. In the short run, with a given number of firms in the industry, there are positive profits when demand conditions are favourable. In the long run, these profits attract new entrants and equilibrium is realized when profits are at their normal level. But entry into an industry is 'a risky business, with a real possibility of irreversible loss'. Thus, inevitably, entry decisions are influenced by optimistic or pessimistic expectations about the future level of demand. In other words, entry occurs when animal spirits are favourable. The considerations for entry decisions can be immediately extended and applied to investment decisions (Solow, 1998, p. 24).[4]

In the following sections, we look at some of the aspects and issues mentioned above. Section 8.2 is concerned with short and long-period equilibria in monopolistic competition; section 8.4 deals with a simplified New Keynesian macroeconomic model with imperfect competition, which is largely used in modern textbooks and in the debate on economic policy. The relationship between mainstream macroeconomics and the Keynesian-Kaleckian approach is discussed in section 8.4. Section 8.5 concludes.[5]

8.2 EQUILIBRIA UNDER MONOPOLISTIC COMPETITION

8.2.1 The Short Period

In most mainstream macroeconomic models assuming monopolistic competition, the households' demand for consumption as well as their supply of labour are derived from the maximization of their inter-temporal utility function.[6] This aspect, which undoubtedly is very far from the Keynesian-Kaleckian approach, is not dealt with here. Attention is instead focused on firms' behaviour.

Let us start by considering real aggregate demand, $\bar{y}$:[7]

$$\bar{y} = m - \bar{p} \qquad (8.1)$$

where m is the nominal money supply and $\bar{p}$ is the average price level.

Let us then consider one of the many firms in the economy. This firm faces a downward-sloping demand curve that depends on real aggregate demand ($\bar{y}$) the average price level ($\bar{p}$) and the price p set by the firm itself:

$$q = -k(p - \bar{p}) + \bar{y} \tag{8.2}$$

q is the quantity demanded and k denotes the degree of competition in the economy. Technology is such that the cost of producing the quantity q^s is $(1 + c_1)q^s$, with $c_1 > 0$. The fact that the individual firm takes account of the average price, which derives from the other firms' price decisions, denotes strategic complementarity, or interdependence.[8]

The firm's real profits are:

$$\Pi = \exp(p - \bar{p}) \exp(q^s) - \exp[(1 + c_1)q^s] \tag{8.3}$$

which are maximized with respect to p, subject to $q^s \leq q$. By solving the firm's maximization problem, the price p is determined. It depends on the marginal cost, the degree of competition k, the money supply and the average price $\bar{p}$.[9]

When the economy as a whole is in equilibrium, the firms' individual prices must be equal; in other words, individual prices p must equal the average price $\bar{p}$. From this, it follows that

$$\bar{p} = 1/c_1 \left[\log (1 + c_1) + \log (k/k - 1) \right] + m \tag{8.4}$$

The equilibrium output is:

$$\bar{y} = 1/c_1 \left[\log (1 + c_1) + \log (k/(k - 1)) \right] + m \tag{8.5}$$

These results can be compared with the results under the hypothesis of perfect competition, which amounts to k going to infinity. Equations (8.4) and (8.5) show that the monopolistically competitive equilibrium is characterized by higher prices, lower output and, hence, lower employment.[10]

The equilibrium under monopolistic competition can be expressed also in terms of strategic interdependence among firms. In the model, the firm takes the average price as given and it ignores the effects of its price setting on the average price. This, in particular, means that the firm's individual price is not reduced in order to increase demand.[11] If the firm took into account that a reduction of its price also implies a reduction of the average price, this would lead to a generalized price reduction, which, with a given money supply m, would produce real balance effects, that is an increase in aggregate demand, output and employment.[12]

The firm's equilibrium under monopolistic competition can be represented graphically in the traditional way (Figure 8.1). The firm produces the output *OE*, which is sold at the price *OP* , larger than its marginal cost. The firm realizes a positive profit (represented by the rectangle *ABPC* in Figure 8.1). At equilibrium, the firm produces at decreasing unit costs, which means that it is

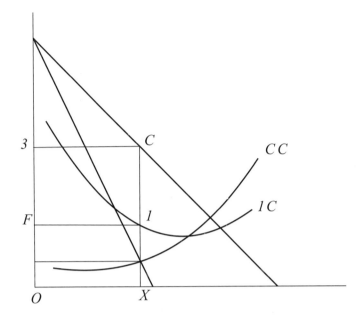

Figure 8.1   The firm's equilibrium in monopolistic competition

producing below full capacity (interpreted as optimum capacity, associated with the minimum unit cost). The firm is demand-constrained, in the sense that if, at the current price, the demand for its good were larger, it would produce more because its price is above its marginal cost.

8.2.2 The Long Period

The equilibrium depicted above is a typical short-period equilibrium with extra-profits in monopolistic competition. But the analysis can be extended to the long period. Extra profits attract new firms into the industry and their entry brings the industry to long-period equilibrium, with profits at their normal level. The entry of new firms makes the demand curve faced by each individual firm shift down and to the left until it becomes tangent to the average total cost (Figure 8.2). At the output *OE*, profits are at their normal level. The tangency condition implies that, in equilibrium, the average cost is decreasing and larger than its minimum, so that each firm in the industry is experiencing excess capacity, that is it produces less than its optimal output (*OF* in Figure 8.2), which is the output that the firm would produce in perfect competition.

The industry long-period equilibrium has been determined under the assumption that entry into an industry in monopolistic competition is essentially the

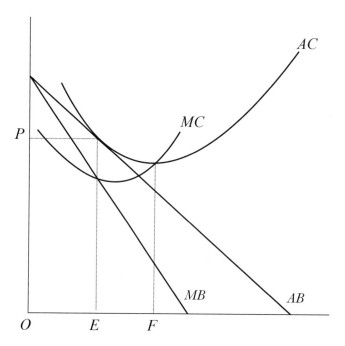

Figure 8.2   Long-period equilibrium with excess capacity

same process as in perfect competition. However, several economists have argued that this is not the case. Solow (1998, pp. 21–5) points out that increasing returns imply that the new firm must have a non-trivial size and this, in turn, implies that potential losses are significant, so that entry is a 'risky business'.[13]

Moreover, if the reactions of the incumbent firms are considered, there is a high probability that the new firms will suffer losses in the initial period of their existence. Incumbent firms could reduce their prices, increase advertising, and so on (Solow, 1998, p. 23). Thus, entry into an industry is highly risky and Solow concludes that entry occurs only when animal spirits are highly favourable. What applies to the entry of new firms into an industry can be extended to investment by existing firms.[14] Increasing returns imply that investment in new capacity must be large and, hence, subject to the risk of incurring large losses.

Others have also developed the analysis of entry into industries in conditions of monopolistic competition by focusing on strategic interdependence and abandoning the simplistic idea that entry occurs in a similar way to that under perfect competition.[15] All these analyses, though different in several respects and results, lead to the conclusion that, in monopolistic competition, the entry of new firms and/or the investment by existing firms is a complex process that cannot be reduced to the simple, mechanical process that is typical of perfect competition.[16] Unfortunately, however, the acknowledgment of the complex nature of firms' long-period decisions has not led to significant developments of a macroeconomic theory of investment. Investment, when introduced into macroeconomic models, is often simply taken as an inverse function of the interest rate.

8.3   THE NEW KEYNESIAN WORKHORSE

In recent years, New Keynesian economists have developed many macroeconomic models with imperfect or monopolistic competition. Here, we refer to a highly simplified basic model, which is largely used in textbooks and also in the debate on policy.[17]

This simplified medium-period model, denoted as a 'workhorse' (Clarida et al., 1999), assumes that both firms and workers are price setters because of some imperfections in the markets. As in the model of section 8.2, this implies that the quantities produced are demand-constrained. As to policy, attention is focused on monetary policy, which is assumed to be conducted by the central bank through variations of the interest rate rather than variations of the quantity of money.[18]

The basic features of the model are expressed by three equations:[19]

1.   an aggregate demand function, which can be regarded as the equivalent of the *IS* schedule of traditional Keynesian models;
2.   an expectation-augmented Phillips curve;
3.   a 'monetary rule', which expresses the behaviour of the central bank.

The *IS* function can be expressed in terms of deviations of the actual level of output from what is often called its natural equilibrium level. Starting from the equation of aggregate demand

$$y = A - ar$$

(with *A* denoting all the exogenous components of aggregate demand and *r* the real interest rate) we obtain

$$y - y_e = - a(r - r_e) \tag{8.6}$$

where y_e denotes the natural equilibrium level of output and r_e is the real interest rate associated with it. y_e is defined as the level of output at which inflation is constant.

The second equation is an expectation-augmented Phillips curve:

$$\pi = \pi_{-1} + \alpha(y - y_e) \tag{8.7}$$

Expected inflation is set equal to inflation in the previous period, π_{-1}.

The monetary rule can be written as

$$y - y_e = -b(\pi - \pi^T) \tag{8.8}$$

where π^T is the rate of inflation targeted by the central bank.

From equations (8.6) to (8.8), it is obvious that insofar as the economy does not deviate from y_e it experiences a constant inflation rate. If the economy deviates from y_e and, in particular, it is $y > y_e$, an inflationary process starts. The Phillips curve (8.7) describes the dynamics of the process. The central bank's interventions ensure that the economy is brought back to its natural equilibrium every time it is hit by a shock of any type and inflation deviates from its target.

The natural equilibrium level of output, y_e, is essentially determined by the interaction of workers and employers, who set wages and prices respectively. The money wage rate is set, through bargaining, at a level W that depends on the expected price level, P^e, and the level of employment, L:

$$W = P^e b(L) \tag{8.9}$$

with both $dW/dP^e > 0$ and $dW/dL > 0$. From (8.9) we obtain

$$w^B = W/P^e = b(L) \tag{8.10}$$

which is the real wage rate that workers aim for, when they bargain at the level of employment L.[20]

Firms set prices by applying a mark up μ to their unit prime cost, which is given by the unit labour cost W/λ (with λ denoting the productivity of labour), so that

$$P = (1 + \mu)(W/\lambda)$$

from which we obtain

$$w^F = W/P = \lambda/(1 + \mu) \tag{8.11}$$

w^F is the real wage rate determined by the firms' price setting. If it is assumed that firms set the price P after nominal wages have been set through bargaining, the actual real wage rate earned by workers is always w^F. Only firms as a whole can determine the actual real wage rate.

The w^F function can be either decreasing or flat with respect to L and output. Its shape depends on the hypotheses made on the behaviour of λ and μ with respect to changes in L. If it is traditionally assumed that labour productivity is decreasing in L, the w^F function is decreasing in L if μ is kept constant by firms. This means that the real wage rate set by firms decreases as the level of employment rises. If while λ decreases, the mark up behaves in such a way as to compensate for the effect of a lower λ, the w^F function can be flat (Carlin and Soskice, 2006, p. 49). Finally, if the average prime cost is assumed to be constant over the business cycle and firms are assumed to apply a constant mark up to their average prime cost, the w^F function is flat as well.[21] Often, at least for the sake of simplicity, the hypothesis of a flat w^F is made. The main implication of a perfectly elastic w^F is that the *actual* real wage rate earned by workers is constant at whatever level of employment.

Regardless of the assumption on the shape of the w^F function, the labour market is in equilibrium when w^B and w^F intersect, that is to say when the claims on the real output per head by workers and employers are compatible with one another. It has to be $w^B = w^F$. This, of course, means that the level of prices expected by workers coincides with the actual level of prices set by firms, which amounts to

$$b(L) = \lambda/(1 + \mu) \tag{8.12}$$

By solving (8.12) in L, we obtain the equilibrium level of employment L_e. Given the economy's aggregate short-period production function, the equilibrium level of output is determined as well,

$$y_e = f(L_e) \tag{8.13}$$

If N is the total labour force, the equilibrium rate of unemployment, or natural rate of unemployment, or non-accelerating inflation rate of unemployment (NAIRU), is:

$$u_e = (N - L_e)/N \tag{8.14}$$

If the economy deviates from its natural level of unemployment and, in particular, if the actual rate of unemployment is smaller than u_e, an inflationary process starts.

u_e is the equilibrium level of unemployment under monopolistic competition, which is higher than the equilibrium rate that would obtain in an economy in which workers do not have the market power that makes the w^B curve lie above the competitive labour supply curve. This unemployment differential is defined as 'involuntary unemployment'.[22]

8.4 THE MAINSTREAM AND THE KALECKIAN APPROACH

In the previous chapter, Kalecki's macroeconomic theory was seen and presented as the response to the problems and issues left unsolved by Keynes as well as Marx. The current macroeconomic mainstream can be seen as a response to the problems and difficulties encountered by Keynesian macroeconomics, even though it is the Keynesian macroeconomics of the second half of the twentieth century, which was quite far from Keynes's original approach. In this section we look at the methodological and analytical relationships between these two approaches by concentrating on the issue of market forms, which plays an important role in both.[23]

The New Keynesian approach to macroeconomics has its origin in the debate on the microfoundations of macroeconomics, which developed from the question whether the Keynesian results at the macro level were compatible with the traditional hypotheses at the micro level.[24] More precisely, New Keynesian macroeconomics is the reaction to the so-called New Classical Macroeconomics, which was characterized by the radical rejection of the Keynesian tradition.

New Classical Macroeconomics, in the wake of Monetarism, reacted to the alleged contradiction between micro and macro theory by developing microfounded models that fully embody the traditional neoclassical hypotheses of maximizing agents operating in conditions of perfect competition.[25] The results obtained in this way, are obviously very far from the Keynesian results, may be logically consistent and rigorous but, not surprisingly, also largely unable to give an acceptable account of the behaviour of actual economies.

The New Keynesian approach is the reaction to the failures of New Classical Macroeconomics. New Keynesian models are able to yield so-called 'Keynesian results'. These results crucially depend on the abandonment of the hypothesis of perfect competition. Also the results of the 'old' Keynesian models of the neoclassical synthesis were contingent on the existence of imperfections, but in the New Keynesian models the agents' behaviour in imperfect markets is explained through microeconomic foundations rather than being simply assumed (see, for example, Blanchard, 2000, 2008).

Since both the Kaleckian and the New Keynesian approaches are characterized by the rejection of the hypothesis of free or perfect competition, this might appear as a significant similarity. In reality, the differences between the two theoretical strands remain relevant. Below, we briefly outline those differences that seem to be most important.

8.4.1 Methodology and Analysis

The methodological stance underlying a typical mainstream model can be summarized as follows.

1. Build a neoclassical model of an economy in perfect competition, with (representative) rational agents that maximize utility and profits over an inter-temporal range.
2. Find the equilibrium solution of the model.
3. Introduce a number of 'imperfections' into the model.
4. Find the new equilibrium and study the way in which the 'imperfect' model deviates from the 'perfect' model, which is given the role of *benchmark*.
5. Study the policy implications deriving from the introduction of imperfections.[26]

Thus, in this theoretical context, the model that should represent the real world is constructed, so to speak, 'by subtraction', that is by divesting the perfectly competitive benchmark of some of its characteristics (price flexibility, perfect information, and so on).[27]

Also in Kalecki the refusal of perfect or, for that matter, free competition plays an important role. However, Kalecki's 'imperfections' are not the result of a 'subtraction' from the perfectly competitive benchmark.[28] The so-called imperfections of markets are regarded as the outcome of the competitive process itself. In this respect, Marx's contribution and the influence it exerted on Kalecki are very important. Marx showed that the competitive process itself leads to the creation of monopolistic positions, which can become permanent.[29]

Consequently, the Kaleckian model of the economy need not be compared to an abstract model of perfect competition. The model aims to represent the world as it is, a world in which firms, and economic agents in general, enjoy a certain degree of market power that derives from the evolution and transformation of competitive markets rather than from special *ad hoc* hypotheses.

Another important difference between the New Keynesian macroeconomic model and the Marxian-Keynesian-Kaleckian approach concerns investment and the role it plays in the determination of underemployment equilibria. In the mainstream macroeconomic model with monopolistic competition, aggregate demand is basically derived from the maximization of the households' inter-temporal utility function. Much less attention is paid to investment and to firms' long-period decisions.[30] Very often, New Keynesian models do not consider investment, for the sake of simplicity. But this simplification has the important implication that, in the model, what essentially prevents the economy from achieving the competitive equilibrium are those imperfections that make prices (and, in particular, wages) sticky and diverge from their perfectly competitive values.

Instead, in the Marxian-Keynesian-Kaleckian approach, investment plays the central role in the explanation of the behaviour and dynamics of the economy. No significant 'Keynesian results' can be obtained by considering investment essentially as a redundant variable, which can be ignored. In this perspective, investment theory should be further developed to analyze the way in which non-perfectly competitive markets affect firms' long-period decisions. For example, by following some of the indications and considerations offered by Solow (1998).

There is, however, a feature of the New Keynesian macroeconomics for which it is easier to single out some similarities with the Kaleckian approach. The New Keynesian model, especially in its three-equation version, is characterized by the conflict between workers and firms over the distribution of the economy's output. If the claims over the produced output are incompatible with one another, the economy can experience an inflationary process. There exists a level of output (employment) at which the claims are compatible. At this level of output, the economy is in an equilibrium position.

The conflictual nature of income distribution is also a typical element of the alternative approach we consider in this book. As we saw in Chapter 3, the distributive conflict is at the core of Marx's analysis of capitalism and, in particular, of his explanation of general overproduction crises. On the other hand, while Keynes, at least in *The General Theory*, did not pay much attention to income distribution, Kalecki (for example, 1990b, 1991a) lucidly pointed out the conflict between wages and profits and its implications on policies to bring the economy towards full employment.[31]

At this level, therefore, it is possible to find a point of contact between the New Keynesians and the non-mainstream approach. This similarity, however, is somewhat hidden by the way in which the New Keynesian equilibrium is interpreted. From the model in section 8.4, it is evident that any equilibrium level of output, y_e, is associated to a corresponding equilibrium interest rate, r_e. Many mainstream as well as Post Keynesian macroeconomists tend to identify this interest rate with the Wicksellian natural interest rate, so that y_e is the 'natural' level of output.[32] However, in our opinion, this sort of interpretation is not correct.

It can be immediately seen from section 8.3 that the determination of the non-inflationary equilibrium does not require any recourse to the Wicksellian natural interest rate. The equilibrium interest rate, r_e, of the New Keynesian model is non-inflationary, like the Wicksellian natural rate, but the similarities end here. In fact, Wicksell's natural interest rate is associated with an economy working in conditions of perfect competition with the factors remunerated at their marginal productivity (see, for example, Wicksell, 1936, pp. 102–21). The three-equation equilibrium (r_e, y_e) deviates from the perfectly competitive benchmark equilibrium (r^*, y^*), which could be properly defined as Wicksellian.

Thus, the equilibrium determined by the three-equation model can be interpreted in a different sense, which is closer to the Kaleckian approach. In a non-perfectly competitive economy, and given the market power of workers and firms, given the economic and social context,[33] there exists a unique level of output and employment (unemployment) at which inflation is constant, that is at which the workers' and firms' claims on output are compatible.[34] This, however, cannot be defined as a state of the economy determined exclusively by the fundamental factors that determine neoclassical equilibria. Since the market power of the agents is affected also by social, political and historical factors, so is the resulting non-inflationary macroeconomic equilibrium.[35]

The nature of the imperfectly competitive equilibrium has another important implication. When the assumption of a given and constant equilibrium level of the output (y_e) is lifted and is allowed to grow over time, the standard approach is to consider a growth rate that is determined by a neo-classical growth model. If the medium-run equilibrium of the three-equation model is interpreted in the alternative way suggested above, it is evident that the growth of y_e cannot be simply explained by any standard model of growth. Since other factors than those embodied in mainstream growth models contribute to determine the movements of y_e from one period to the next, the dynamics of the neoclassical perfectly competitive economy can also constantly diverge from the dynamics of the non-competitive economy of the New Keynesian model.

Thus, the three-equation model can be interpreted, at least to a certain extent, in a different way from the mainstream and in a way that is more directly related to the Marxian-Keynesian-Kaleckian approach. The model tells us that the levels of output and employment are demand-determined, but also that the growth of production and employment through the expansion of demand is constrained by inflationary processes that can be triggered by increases in wages and prices that are incompatible with one another. In other words, the economy is characterized by the existence of a *critical* level of output, and employment, beyond which it cannot go without giving rise to growing inflation. Such a critical level of output is by no means 'natural', but affected by social, political and historical factors.[36]

8.4.2 Policy

The methodological and analytical differences between the current mainstream and the alternative approach have, of course, implications also at the policy level. The policy indications that can be derived from the two models can be remarkably different. Let us start from the most obvious difference, which directly stems from the two models' different methodological stance. The mainstream prevailing idea that the model of imperfect competition has to be contrasted with the perfectly competitive benchmark brings with itself the temptation to see policies as the instrument to eliminate or reduce the imperfections. The closer the economy is to perfect competition, the closer its equilibrium is to optimality (full employment, constant inflation and so on). So-called 'supply-side' policies, aiming to reduce market rigidities, are an example of this sort of approach.

On the other hand, in a Marxian-Keynesian-Kaleckian context, attempts to bring the economy to a state of perfect competition do not make much sense. The 'imperfect' world in which we live is the outcome of the competitive process itself, because actual competition is a dynamic process very different from the abstract world assumed in neoclassical economics. Policies to curb the monopolistic power of particular firms and/or sectors can be necessary, indeed desirable, but it should never be forgotten that competitive conditions tend to evolve dynamically towards situations characterized by the presence of significant monopolistic or oligopolistic elements.

The mainstream, of course, is also concerned with policies to cope with the imperfect world as it is, given its structural features.[37] At this level, it could be easier to find some points of contact with the Kaleckian approach. Since in both models firms are demand-constrained, both approaches allow for fiscal policies to raise the aggregate demand either via increases in spending or tax cuts. Fiscal policy is effective, but this statement needs important qualifications.

In the mainstream model, fiscal policies are justified and necessary when the economy is below its natural equilibrium and when the interest rate is so close to zero that monetary policies are ineffective. In no case, is the use of fiscal policies or, for that matter, of monetary policies justified to try to push the economy beyond its natural equilibrium. In fact, attempts to push the economy beyond its natural equilibrium through increases in the aggregate demand would trigger an inflationary process. The natural equilibrium can be changed only through supply-side (structural) policies.

That, in any given situation, there exists a critical level of output and employment beyond which the economy cannot go without experiencing increasing inflation is acknowledged also by the Marxian-Keynesian-Kaleckian tradition. This, however, does not imply that demand policies cannot be used to shift the 'natural' equilibrium. Once it is recognized that the so-called natural equilibrium is significantly affected and determined by historical, social and institutional factors, policies on the demand side can be viable and effective if they are accompanied by interventions to keep under control those factors that prevent the economy from expanding without inflation. Incomes policies obviously come to mind.[38]

Whereas the mainstream concentrates on monetary policy as the instrument to ensure a constant inflation rate, the alternative approach concentrates instead on the necessity to control the dynamics of wages and prices through different policies. As a consequence, differently from the mainstream conviction, expansionary demand policies, accompanied by adequate distributive measures, can produce *stable* higher equilibrium levels of output and employment. In other words, price stability can be achieved at a lower social cost than that associated with mainstream policies.

8.5 CONCLUSION

The salient features of the current mainstream macroeconomic model have been presented and contrasted with the alternative approach suggested in this book. Although both approaches adopt a hypothesis of non-perfectly competitive markets, their differences remain significant. However, the present gap between the two approaches is undoubtedly narrower than the distance from the New Classical Macroeconomics of the 1970s and 1980s.

The road to walk to cover the distance from the current mainstream is very long, maybe endless, because the existing differences are not only analytical but quite often also ideological and political. However, it is worth making the effort to walk along this road, with the objective to achieve a better comprehension of the world in which we live and to produce better tools to improve it.

On the one hand, a less arrogant and sectarian attitude of the mainstream towards other traditions of thought could help improve the analysis of the actual economy. New insights into the working of the economy could come from different perspectives rather than the uncritical reproduction of essentially the same model, enriched by some minor variations. On the other hand, a more open attitude towards the mainstream by heterodox economists might help break the isolation in which they find themselves in most cases. The weaknesses of the mainstream could be overcome by showing that there is a viable alternative to it, but this requires the ability to communicate with the economists in the mainstream and point out alternative ways to deal with the problems at hand.

NOTES

1. For a more exhaustive survey, see Dixon and Rankin (1995).
2. Here, this aspect is not given particular attention. On price stickiness see, for example, Akerlof and Yellen (1985) and Mankiw (1985).
3. 'A perfectly competitive firm needs to form expectations only about the market price of its products ... [a] monopolistically competitive firm does not have to predict a price; it sets its

own price. ... It has to predict the location and shape of its demand curve' (Solow, 1998, p. 16).

4. On the grounds of the above considerations, Solow (1998) develops his own model of monopolistic competition with a Keynesian flavour. See also Hahn and Solow (1995).

5. Sections 8.3 and 8.4 are partly based on Sardoni (2010).

6. See, for example, Blanchard and Fischer (1989, pp. 372–504), Benassy (1991, 2002), Nishimura (1992), Woodford (2003), Carlin and Soskice (2006, pp. 563–636), who pay particular attention to the labour market, and Galí (2008).

7. The following equations are derived from Nishimura (1992). All variables are in log terms.

8. Notice the similarity between (8.2) and Kalecki's price equation in Appendix C.

9. See Nishimura (1992, p. 10), for the exact value that p takes.

10. When k goes to infinity, the price $\bar{p}$ reduces to $\bar{p}^* = (1/(c-1)) [(\log(1+c_1)] + m$ which is certainly smaller than $\bar{p}$ in (8.4). The output $\bar{y}^*$, associated to $\bar{p}^*$, is larger than $\bar{y}$ in (8.5).

11. Moreover, firms exclude the possibility of a concerted price reduction, because of a free-rider problem. If other firms reduce their prices and the firm under consideration does not, the latter will realize more profits. Therefore, all firms behave in the same way and prices are not cut.

12. This model retains classical features. In fact, in this economy there is no nominal or real rigidity and money is also neutral in the short period. Changes in m produce only a proportional increase in the price level, as it clearly appears from (8.4) and (8.5).

13. Schmalensee (1981), however, argues that economies of scale are generally of little importance as a barrier to the entry of new firms into an industry.

14. In both cases, we are dealing with decisions to increase the existing productive capacity; in the first case through the increase in the number of firms, in the second case through the growth of the dimensions of existing firms.

15. Recent analyses, however, yield results that are not always concordant. Spence (1977, 1979), for example, concludes that long-period equilibria are characterized by excess capacity and extra profits; whereas Dixit (1980) finds that in many cases the industry reaches an equilibrium with the full use of existing capacity. In these models, incumbent firms deter the entry of new firms by increasing their capacity through investment.

16. Analogous conclusions had been reached in the 1930s, when the 'tangency solution' was first found. This solution is contingent on the hypothesis of free entry, but the entry process under conditions of non-perfect competition is significantly more complex than the process postulated under perfect competition. See Sardoni (1999) for a reconstruction of the debate in the 1930s.

17. See, for example, the textbooks by Carlin and Soskice (1990, 2006) and Blanchard (1997); see Clarida et al. (1999), Meyer (2001), Woodford (2003), Galí and Gertler (2007) and Galí (2008) for examples of the model used to deal with monetary policy.

18. This is a significant difference from older macroeconomic models in which the central bank is assumed to conduct its policy through changes in the quantity of money. In New Keynesian models, the quantity of money is an endogenous variable, a feature that, to a certain extent, resembles the approach to money and monetary policy typical of many Post Keynesian (Kaldorian) models. Here, we do not deal with this aspect of the relationship between the two approaches. For some considerations on this topic see Sardoni (2007, 2008).

19. The model is often denoted also as the 'three-equation' model.

20. The real wage rate w^B in (8.9) is higher than the real wage rate associated with the same level of employment in perfect competition because workers (unions) have a certain degree of market power.

21. Notice, also in this case, the similarity with the Kaleckian hypothesis of constant short-period returns.

22. See Carlin and Soskice (2006, pp. 51–3) for a graphical representation of voluntary and involuntary unemployment.

23. For a more general comparison between New Keynesian economics and the Post Keynesian and Kaleckian approaches, see, for example, the contributions in Rotheim (1997).

24. On the debate on the microfoundations of macroeconomics, which started in the 1970s, see, for example, Harcourt (1977) and Weintraub (1979).

25. Solow (1998) argues that the New Classical response was not so much an attempt at providing macroeconomics with its missing microfoundations, which were present also in *The General Theory*. The New Classical response rather derives from the desire to base macroeconomics on particular and specific microfoundations, characterized by a fully rational and omniscient representative agent and perfectly competitive markets.

26. The structure and organization of Blanchard and Fischer (1989) is perhaps the clearest example of this type of approach.

27. Blanchard has some doubts about the current practice of using the perfectly competitive benchmark, which he justifies on the grounds of ease of communication in the profession. The 'utterly' unrealistic case of perfect competition is given the status of benchmark 'because most current research is organized in terms of what happens when one relaxes one or more assumption in that model. This may change one day. But for the time being, this approach provides a common research strategy and makes for easier communication among macroeconomic researchers.' (Blanchard, 2000, p. 580n).

28. Kalecki rather regarded the competitive hypothesis as a special case (see, for example, Kalecki, 1990c).

29. Schumpeter (1954, pp. 972–85), though belonging to the neoclassical tradition, viewed competition in a way that was close to Marx. Schumpeter also criticized the neoclassical concept of perfect competition for being static in its nature.

30. See Blanchard (2008) for some comments on the role of investment in New Keynesian models.

31. More recently, other non-mainstream economists have developed analyses of the distributive conflict, which explains the dynamics of prices as well as of effective demand. See, for example, Sylos Labini (1967, 1974); Rowthorn (1977); Bhaduri and Marglin (1990), Harcourt (2006). Others have also used a non-neoclassical Phillips curve (see, for example, Palley, 2003) and a non-neoclassical notion of NAIRU (Stockhammer, 2008).

32. Woodford (2003) is the economist who most emphasizes the Wicksellian characteristics of the current dominant paradigm in macroeconomics. Also in a recent book (Fontana and Setterfield, 2009), devoted to a comparison between the mainstream and the Post Keynesian teaching of macroeconomics, several contributors refer to the New Keynesian equilibrium as a Wicksellian equilibrium (see, for example, Tamborini, 2009; Smithin, 2009).

33. By economic and social context we mean the structural features of the economy (the level and composition of productive capacity as well as labour force, the level of productivity, and so on) and the socio-political institutions and arrangements (welfare system, unemployment benefits, unions' organization, etc.).

34. There can be multiple equilibria in an open economy with a floating exchange rate.

35. Moreover, it should be pointed out that the New Keynesian model does not contain any endogenous factors ensuring that the economy tends to its equilibrium when hit by a shock. In fact, to ensure that the economy tends to its equilibrium, it is necessary to assume a non-inflationary stance of the central bank.

36. Blanchard (1997, p. 310), again, underlines the non-natural character of the equilibrium derived from the New Keynesian model, even though he keeps using the term 'natural' for ease of communication.

37. The policies concerned with the economy 'as it is' can be defined as short-medium term policies, whereas policies aimed at modifying the structure of the economy (such as increasing the degree of competition, reducing the rigidity of prices and wages, and so on) can be regarded as long-term policies.

38. See, for example, Weintraub (1978) and Harcourt (2001, pp. 66–80).

9. Concluding remarks

This chapter presents some final remarks concerning a number of topics that have a central place in the book. They essentially relate to the problem of realism in economic theorizing.

9.1   THE 'ECONOMIC MACHINE': THE SCIENTIFIC DISCOVERIES OF MARX AND KEYNES

Classical political economists developed and used the concept of the 'economic machine'.[1] This machine works according to laws which can be understood and studied in a scientific way. They regulate the process by which the machine reproduces itself and grows, and this process fundamentally represents the general (social) interest because all actors within the system (individuals or, rather, social classes) benefit from it.

In this framework, each class pursues its own specific interests and, in doing so, it acts in the general interest as well. In other words, there is a fundamental convergence of individual interests and the general interest. In particular, the capitalist class in pursuing its interest enables the machine to reproduce and grow and, as a result, to provide benefits for all. The laws that regulate the working of the machine force individual capitalists to behave in this way.

Adam Smith was the classical economist who was most firmly convinced of all this.[2] Marx, too, believed that the economy and the social system can be regarded as a gigantic machine, but he also brought a fundamental new insight; namely, that this machine cannot possibly work without using money, which performs several different roles.

Once money is introduced, the analytical picture is radically altered. In so far as money has no significant role, the entrepreneurial class is 'forced' to behave according to the general interest; as soon as money is assumed to play a central and crucial role, entrepreneurs are given a greater degree of 'freedom'. They are no longer compelled to respect the laws of the machine, in that the pursuit of their interests (profits) is no longer necessarily associated with production, investment and growth at the highest possible levels. The existence of money gives them the option of choosing not to invest whenever this is expected to be more advantageous.

Perhaps the best illustration of Marx's approach is his attitude towards the study of the conditions for the reproduction of the system as a whole and his theory of crises. Through his schemes of reproduction, Marx showed the laws that must be respected if the 'machine' is to reproduce itself and grow. However, the tendency of entrepreneurs to maximize profits and their 'freedom' with regard to these laws, do not ensure that the laws actually will be respected. In fact, it is much more likely that there will be disturbances that impede the ordered process of reproduction and growth.

Neoclassical economics had a fundamentally different vision of the economic machine and of the laws that regulate its working, but it shared with classical political economy confidence in the compatibility or convergence of individual interests and the general interest. Neoclassical economics, indeed, went far beyond classical political economy, for it held that each and every individual behaves in such a way that the general interest is achieved in the form of a (general) equilibrium position at which everyone maximizes benefits and cannot get better off.

Keynes, in his critique of the neoclassical vision of the economic machine, played much the same role as Marx had done with respect to classical economics.[3] The capitalist economic machine cannot possibly function without money: once money is made an integral part of the analytical picture, individual actions (guided by the pursuit of individual interests) may produce results and effects that are contrary to the general interest; that is to say, these actions prevent the system as a whole from finding its equilibrium at a point on the boundary of feasible optimum equilibria. Money, again, is the scientific tool which Keynes used to discard his predecessors' theories.

Thus, both Marx and Keynes believed that the working of the machine cannot be studied and understood without taking money and its specific role into account. Taking money into account enabled them to explain how individual interests and the general interest can contradict each other. Money gives the entrepreneurial class a higher degree of 'freedom', such that it can pursue its own interest without pursuing the more general interest. Marx's and Keynes's concepts of money and their introduction into the analytical framework constitute scientific discoveries – that is to say, innovations at the theoretical level that open the door to a new vision of the object under consideration (the economic machine). They built theories based upon a process of abstraction which gives an account of fundamental characteristics of the 'machine' that their predecessors regarded as secondary or utterly irrelevant.

Both Marx and Keynes looked at the fundamental and essential properties of money and located the possibility of aggregate demand diverging from aggregate supply at the most abstract level of analysis. Kalecki carried out his analysis at a less abstract level than Marx and Keynes. Kalecki's approach, however, not only retains the same essential characteristics as Marx's and Keynes's, it also provides the solution to some important problems left unsolved by them.

Marx, Keynes and Kalecki can be said to have developed more 'realistic' analyses of the working of the machine than those offered by their classical or neoclassical predecessors. In their analyses, they took account of factors previously overlooked, to understand the laws that regulate the working of the economy. The sense in which a theory can be regarded as more realistic, however, requires some further considerations.

9.2   THE QUEST FOR REALISM: FROM MARX TO KEYNES, AND KALECKI

The use of terms like 'realism' and realistic theory can be somewhat ambiguous, so they need to be clearly defined before it can be argued that the theories of Marx, Keynes and Kalecki are more realistic than those of their respective predecessors.

Theoretical reasoning, in whatever discipline, is not and cannot be realistic in the sense of providing a full, detailed description of the object under investigation, as it appears to observation. Theory, in other words, cannot be a reproduction of reality on a 'one-to-one' scale.

Theory has to grasp the essential and fundamental characteristics of its object of study through a process of abstraction. In the course of this process, accidental and contingent aspects are taken out of consideration. In this way, theory 'reproduces' reality, in that it provides an analysis of the object describing its fundamental characteristics – all those properties that make it 'similar' to others and all those that make it distinct and specific. Marx expressed this as follows. The concrete (that is reality)

> appears in the process of thinking ... as a process of concentration, as a result, not as a point of departure, even though it is the point of departure in reality and hence also the point of departure for observation and conception ... . [T]he abstract determination leads towards a reproduction of the concrete by way of thought. (Marx, 1973, p. 101)

But the process of abstraction is very difficult and potentially dangerous. While accidental and contingent aspects of the object must be weeded out, no fundamental and specific characteristics must be overlooked or mistaken for accidental or irrelevant ones. If, in the process of abstraction, some fundamental aspects of the object get lost, theory ceases to be realistic: the reproduction of the object it provides no longer fits the actual, concrete object.

Marx referred to the case of the concept of production, which is an abstraction. The concept of capitalist production must be such as to include not only those determinations (aspects) of production that are common to all social and economic systems, but also, and above all, those that are specific to production in a capitalist economy. Otherwise, economic analysis cannot possibly provide a satisfactory understanding of the essential features of the system under consideration.[4]

Marx's critique of Ricardo's theory of effective demand and crises is a natural consequence of this approach. In working out his concept of capitalist economy, Ricardo failed to understand that money, and its specific role, cannot be regarded as something that can be left out of consideration in specifically treating the capitalist economy. Neglecting this, Ricardo could liken the capitalist process of exchange to barter and so fail to see that aggregate demand can fall short of aggregate supply, and give rise to the consequences that Marx studied. From this point of view, Ricardo's theory lacks realism, that is to say, it is inadequate to provide a satisfactory 'reproduction' of the actual world. Marx's theory, in so far as it brings money into its analytical framework, represents an advance and allows us to perceive some fundamental and peculiar characteristics of actual capitalist economies.

Keynes, certainly, was not familiar with Marx's methodology, but it is quite clear that his methodological criticism of his predecessors, at least in the 1933 draft, closely resembles Marx's criticism of Ricardo. Keynes, like Marx, pointed out that his predecessors failed to realize that the analysis of capitalist economies cannot possibly be carried out by assuming that they behave like a 'neutral economy'. The latter is an unrealistic abstraction. The wrong process of abstraction led neoclassical economists (and classical economists, for that matter) astray and prevented them from understanding the real nature of a capitalist (monetary entrepreneur) economy.

Keynes, however, went further than Marx on the road to realism. Whereas Marx's theory can only explain unemployment due to lack of effective demand under quite exceptional conditions, Keynes argued that, because of its inherent characteristics, a capitalist economy can also experience unemployment due to insufficient effective demand in more 'normal' conditions than general crises of overproduction. But it is somewhat paradoxical that Keynes could achieve a more realistic account of the way in which the economy works in spite of the fact that his analysis is based on hypotheses about individual firms' behaviour that, on the whole, are less realistic than Marx's.

In Keynes's analysis, upward-sloping short-period supply curves and downward-sloping investment functions play a crucial role, but both these aspects prove unable to represent the reality of actual production and investment decisions. In this sense, Kalecki's theory represents a further advance upon Keynes and Marx. Kalecki based his analysis on foundations that better represent reality. In particular, Kalecki developed his analysis by abandoning the hypothesis of perfect as well as free competition, which he regarded as inadequate to deal with the problems at hand.

In conclusion, Marx's, Keynes's and Kalecki's theories are more realistic than their respective predecessors' theories not because they enlarged the scope of their analyses to take account of details and (accidental and contingent) aspects that others had overlooked. They are more realistic because they are founded upon a set of abstractions able to embrace essential, inherent characteristics of a capitalist economy that other economists had failed to grasp (with the consequence that their theories were in open contradiction to actual reality).

9.3   THE ABANDONMENT OF PERFECT COMPETITION

The concept of perfect or free competition is an abstraction that can be wrong when dealing with salient features of the actual economy, in particular when dealing with the problem of unemployment and effective demand.[5]

Marx and Keynes carried out their analyses under the assumption of competition for different reasons. Marx probably thought that his concept of free competition was, on the whole, an adequate abstraction in so far as it allowed him to give an account of the process which had to lead to concentration, monopolies, and so on. But he failed to realize that under his assumption of free competition the economy should have reached a completely monopolistic situation, which is an unrealistic analytical conclusion.

Keynes, on the other hand, accepted the hypothesis of free competition because he wanted to achieve his fundamental results working with the assumptions and hypotheses most favourable to, and most widely accepted by, the mainstream of his times. But Keynes, too, failed to realize that the hypothesis of free competition – even allowing for uncertainty – could be retained only at the cost of making other hypotheses and assumptions on the behaviour of individual firms that can hardly be regarded as acceptable.

Kalecki parted from Marx's and Keynes's hypotheses and from the outset put his analysis of effective demand in a framework in which it is possible to explain underemployment rest states, as well as the co-existence of firms of different size and industries with different degrees of monopoly. With him, a further step towards a 'realistic' theory of capitalist economies was taken.

If we turn to look at the evolution of mainstream macroeconomics, we also start from 'Keynesian results' that while able to represent the actuality of unemployment and other important features of reality, were analytically flawed. From the mainstream point of view, the major Keynesian weakness was the lack of rigorous microfoundations. The new classicals gave macro-economics more coherent and rigorous microfoundations, but at the cost of the utter unrealism of their results. New Keynesians have been trying to provide more realistic analyses of the economy, and by abandoning the hypothesis of perfect competition, New Keynesian models can yield results that appear closer to reality. In this sense, the New Keynesian approach may also be said to represent a step towards realism of analysis.

The idea to ground macroeconomic analysis on a hypothesis of non-perfect competition is criticized by several Post Keynesian economists (see, for example, Davidson, 2000, 2002). They argue that, in this way, both New Keynesians and Kaleckians explain unemployment through the existence of imperfections introduced into the model in an *ad hoc* way; whereas unemployment due to lack of effective demand can be explained regardless of market imperfections. This line of criticism, however, can be misleading, because it is based on a misunderstanding of the meaning of competition or, more precisely, of perfect competition.

There is no doubt, in our opinion, that if the economy had the features of neoclassical perfect competition, it would necessarily give rise to full employment equilibria. The mainstream models refer to this benchmark. When Post Keynesians hold that the economy can also find unemployment equilibria with competitive markets, they refer to a sort of competition that cannot be reduced to the neoclassical notion.[6] For many Keynesians (see, for example Chick, 1992), the assumption of competitive markets amounts to assuming that firms are small (they are price-takers) and that prices and wages are flexible. Within this specific competitive context, underemployment equilibria can be demonstrated, but this does not seem to be a fully satisfactory solution to the problem of market forms.[7] As we argued in the previous chapters, Keynesian results within a competitive framework are untenable once Keynes's assumptions on short-period returns, supply functions and firms' ability to foresee the macroeconomic effects of their investment are removed and replaced by more satisfactory and consistent hypotheses.

Moreover, one should never forget that the real world is not characterized by perfectly competitive markets, so that the assumption of free or perfect competition should be regarded, at most, as a useful way to criticize other models and not as an acceptable representation of the economy as it is.[8] Kalecki seems to provide the most satisfactory answer to these issues. He provides the demonstration of the possibility of underemployment due to insufficient effective demand by grounding his analysis on microeconomic foundations that are not only more coherent and rigorous than Keynes's but also more realistic, as they better reflect the way in which the economy actually works.

9.4   UNDEREMPLOYMENT EQUILIBRIA AND ACTUAL DYNAMIC PROCESSES

Throughout the book the central focus has been on the problem of underemployment equilibria and the possibility of demonstrating that the economy can tend towards them. A significant line of division betweeen Marx and Keynes was drawn with respect to this issue. We argued that Marx's analytical results should be regarded as less realistic than Keynes's, for Marxian theory is not able to give an account of underemployment rest states.

The emphasis laid on this issue requires some further clarification. The crucial question is: in what sense can Keynes's analytical results be said to be more realistic than those of Marx? The answer is that they are more realistic not because they provide a demonstration that underemployment equilibria are actually experienced by the economy, but because, in proving that they are possible, they allow us to advance the analysis of actual economies and to study their dynamics in a more adequate way.

Marx's analysis allows us only to demonstrate that the capitalist process of growth has a cyclical character and that, after a crisis, it tends again to the full utilization of the existing productive capacity. In so far as this analysis allows us to give an account of cycles, it is realistic because it provides an explanation of phenomena which indeed are inherent in capitalist economies. But in so far as it implies that the full utilization of capacity has to be reached, it lacks realism. Within such a framework, it would be hard to avoid the conclusion that the 'true' equilibrium position is the full-utilization position, though the economy may be subject to fluctuations around it. In other words, the economy oscillates around its long-period trend, which is characterized by the full utilization of capacity but not necessarily of labour.

To prove the possibility of 'underemployment equilibria', however, does not imply either that an underemployment equilibrium is actually reached by the economy, or that if it is reached, the economy will not move from it.[9] The economy may well move away from an underemployment equilibrium position to another position (with higher or lower levels of employment), or it may fluctuate around it for a certain span of time. But the economy could also remain in its rest state for protracted periods of time.[10]

Keynes, indeed, was convinced that underemployment equilibria represent, so to speak, 'centres of gravitation' as the economy itself experiences a cyclical process. But this piece of analysis is carried out at another level of abstraction, from a standpoint closer to actuality. Keynes's explanation of this point is set out in Chapter 18 of his *General Theory* (1936, pp. 245–54), where he presented a summary of the theory. After pointing out the variables that determine the equilibrium position of the economy in a general abstract model, he looks more closely at the actual world. In the real world, he observed: 'the actual phenomena of the economic system are also coloured by certain special characteristics of the propensity to consume, the schedule of the marginal efficiency of capital and the rate of interest, about which we can safely generalise from experience, *but which are not logically necessary'* (Keynes, 1936, p. 249; emphasis added).

At this stage of the analysis it is no longer a question of inevitability, of logical necessity (or logical consequentiality of results), but of empirical observation of how those variables behave in reality. This led Keynes to conclude:

> the outstanding features of our actual experience; – namely, that we oscillate, avoiding the gravest extremes of fluctuation in employment and in prices in both directions, round an intermediate position appreciably below full employment and appreciably above the minimum employment a decline below which would endanger life. But we must not conclude that the mean position ... is, therefore, established by laws of necessity. The unimpeded rule of the above conditions[11] is *a fact of observation concerning the world as it is or has been, and not a necessary principle which cannot be changed.* (Keynes, 1936, p. 254; emphasis added)

Keynes's further approach to reality comes after his general abstract model, which aims to dismantle the idea that, in principle, the economy must tend to full employment. Without such a prior analytical step, any description of fluctuations around mean positions would be lacking sound theoretical foundations. It might possibly correspond to observation but would be subject to rejection from a general point of view, in that the empirical reasons why full employment is not actually experienced are innumerable.

Thus, to provide a rigorous demonstration of the possibility of underemployment equilibria is of vital importance. It is no help to argue that in reality the economy never experiences equilibrium positions. Both Marx's and Keynes's inability to offer a rigorous and consistent proof that underemployment equilibrium is possible is a serious flaw in their analyses. By solving the problems left unsolved by Keynes as well as Marx, Kalecki provided a more satisfactory demonstration of underemployment equilibria.

This interpretation of Kalecki, however, requires some further clarification because it could engender misunderstanding. It is undeniable that Kalecki, throughout his works, mainly concentrated on cycles and dynamics rather than on rest states or equilibrium positions. This has led some authors to hold that his is best described as a 'non-equilibrium approach' (Sawyer, 1985, pp. 191–2) and others to hold that it is essentially different from Keynes's approach (Patinkin, 1982, pp. 58–78). But, in our opinion, this does not imply that Kalecki disregarded the crucial importance of showing the existence of underemployment equilibria.[12]

Although it may be true that before *The General Theory* Kalecki did not pay particular attention to the problem of equilibrium (Asimakopulos, 1983), in the following years he changed his attitude. Kalecki's 1936 review of *The General Theory* and an article written in 1937, and revised in 1939, clearly indicate such a change.[13] As we saw in Chapter 6, in 1936, Kalecki criticized Keynes's theory of investment precisely for the reason that it was unable to give an account of short-period equilibria. This criticism would be difficult to explain if Kalecki was not concerned with equilibrium. After all, if he was exclusively interested in trade cycles, the individuation of a Wicksellian cumulative process could have been regarded as a satisfactory result. Most of the points made in 1936 were reconsidered by Kalecki in his 1937 and 1939 works, in which he determines an equilibrium level of income that does not imply full employment. Kalecki repeatedly stressed that cycles do not necessarily have their peak at full-employment positions, and to be able to hold this he needed to demonstrate that the economy can find a position of rest at any level of employment and utilization of capacity.

The reason Kalecki mainly concentrated on trade cycles is that he generally carried out his analysis at a level closer to actual reality than did Keynes. In *The General Theory*, Keynes's primary intent was to criticize the dominant theory of employment; only later did he plan to develop more concrete analyses of, and policies for, the actual economy.[14] In contrast, Kalecki had a more immediate and direct concern for actual reality. At this level of analysis, it can be more relevant to show that underemployment equilibria are not permanent states but rather centres of gravitation.

Kalecki's more direct attention to actual reality, however, is not what makes his analysis more realistic. The claim that Kalecki's analysis of capitalist economies is more realistic than those of Marx and Keynes finds its justification not in his more detailed description of the economy but in his having developed a more correct process of abstraction, one that furnishes a more rigorous model and, hence, an analysis of phenomena that corresponds more closely to reality. The higher degree of realism is essentially contingent on the ability to carry out a more correct and adequate process of abstraction.

NOTES

1. '[I]t was they who first began consciously and consistently to visualize society as a kind of gigantic machine, a vast and intricate mechanism whose innumerable cogs and belts and levers were related to one another in certain defined ways ... . Thus was born the truly revolutionary notion that the things which actually happened in society reflected the working of certain law-governed, mechanistic processes, "autonomous" and "objective" in the sense that they operated independently of the wills of individual men' (Meek, 1977, p. 177).
2. 'Every individual is continually exerting himself to find out the most advantageous employment for whatever capital he can command. It is his own advantage, indeed, and not that of the society which he has in view. But the study of his own advantage naturally, or rather

necessarily, leads him to prefer that employment which is most advantageous to the society' (Smith, 1976, p. 415). Ricardo was no longer as confident as Smith of the compatibility of the interests of all social classes. Ricardo, in particular, was aware of the conflict between rentiers' and capitalists' interests, but he retained the conviction that capitalist entrepreneurs, in pursuing their own interest, also work in the general interest.

3. Chapter 2 of Keynes's 1919 *Economic Consequences of the Peace* (Keynes, 1971a, pp. 5–16) shows that he came to be convinced that the capitalist system did not work any longer in the interest of all classes much earlier than he was able to provide the analytical foundations of his belief.

4. 'Production in general is an abstraction, but a rational abstraction in so far as it really brings out and fixes the common element and thus saves us repetition. Still, this general category ... is itself segmented many times over and splits into different determinations. Some determinations belong to all epochs, others only to a few ... . No production will be thinkable without them ... nevertheless, just those things which determine their development, i.e., the elements which are more general and common must be separated out from determinations valid for production as such, so that in their unity ... their essential difference is not forgotten. The whole profundity of those modern economists who demonstrate the eternity and harmoniousness of the existing social relations lies in this forgetting' (Marx, 1973, p. 85).

5. In his 1926 article, Sraffa, for example, argued that even those markets that seem to best fit the concept of an ideal competitive market embody permanent, structural characteristics that make them essentially different from the neoclassical ideal-type of the perfect market.

6. The fact that they assume uncertainty different from risk is sufficient to characterize the 'Keynesian' competition as different from the Walrasian-Knightian notion.

7. As, for example, in the model of Chapter 6 above. From this point of view, our position is different from that taken by Marris (1991), for whom perfect competition is in no case compatible with Keynesian results.

8. Reddaway put the issue in the right terms: 'I regard the existence of imperfect competition as such an obvious assumption if one is talking of the real world that one should put it down but it is not one for which you have to make an apology, you have to apologise when you are assuming perfect competition which manifestly does not exist' (1985, pp. 96–7).

9. 'If we suppose a state of expectation to continue for a sufficient length of time for the effect on employment to have worked itself out ... completely ... the steady level of employment thus attained may be called the long-period employment corresponding to that state of expectation. It follows that, *although expectation may change so frequently that the actual level of employment has never had time to reach the long-period employment corresponding to the existing state of expectation, nevertheless every state of expectation has its definite corresponding level of long-period employment* ' (Keynes, 1936, p. 48; emphasis added).

10. To remind Kahn (1989, pp. xxiii–v), the short-period can become considerably long.

11. The conditions that ensure fluctuations of this kind are: (a) the multiplier is larger than 1 but not very large; (b) the response of investment to moderate changes in the rate of interest and/or in the expected returns is moderate; (c) the response of money-wages to moderate changes in employment is moderate as well; (d) a higher (lower) rate of investment which continues for a number of years reacts negatively (positively) on the marginal efficiency of capital (see Keynes, 1936, pp. 250–3).

12. For more details on differing interpretations of Kalecki, see Sardoni (1995).

13. The 1937 article (Kalecki, 1937) was reprinted with considerable changes in Kalecki (1939). We refer to this latter version.

14. The main purpose of *The General Theory* is 'to deal with difficult questions of theory, and only in the second place with the applications of this theory to practice' (Keynes, 1936, p. xxi).

Appendix A: A formalization of Marx's schemes of reproduction

The conditions for a balanced process of simple or expanded reproduction were determined by Marx through numerical examples. Here, we use a more general model that, although differing from Marx's original analysis in several respects, retains the same basic features as Marx's schemes.[1]

Let us consider an n-sector economy which produces consumer and capital goods (final goods). Each good can be either consumed or used up as a means of production. Moreover, for simplicity, it is assumed that all the goods are basic commodities, that is that each good is used, directly or indirectly, to produce all the others (Sraffa, 1960). Wages are paid at the end of the period of production; the workers' propensity to consume is equal to 1. There is no technical change and returns to scale are constant. Goods exchange at their prices of production (natural or normal prices).[2]

Let $\mathbf{Y_t}$ be a positive $(n \times 1)$ vector, whose generic element $y_{i,t}$ ($i = 1, 2, \ldots, n$) is the output of the i–th sector at t. The $(n \times n)$ matrix $\mathbf{X_t}$ is the matrix of inputs $x_{ij,t}$ ($i, j = 1, 2, \ldots n$).[3] The price system of the economy is

$$\mathbf{Y_t p_t} = \mathbf{X_t p_t}\,(1 + r_t) + \mathbf{L_t} w_t$$

where $\mathbf{p_t}$ is the vector of the prices of production; $\mathbf{L_t}$ is the vector of the quantities of labour employed in the n sectors; w_t is the wage rate and r_t is the uniform rate of profits exogenously fixed. It is assumed that the matrix $\mathbf{X_t}$ and the vector $\mathbf{Y_t}$ have all the properties that ensure the positivity of prices. In particular, it is assumed that the n outputs $y_{i,t}$ are such that there is a positive (physical) surplus $s_{i,t}$ of all the n goods, that is

$$y_{i,t} = \sum_{j=1}^{n} x_{ij,t} + s_{i,t} \tag{A.1}$$

$$s_{i,t} > 0$$

$$(i = 1, 2, \ldots n)$$

The outputs $y_{i,t}$ are those associated with the full utilization of the existing capacity at t in the n sectors. This assumption derives from our analysis of Marx's microfoundations in Chapter 3.

Let us now denote by $\mathbf{CW_t}$ a $(n \times 1)$ vector whose generic element $cw_{i,t}$ denotes the workers' consumption of the i–th good at t.[4] $\mathbf{CW_t}$ is assumed to be smaller than $\mathbf{S_t}$, the vector of sectoral surpluses:

$$0 < \mathbf{CW_t} < \mathbf{S_t}$$

Finally, let us denote by $\mathbf{CK_t}$ a $(n \times 1)$ vector whose generic element $ck_{i,t}$ is the capitalists' consumption of the i–th good in t.[5] In order to concentrate on expanded reproduction, $\mathbf{CK_t}$ is assumed to be:

$$0 \leq \mathbf{CK_t} < (\mathbf{S_t} - \mathbf{CW_t})$$

Marx's problem can be expressed in the following way. At time t, given the vector $\mathbf{Y_t}$ of outputs, find the n sectoral rates of growth that ensure that there is no excess supply (demand) of any good and that all goods are sold at their normal prices. Let $\mathbf{g}$ be the vector whose elements are such rates of growth. A process of expanded reproduction occurs when all the elements of $\mathbf{g}$ are positive.

If expanded reproduction takes place from t to $(t + 1)$, the n outputs must all grow, that is

$$y_{j,t+1} = (1 + g_j)y_{j,t} \tag{A.2}$$

$$(j = 1, 2, \ldots n)$$

where g_j is the growth rate of the j–th sector. Moreover, if there is no technical change and returns to scale are constant, inputs in all sectors grow at the same rate as the output:

$$x_{ij,t+1} = (1 + g_j)x_{ij,t} \tag{A.3}$$

$$(i, j = 1, 2, \ldots n)$$

$x_{ij,t}$ is the (physical) amount of the i–th good used at t as a capital good to produce the output $y_{j,t}$. This amount of the good must be replaced in order to reconstitute the productive capacity of the j–th sector. So $x_{ij,t+1}$ comprises the replacement investment in the i–th good $x_{ij,t}$ by the j–th sector, and $g_j x_{ij,t}$ is the additional input of the same good, or net investment.

In order to have the equality between demand and supply in each sector, it must be that

$$y_{i,t} = \sum_{j=1}^{n} x_{ij,t+1} + cw_{i,t} + ck_{i,t}$$

$$(i = 1, 2, \ldots n)$$

which, from (A.3), can be written as

$$y_{i,t} = \sum_{j=1}^{n} x_{i,t} (1 + g_j) + cw_{i,t} + ck_{i,t} \qquad (A.4)$$

$$(i = 1, 2, \ldots n)$$

or, in matrix form and recalling (A.1)

$$\mathbf{g} = \mathbf{X}^{-1} (\mathbf{S_t} - \mathbf{CW_t} - \mathbf{CK_t}) \qquad (A.5)$$

The elements of the vector $\mathbf{g}$ are the sectoral rates of growth that ensure the equality between demand and supply of each good. Here, it is assumed that $\mathbf{g}$ exists and is positive.[6] It is evident that, if the actual growth rate of one or more of the n sectors is lower than the rate that fulfills (A.5), all the sectors producing inputs for this sector experience an excess supply of their outputs.[7]

The conditions for aggregate equilibrium, the equality between aggregate supply and demand, can be easily derived. It must be

$$\sum_{j=1}^{n} y_j p_j = \sum_i \sum_j x_{ij,t} p_j + \sum_i \sum_j g_j x_{ij,t} p_j + \sum_i cw_{i,t} p_i + \sum_i ck_{i,t} p_i \qquad (A.6)$$

(the time subscript t is omitted for simplicity).

By setting

$$Y = \sum_{j=1}^{n} y_j p_j \text{ (gross domestic product)}$$

$$I = \sum_i \sum_j (x_{ij,t} + g_j x_{ij,t}) p_j \text{ (gross investment)}$$

$$C = \sum_i (cw_{i,t} + ck_{i,t}) p_i \text{ (total consumption)}$$

we obtain

$$Y = C + I \qquad (A.7)$$

Since it is also true that

$$Y = W + \Pi = W + c\Pi + s\Pi \tag{A.8}$$

where Π is gross profits (that is inclusive of depreciation), $W + c\Pi$ is aggregate consumption and $s\Pi$ is gross saving. From (A.7) and (A.8) we derive

$$s\Pi = I \tag{A.9}$$

which expresses the aggregate equilibrium condition by pointing out the necessary equality between saving and investment. Aggregate saving coincides with the level of capitalists' saving because the workers' average, and marginal propensity to consume is 1.

NOTES

1. See Sardoni (1981, 2009) for a more detailed exposition of the relationship between Marx's original schemes and a model of the same type as that used here.
2. The process of circulation of the goods produced by the n sectors of the economy requires the use of money. Here, however, we are not concerned with this issue, which is considered in Chapters 2 and 3.
3. The i–*th* row of $\mathbf{X}_t$ denotes the different uses of the good i as an input by the n sectors to produce their outputs; its j–*th* column denotes the inputs of the n goods used by the sector j to produce its output.
4. It must be $L_t w_t = \mathbf{CW}_t \mathbf{p}_t$, since the workers' propensity to consume is 1.
5. If $0 \le \beta < 1$ is the capitalists' propensity to consume, it is $\beta \mathbf{X}_t \mathbf{p}_t r_t = \mathbf{CK}_t \mathbf{p}_t$.
6. The solutions for (A.5) ensure that there is no sectoral excess supply or demand, but they do not ensure that there is a process of expanded reproduction. In fact, there is no reason why the vector $\mathbf{g}$ must necessarily be positive. A proof that positive solutions exist is provided in Sardoni (2009, pp. 172–3).
7. An actual growth rate $0 \le \bar{g}_j < g_j$ ($j = 1, 2, \dots n$) means that the j–*th* sector, from t to ($t + 1$), grows less than it is required for a balanced process of expanded reproduction. If $\bar{g}_j < 0$, the j–*th* sector reduces its output at ($t + 1$).

Appendix B: Effects of wage changes in Keynes's model

Proposition 1 At $p = p^*$ and $r = r^*$, it is

$$\partial p/\partial r > 0$$

From (5.14), let us consider the implicit function

$$K(c, p, r, w) \equiv F(p, w) - M(c, p, r, w) = 0$$

From (5.8) and (5.11), and remembering that in equilibrium $p = p^e$, $M(c, p, r, w)$ can be also written as

$$M(c, p, r, w) = cF(p, w) + cG(r, p, w, i, E)$$

with $G(r, p, w, i, E) = rI/p$.

Since it is $\partial G/\partial p < 0$ and $\partial G/\partial r > 0$, then

$$\partial p \partial r = -(\partial K/\partial r)/(\partial K/\partial p) = -[s(\partial F/\partial r) - c(\partial G/\partial r)]/[s(\partial F/\partial p) - c(\partial G/\partial p)]$$

with $s = (1 - c)$.

Since it is $\partial F/\partial r = 0$, $\partial G/\partial r > 0$, $[s(\partial F/\partial r) - c(\partial G/\partial r) > 0$, $[s(\partial F/\partial p) - c(\partial G/\partial p)] > 0$, then

$$\partial p/\partial r > 0 \tag{B.1}$$

Proposition 2 At $p = p^*$ and $r = r^*$, it is

$$\partial r/\partial w > 0$$

$$\partial p/\partial w > 0$$

The sign of $\partial r/\partial w$ can be easily determined from (5.15). Let us consider the implicit function

$$R(r, w, i, E) \equiv G(r, w) - H(r, i, E) = 0$$

It is

$$\partial r/\partial w = - (\partial R/\partial w)/(\partial R/\partial r) = - [(\partial G/\partial w) - (\partial H/\partial w)]/[(\partial G/\partial r) - (\partial H/\partial r)]$$
$$= (\partial G/\partial w)/[(\partial G/\partial r) - (\partial H/\partial r)]$$

as $\partial H/\partial w = 0$.

Since it is $\partial G/\partial w < 0$, $\partial G/\partial r > 0$ and $\partial H/\partial r < 0$,

$$\partial r/\partial w > 0 \qquad\qquad (B.2)$$

The sign of $\partial p/\partial w$ is immediately obtained. Since $\partial r/\partial w > 0$ and, from Proposition 1, $\partial p/\partial r > 0$, it necessarily is

$$\partial p/\partial w > 0 \qquad\qquad (B.3)$$

Appendix C: Price determination and income distribution in Kalecki

Kalecki's analysis of the determination and variations of the wage share is based on his analysis of price formation. He assumes that imperfect competition prevails in the industry and that prices are cost-determined. In agriculture and in the production of raw materials, competitive conditions prevail, so that prices are demand-determined.

C.1   PRICE DETERMINATION

Individual industrial firms, which are not assumed to maximize profits in 'any precise sort of manner' (Kalecki, 1965, p. 12), fix their prices by applying a mark up to their average prime cost by taking account of the behaviour of 'contiguous' firms, that is firms that produce similar goods. If u is the unit prime cost (the unit wage cost plus the unit cost of raw materials), the firm fixes its price by taking account of u and the prices fixed by all the contiguous firms:

$$p = mu + n\bar{p} \qquad (C.1)$$

$$m, n > 0$$

$\bar{p}$ is the weighted average of the prices fixed by all the firms producing similar goods. If u increases, p can rise in the same proportion only if also $\bar{p}$ rises in the same proportion as u. The values taken by m and n reflect what Kalecki calls the *degree of monopoly*, which is increasing in the values taken by the ratio $m/(1-n)$ (Kalecki, 1965, pp. 13–4).

The average price for the whole industry can be written as

$$\bar{p} = \bar{m}/(1 - \bar{n})\bar{u} \qquad (C.2)$$

with $\bar{m}/(1 - \bar{n})$ reflecting the degree of monopoly in the industry.[1]

C.2 THE DETERMINATION OF THE WAGE SHARE

On these grounds, Kalecki first sets out to determine the wage share in the value added of the industry. The industry's value added is the value of its total production minus the cost of raw materials and it is equal to the sum of wages (W) and profits (P).[2] Therefore,

$$P = O - M - W$$

(with O denoting the value of the industry produce and M denoting the cost of raw materials), which can be written as

$$P = (k - 1)(W + M) \tag{C.3}$$

with $k = O/(W + M)$, which depends on the industry's degree of monopoly.

The ratio of wages to the industry value added is

$$w = W/[W + (k - 1)(W + M)] = 1/[1 + (k - 1)(j + 1)] \tag{C.4}$$

with $j = M/W$. Therefore, the wage share in the value added of the industry depends on the degree of monopoly and on the ratio of the cost of raw materials to the wage cost.

The wage share in the value added of the whole manufacturing sector can be expressed with a similar formula by substituting k and j in (C.4) with ratios that reflect the composition effect deriving from aggregating different industries (Kalecki, 1965, pp. 28–9).

At this stage, it is possible to determine the wage share in the gross national income by considering also agriculture, mining and the service sector. As to agriculture and mining, they produce raw materials whose price is demand-determined and the wage share in the value added mainly depends on the ratio of the prices of raw materials to the unit wage cost. As to the service sector, Kalecki assumes that in this case the wage share in the value added is negligible.[3] Therefore, 'broadly speaking, the degree of monopoly, the ratio of prices of raw materials to unit wage costs and industrial composition are the determinants of the relative share of wages in the gross income of the private sector' (Kalecki, 1965, p. 30).

NOTES

1. $\bar{u}$ is the industry's average unit prime cost, $\bar{m}$ and $\bar{n}$ are obtained as the weighted average of the single firms' ms and ns.
2. For simplicity, overheads are not considered here.
3. In the service sector, labour's remuneration is mostly salaries.

Bibliography

Ackley, G. (1961), *Macroeconomic Theory*, London: Macmillan.

Akerlof, G.A. and J.L. Yellen (1985), 'A near-rational model of the business cycle, with wage and price inertia', *Quarterly Journal of Economics*, **100** (5), 823–38.

Alexander, S.S. (1940), 'Mr. Keynes and Mr. Marx', *Review of Economic Studies*, **7** (2), 123–35.

Armstrong, P. and A. Glyn (1980), 'The law of the falling rate of profit and oligopoly: a comment on Shaikh', *Cambridge Journal of Economics*, **4** (1), 69–70.

Asimakopulos, A. (1971), 'The determination of investment in Keynes's model', *Canadian Journal of Economics*, **4**, 382–8.

Asimakopulos, A. (1977), 'Profits and investment: a Kaleckian approach', in G.C. Harcourt (ed.), Th*e Microeconomic Foundations* of *Macroeconomics*, London: Macmillan, pp. 328–42.

Asimakopulos, A. (1982), 'Keynes' theory of effective demand revisited', *Australian Economic Papers*, **21**, 18–36.

Asimakopulos, A. (1983), 'Anticipations of Keynes's General Theory?', *Canadian Journal of Economics*, **16** (3), 517–30.

Asimakopulos, A. (1984), 'The General Theory and its Marshallian micro-foundations,' *Metroeconomica*, **36** (2–3), 161–75.

Asimakopulos, A. (1985), 'The role of finance in Keynes's General Theory', *Economic Notes*, **0** (3), 5–16.

Asimakopulos, A. (1991), *Keynes's General Theory and Accumulation*, Cambridge: Cambridge University Press.

Baumol, W.J. (1977), 'Say's (at least) eight laws, or what Say and James Mill may really have meant', *Economica*, **44**, 145–62.

Benassy, J.P. (1991), 'Monopolistic competition,' in W. Hildebrand and H. Sonnenschein (eds), *Handbook of Mathematical Economics, vol. 4*, Maryland Heights, MO: Elsevier Science Publishers B.V., pp. 1996–2045.

Benassy, J.P. (2002), *The Macroeconomics of Imperfect Competition and Nonclearing Markets. A Dynamic General Equilibrium Approach*, Cambridge MA: MIT Press.

Bhaduri, A. and S.A. Marglin (1990), 'Unemployment and the real wage: the economic basis for contesting political ideologies', *Cambridge Journal of Economics*, **14** (4), 375–93.

Bharadwaj, K.R. (1976), *Classical Political Economy and Rise to Dominance of Supply and Demand Theories*, New Delhi: Longman.

Bharadwaj, K.R. (1978), 'The subversion of classical analysis: Alfred Marshall's early writing on value,' *Cambridge Journal of Economics*, **2**, 253–71.

Bibow, J. (1995), 'Some reflections on Keynes's "finance motive" for the demand for money', *Cambridge Journal of Economics*, **19** (5), 647–66.

Blanchard, O.J. (1997), *Macroeconomics*, 1st edn, Upper Saddle River, NJ: Prentice-Hall, Inc.

Blanchard, O.J. (2000), 'What do we know about macroeconomics that Fisher and Wicksell did not?', *De Economist*, **148** (5), 571–601.

Blanchard, O.J. (2008), 'The state of macro', National Bureau of Economic Research working paper no. 14259, Cambridge MA.

Blanchard, O.J. and S. Fischer (1989), *Lectures on Macroeconomics*, Cambridge MA: MIT Press.

Bleaney, M. (1980), 'Maurice Dobb's theory of crisis: a comment', *Cambridge Journal of Economics*, **4** (1), 71–3.

Brown, V. (1991), 'On Keynes's inverse relation between real wages and employment: a debate over excess capacity', *Review of Political Economy*, **3**, 439–66.

Carlin, W. and D. Soskice (1990), *Macroeconomics and the Wage Bargaining*, Oxford: Oxford University Press.

Carlin, W. and D. Soskice (2006), *Macroeconomics. Imperfections, Institutions and Policies*, 1st edn, Oxford: Oxford University Press.

Casarosa, C. (1981), 'The microfoundations of Keynes's aggregate supply and expected demand analysis', *Economic Journal*, **91** (361), 188–94.

Chamberlin, E.H. (1962), *The Theory of Monopolistic Competition: A Reorientation of the Theory of Value*, 8th edn, Cambridge, MA: Harvard University Press.

Chick, V. (1978), 'The nature of the Keynesian revolution: a reassessment', *Australian Economic Papers*, **17**, 1–20.

Chick, V. (1983), *Macroeconomics After Keynes*, Cambridge, MA: MIT Press.

Chick, V. (1992), 'The small firm under uncertainty: a puzzle of The General Theory', in B. Gerrard and J. Hillard (eds), *The Philosophy and Economics of J.M. Keynes*, Aldershot: Edward Elgar, pp. 149–64.

Clarida, R., J. Galí and M. Gertler (1999), 'The science of monetary policy: a New Keynesian perspective', *Journal of Economic Literature*, **37** (4), 1661–1707.

Coddington, A. (1983), *Keynesian Economics: The Search for First Principles*, London: Allen and Unwin.

Corry, B.A. (1959), 'Malthus and Keynes – a reconsideration', *Economic Journal*, **69** (276), 717–24.

Dasgupta, A.K. (1983), *Phases of Capitalism and Economic Theory*, Oxford: Oxford University Press.

Davidson, P. (1978), *Money and the Real World*, 2nd edn, London: Macmillan.

Davidson, P. (1983), 'The marginal product curve is not the demand curve for labor and Lucas's labor supply function is not the supply curve for labor in the real world', *Journal of Post Keynesian Economics*, **6** (1), 105–17.

Davidson, P. (1994), *Post Keynesian Macroeconomic Theory*, Cheltenham, UK and Brookfield, USA: Edward Elgar.

Davidson, P. (1995), 'The Asimakopulos view of Keynes's *General Theory*', in G.C. Harcourt, A. Roncaglia and R. Rowley (eds), *Income and Employment in Theory and Practice*, The Jerome Levy Economics Institute Series, London: Macmillan, pp. 40–66.

Davidson, P. (2000), 'There are major differences between Kalecki's theory of employment and Keynes's general theory of employment interest and money,' *Journal of Post Keynesian Economics*, **23** (1), 3–25.

Davidson, P. (2002), 'Keynes versus Kalecki: responses to López and Kriesler,' *Journal of Post Keynesian Economics*, **24** (4), 631–41.

Dillard, D. (1984), 'Keynes and Marx: a centennial appraisal', *Journal of Post Keynesian Economics*, **6** (3), 421–32.

Dixit, A. (1980), 'The role of investment in entry-deterrence,' *Economic Journal*, **90** (357), 95–106.

Dixon, H. and Rankin, N. (1995), 'Imperfect competition and macroeconomics: a survey', in H. Dixon and N. Rankin (eds), *The New Macroeconomics*, Cambridge: Cambridge University Press, pp. 34–62.

Dow, C.S. (1997), 'Endogenous money,' in G.C. Harcourt and P. Riach (eds), *A 'Second Edition' of The General Theory*, vol. 2, London and New York: Routledge, pp. 61–78.

Dunlop, J.T. (1938), 'The movement of real and money wage rates', *Economic Journal*, **48** (191), 413–34.

Eatwell, J.L. (1982), 'Competition', in I. Bradley and M. Howard (eds), *Classical and Marxian Political Economy*, London: Macmillan, pp. 203–228.

Eichner, A.S. (1976), *The Megacorp and Oligopoly*, Cambridge: Cambridge University Press.

Fan-Hung (1939), 'Keynes and Marx on the theory of capital accumulation, money and interest', *Review of Economic Studies*, **7** (1), 28–41.

Fontana, G. and M. Setterfield (eds) (2009), *Macroeconomic Theory and Macroeconomic Pedagogy*, London: Palgrave Macmillan.

Galí, J. (2008), *Monetary Policy, Inflation, and the Business Cycle*, Princeton, NJ: Princeton University Press.

Galí, J. and M. Gertler (2007), 'Macroeconomic modeling for monetary policy evaluation,' *Journal of Economic Perspectives*, **21** (4), 25–45.

Garegnani, P. (1978), 'Notes on consumption, investment and effective demand: I', *Cambridge Journal of Economics*, **2** (4), 335–53.

Graziani, A. (1984), 'The debate on Keynes' finance motive', *Economic Notes*, **0** (1), 1–33.

Hahn, F.H. and R. Solow (1995), *A Critical Essay on Modern Macroeconomic Theory*, Cambridge MA: MIT Press.

Hamouda, O.F. and G.C. Harcourt (1988), 'Post Keynesianism: from criticism to coherence?', *Bulletin of Economic Research*, **40**, 1–33.

Harcourt, G.C. (ed.) (1977), *The Microeconomic Foundations of Macroeconomics*, London: Macmillan.

Harcourt, G.C. (1981), 'Marshall, Sraffa and Keynes: incompatible bedfellows?', *Eastern Economic Journal*, 5, 39–50.

Harcourt, G.C. (1982), 'The Sraffan contribution: an evaluation', in I. Bradley and M.C. Howard (eds), *Classical and Marxian Political Economy. Essays in Honour of R.L. Meek*, London: Macmillan, pp. 255–75.

Harcourt, G.C. (1983), 'On Piero Sraffa's contributions,' in P.D. Groenewegen and J. Halevi (eds), *Altro Polo, Italian Economics – Past and Present*, Sydney, NSW: Frederick May Foundation for Italian Studies, pp. 117–28.

Harcourt, G.C. (1992), 'Theoretical methods and unfinished business', in C. Sardoni (ed.), *On Political Economists and Modern Political Economy. Selected Essays of G.C. Harcourt*, London and New York: Routledge, pp. 235–49.

Harcourt, G.C. (1995), 'The structure of Tom Asimakopulos's later writings,' in G.C. Harcourt, A. Roncaglia and R. Rowley (eds), *Income and Employment in Theory and Practice*, The Jerome Levy Economics Institute Series, London: Macmillan, pp. 1–16.

Harcourt, G.C. (2001), *Selected Essays on Economic Policy*, London: Palgrave Macmillan.

Harcourt, G.C. (2006), *The Structure of Post-Keynesian Economics*, Cambridge: Cambridge University Press.

Harcourt, G.C. and P. Kenyon (1976), 'Pricing and the investment decision', *Kyklos*, **29** (3), 449–77.

Harcourt, G.C. and C. Sardoni (1994), 'Keynes's vision: method, analysis and tactics', in J.B. Davis (ed.), *The State of Interpretation of Keynes*, Dordrecht, the Netherlands and Boston, MA: Kluwer Academic Press, pp. 131–52.

Harrod, R.F. (1930), 'Notes on supply,' *Economic Journal*, **40** (158), 232–241.

Harrod, R.F. (1975), *The Life of John Maynard Keynes*, London: Macmillan.

Hein, E. (2006), 'Money, interest and capital accumulation in Karl Marx's economics: a monetary interpretation and some similarities to Post-Keynesian approaches,' *European Journal of the History of Economic Thought*, **13** (1), 113–40.

Hicks, J.R. (1936), 'Mr. Keynes' theory of employment', *Economic Journal*, **46** (182), 238–53.

Hicks, J.R. (1937), 'Mr. Keynes and the "Classics"', *Econometrica*, **5** (2), 147–59.

Hicks, J.R. (1939), *Value and Capital. An Inquiry into some Fundamental Principles of Economic Theory*, Oxford: Oxford University Press.

Hicks, J.R. (1982a), 'IS-LM – an explanation,' in *Money, Interest & Wages*, vol. 2 of *Collected Essays on Economic Theory*, Oxford: Basil Blackwell, pp. 318–31.

Hicks, J.R. (1982b), 'Time in economics,' in *Money, Interest & Wages*, vol. 2 of *Collected Essays on Economic Theory*, Oxford: Basil Blackwell, pp. 282–300.

Hollander, S. (1962), 'Malthus and Keynes: a note', *Economic Journal*, **72** (286), 355–9.

Kahn, R.F. (1931), 'The relation of home investment to unemployment', *Economic Journal*, **41** (162), 173–198.

Kahn, R.F. (1984), *The Making of Keynes' General Theory*, Cambridge: Cambridge University Press.

Kahn, R.F. (1989), *The Economics of the Short Period*, London: Macmillan.

Kalecki, M. (1935), 'A macrodynamic theory of business cycles', *Econometrica*, **3** (3), 327–44.

Kalecki, M. (1937), 'A theory of the business cycle', *Review of Economic Studies*, **4** (2), 77–97.

Kalecki, M. (1938), 'The determinants of distribution of national income', *Econometrica*, **6** (2), 97–112.

Kalecki, M. (1939), *Essays in the Theory of Economic Fluctuations*, London: Allen & Unwin.

Kalecki, M. (1965), *Theory of Economic Dynamics*, 2nd edn, London: Allen and Unwin.

Kalecki, M. (1968), 'The Marxian equation of reproduction and modern economics', *Social Science Information*, **7**, 73–9.

Kalecki, M. (1971), *Selected Essays on the Dynamics of the Capitalist Economy. 1933–1970*, Cambridge: Cambridge University Press.

Kalecki, M. (1990a), 'The essence of the business upswing', in J. Osiatyński (ed.), *Capitalism. Business Cycles and Full Employment*, vol. 1 of *Collected Works of Michal Kalecki*, Oxford: Clarendon Press, pp. 188–94.

Kalecki, M. (1990b), 'Political aspects of full employment,' in J. Osiatyński (ed.), *Capitalism. Business Cycles and Full Employment*, vol. 1 of *Collected Works of Michal Kalecki*, Oxford: Clarendon Press, pp. 347–56.

Kalecki, M. (1990c), 'Some remarks on Keynes's theory', in J. Osiatyński (ed.), *Capitalism. Business Cycles and Full Employment*, vol. 1 of *Collected Works of Michal Kalecki*, Oxford: Clarendon Press, pp. 223–32.

Kalecki, M. (1991a), 'Class struggle and distribution of national income', in J. Osiatyński (ed.), *Capitalism: Economic Dynamics*, vol. 2 of *Collected Works of Michal Kalecki*, Oxford: Clarendon Press, pp. 96–103.

Kalecki, M. (1991b), 'Money and real wages,' in J. Osiatyński (ed.), *Capitalism: Economic Dynamics*, vol. 2 of *Collected Works of Michal Kalecki*, Oxford: Clarendon Press, pp. 21–50.

Kalecki, M. (1991c), 'Trend and the business cycle', in J. Osiatyński (ed.), *Capitalism: Economic Dynamics*, vol. 2 of *Collected Works of Michal Kalecki*, Oxford: Clarendon Press, pp. 433–50.

Keynes, J.M. (1936), *The General Theory of Employment Interest and Money*, 1st edn, London: Macmillan.

Keynes, J.M. (1937a), 'Alternative theories of the rate of interest', *Economic Journal*, **47** (186), 241–252.

Keynes, J.M. (1937b), 'The "ex-ante" theory of the rate of interest', *Economic Journal*, **47** (188), 663–69.

Keynes, J.M. (1937c), 'The general theory of employment', *Quarterly Journal of Economics*, **51** (2), 209–23.

Keynes, J.M. (1939), 'Relative movements of real wages and output', *Economic Journal*, **49** (193), 34–51.

Keynes, J.M. (1971a), *The Economic Consequences of the Peace*, vol. 2 of *The Collected Writings of John Maynard Keynes*, London: Macmillan.

Keynes, J.M. (1971b), *A Treatise on Money. The Pure Theory of Money*, vol. 5 of *The Collected Writings of John Maynard Keynes*, London: Macmillan.

Keynes, J.M. (1973a), *The General Theory and After. Part I, Preparation*, vol. 13 of *The Collected Writings of John Maynard Keynes*, London: Macmillan.

Keynes, J.M. (1973b), *The General Theory and After. Part II, Defence and Development*, vol. 14 of *The Collected Writings of John Maynard Keynes*, London: Macmillan.

Keynes, J.M. (1973c), 'A monetary theory of production', in *The General Theory and After. Part I, Preparation*, London: Macmillan, vol. 13 of *The Collected Writings of John Maynard Keynes*, pp. 408–11.

Keynes, J.M. (1979), *The General Theory and After. A Supplement*, vol. 29 of *The Collected Writings of John Maynard Keynes*, London: Macmillan.

Keynes, J.M. (1983), *Economic Articles and Correspondence. Investment and Editorial*, vol. 12 of *The Collected Writings of John Maynard Keynes*, London: Macmillan.

Knight, F.H. (1921), *Risk, Uncertainty and Profit*, Chicago. IL: University of Chicago Press.

Kregel, J.A. (1976), 'Economic methodology in the face of uncertainty: the modelling methods of Keynes and the Post-Keynesians', *Economic Journal*, **86** (342), 209–25.

Kriesler, P. (1987), *Kalecki's Microanalysis: The Development of Kalecki's Analysis of Pricing and Distribution*, Cambridge: Cambridge University Press.

Lavoie, M. (2006), 'Do heterodox theories have anything in common? A Post-Keynesian point of view', *Intervention*, **3** (1), 87–112.

Mankiw, N.G. (1985), 'Small menu costs and large business cycles: a macroeconomic model', *Quarterly Journal of Economics*, **100** (2), 529–38.

Marris, R.L. (1991), *Reconstructing Keynesian Economics with Imperfect Competition*, Aldershot: Edward Elgar.

Marris, R.L. (1997), 'Yes, Mrs Robinson! *The General Theory* and imperfect competition', in G.C. Harcourt and P.A. Riach (eds), *A 'Second Edition' of The General Theory*, vol. 1, London and New York: Routledge, pp. 52–82.

Marshall, A. (1920), *Principles of Economics*, 8th edn, London: Macmillan.

Marshall, A. (1930), 'The Pure Theory of Foreign Trade. The Pure Theory of Domestic Values', series of reprints of scarce tracts in economics and political science, London: The London School of Economics and Political Science.

Marx, K. (1954), *Capital, Book I*, Moscow: Progress Publishers.

Marx, K. (1956), *Capital, Book II*, Moscow: Progress Publishers.

Marx, K. (1959), *Capital, Book III*, Moscow: Progress Publishers.

Marx, K. (1968), *Theories of Surplus-Value, Part II*, Moscow: Progress Publishers.

Marx, K. (1973), *Grundrisse*, Harmondsworth: Penguin.

McCracken, H.L. (1933), *Value Theory and Business Cycles*, New York: Falcon Press.

McNulty, P.J. (1968), 'Economic theory and the meaning of competition', *Quarterly Journal of Economics*, **82** (4), 639–56.

Meek, R.L. (1977), *Smith, Marx and After*, London: Chapman and Hall.

Meyer, L.H. (2001), 'Does money matter?', Homer Jones Lecture, Federal Reserve Bank of St. Louis, 28 March.

Milgate, M. (1982), *Capital and Employment*, London: Academic Press.

Morishima, M. (1984), *The Economics of Industrial Society*, Cambridge: Cambridge University Press.

Myrdal, G. (1939), *Monetary Equilibrium*, New York: Augustus M. Kelley.

Nakatani, T. (1980), 'The law of falling rate of profit and the competitive battle: comment on Shaikh', *Cambridge Journal of Economics*, **4** (1), 65–8.

Nishimura, K.G. (1992), *Imperfect Competition, Differential Information, and Microfoundations of Macroeconomics*, Oxford: Clarendon Press.

Ohlin, B. (1937a), 'Some notes on the Stockholm theory of savings and investment I', *Economic Journal*, **47** (185), 53–69.

Ohlin, B. (1937b), 'Some notes on the Stockholm theory of savings and investment II,' *Economic Journal*, **47** (186), 221–40.

Okishio, N. (1961), 'Technical change and the rate of profit', *Kobe University Economic Review*, **7**, 85–99.

Palley, T.I. (2003), 'The backward-bending Phillips curve and the minimum unemployment rate of inflation: wage adjustment with opportunistic firms', *Manchester School*, **71** (1), 35–50.

Panico, C. (1980), 'Marx's analysis of the relationship between the rate of interest and the rate of profits', *Cambridge Journal of Economics*, **4** (4), 363–78.

Parrinello, S. (1980), 'The price level implicit in Keynes' effective demand', *Journal of Post Keynesian Economics*, **3** (1), 63–78.

Pasinetti, L.L. (1974), 'The economics of effective demand', in *Growth and Income Distribution, Essays in Economic Theory*, Cambridge: Cambridge University Press, pp. 29–53.

Pasinetti, L.L. (1997), 'The marginal efficiency of investment,' in G.C. Harcourt and P.A. Riach (eds), *A 'Second Edition' of The General Theory*, vol. 1, London and New York: Routledge, pp. 198–218.

Patinkin, D. (1982), *Anticipations of The General Theory?*, Chicago, IL: Chicago University Press.

Pigou, A.C. (1950), *Keynes's General Theory: A Retrospective View*, London: Macmillan.

Reddaway, B.W. (1985), 'Discussion of Kregel,' in G.C. Harcourt (ed.), *Keynes and his Contemporaries*, London: Macmillan, pp. 96–7.

Ricardo, D. (1951), *On the Principles of Political Economy and Taxation*, vol. 1 of *Works and Correspondence of David Ricardo*, Cambridge: Cambridge University Press.

Robertson, D.H. (1936), 'Some notes on Mr. Keynes' general theory of employment', *Quarterly Journal of Economics*, **51** (1), 168–191.

Robinson, J.V. (1934), 'What is perfect competition?' *Quarterly Journal of Economics*, **49** (1), 104–21.

Robinson, J.V. (1951), 'Marx and Keynes', in *Collected Economic Papers, Vol. I*, Oxford: Basil Blackwell, pp. 133–45.

Robinson, J.V. (1960a), '"Imperfect competition" to-day', in *Collected Economic Papers, Vol. II*, Oxford: Basil Blackwell, pp. 239–45.

Robinson, J.V. (1960b), 'Marx, Marshall and Keynes', in *Collected Economic Papers, Vol. II*, Oxford: Basil Blackwell, pp. 1–17.

Robinson, J.V. (1965a), 'Kalecki and Keynes', in *Collected Economic Papers, Vol. III*, Oxford: Basil Blackwell, pp. 92–9.

Robinson, J.V. (1965b), 'Marxism: religion and science', in *Collected Economic Papers, Vol. III*, Oxford: Basil Blackwell, pp. 148–57.

Robinson, J.V. (1969), *The Economics of Imperfect Competition*, 2nd edn, London: Macmillan.

Robinson, J.V. (1973a), 'Michal Kalecki', in *Collected Economic Papers Vol. 4*, Oxford: Basil Blackwell, pp. 87–91.

Robinson, J.V. (1973b), 'On re-reading Marx', in *Collected Economic Papers Vol. 4*, Oxford: Basil Blackwell, pp. 247–68.

Robinson, J.V. (1977), 'Michal Kalecki and the economics of capitalism', *Oxford Bulletin of Economics and Statistics*, **39** (1), 7–17.

Robinson, J.V. (1979), 'History versus equilibrium', in *Collected Economic Papers, Vol. V*, Oxford: Basil Blackwell, pp. 48–58.

Robinson, J.V. (1980a), 'The collected writings of John Maynard Keynes. Volume XXIX: The General Theory and After – a supplement by Donald Moggridge', *Economic Journal*, **90** (358), 391–3.

Robinson, JV. (1980b), 'Marxism and modern economics', in *Further Contributions to Modern Economics*, Oxford: Basil Blackwell, pp. 192–202.

Roemer, J.E. (1979), 'Continuing controversies on the falling rate of profit: fixed capital and other issues', *Cambridge Journal of Economics*, **3** (4), 379–98.

Rotheim, R. (ed.) (1997), *New Keynesian Economics/Post Keynesian Alternatives*, London and New York: Routledge.

Rowthorn, R.E. (1977), 'Conflict, inflation and money', *Cambridge Journal of Economics*, **1** (3), 215–39.

Salter, W.E.G. (1966), *Productivity and Technical Change*, 2nd edn, Cambridge: Cambridge University Press.

Sardoni, C. (1981), 'Multisectoral models of balanced growth and the Marxian schemes of expanded reproduction', *Australian Economic Papers*, **20** (37), 383–97.

Sardoni, C. (1984), 'Some ties of Kalecki to the 1926 Sraffan Manifesto', *Journal of Post Keynesian Economics*, **6** (3), 458–65.

Sardoni, C. (1987), *Marx and Keynes on Economic Recession*, New York: New York University Press.

Sardoni, C. (1994), '*The General Theory* and the critique of decreasing returns', *Journal of the History of Economic Thought*, **16** (1), 61–85.

Sardoni, C. (1995), 'Interpretations of Kalecki', in G. C. Harcourt, A. Roncaglia and R. Rowley (eds), *Income and Employment in Theory and Practice*, London: Macmillan, pp. 185–204.

Sardoni, C. (1997a), 'Keynes and Marx', in G.C. Harcourt and P. Riach (eds), *A 'Second Edition' of The General Theory*, vol. 2, London and New York: Routledge, pp. 261–83.

Sardoni, C. (1997b), 'Wages and employment: a Keynesian model', in R. Rotheim (ed.), *New Keynesian Economics/Post Keynesian Alternatives*, London and New York: Routledge, pp. 107–17.

Sardoni, C. (1998), 'Marx's theory of money and interest: a reconsideration in the light of Robertson and Keynes', in R. Bellofiore (ed.), *Marxian Economics: A Reappraisal – Essays on Volume III of Capital. Method, value and money*, vol. 1, London: Macmillan, pp. 271–85.

Sardoni, C. (1999), 'The debate on excess capacity in the 1930s', in C. Sardoni and P. Kriesler (eds), *Keynes, Post-Keynesianism and Political Economy*, vol. 3 of *Essays in Honour of Geoff Harcourt*, London and New York: Routledge, pp. 259–83.

Sardoni, C. (2007), 'Kaldor's monetary thought: a contribution to a modern theory of money', in M. Forstater, G. Mongiovi and S. Pressman (eds), *Post Keynesian Macroeconomics*, London and New York: Routledge, pp. 129–46.

Sardoni, C. (2008), 'Some notes on the nature of money and the future of monetary policy', *Review of Social Economy*, **66** (4), 523–37.

Sardoni, C. (2009), 'The Marxian schemes of reproduction and the theory of effective demand', *Cambridge Journal of Economics*, **33** (1), 161–73.

Sardoni, C. (2010), 'The new consensus in macroeconomics and non-mainstream approaches', *Intervention*, **7** (2), 255–65.

Sawyer, M.C. (1985), *The Economics of Michal Kalecki*, London: Macmillan.

Schefold, B. (1976), 'Different forms of technical progress', *Economic Journal*, **86** (344), 806–19.

Schmalensee, R. (1981), 'Economies of scale and barriers to entry', *Journal of Political Economy*, **89** (6), 1228–38.

Schumpeter, J.A. (1954), *History of Economic Analysis*, London: Allen and Unwin.

Shackle, G.L.S. (1983), *The Years of High Theory*, Cambridge: Cambridge University Press.

Shaikh, A. (1978), 'Political economy and capitalism: notes on Dobb's theory of crisis', *Cambridge Journal of Economics*, **2** (2), 233–51.

Shaikh, A. (1980), 'Marxian competition versus perfect competition: further comments on the so-called choice of technique', *Cambridge Journal of Economics*, **4** (1), 75–83.

Skouras, T. (1981), 'The economics of Joan Robinson', in R.J. Shackleton and G. Locksley (eds), *Twelve Contemporary Economists*, London: Macmillan, pp. 199–218.

Smith, A. (1976), *An Inquiry into the Nature and Causes of the Wealth of Nations*, vol. 1 and 2 of *The Glasgow Edition of the Works and Correspondence of Adam Smith*, Indianapolis, IN: Liberty Classics.

Smithin, J. (2009), 'Teaching the new consensus model of "Modern Monetary Economics" from a critical perspective: pedagogical issues', in G. Fontana and M. Setterfield (eds), *Teaching the New Consensus Model of "Modern Monetary Economics" from a Critical Perspective: Pedagogical Issues*, London: Palgrave Macmillan, chapter 13, pp. 255–72.

Solow, R. M. (1998), *Monopolistic Competition and Macroeconomic Theory*, Federico Caffè Lectures, Cambridge: Cambridge University Press.

Sowell, T. (1972), *Say's Law. An Historical Analysis*, Princeton, NJ: Princeton University Press.

Spence, A.M. (1977), 'Entry, capacity, investment and oligopolistic pricing,' *Bell Journal of Economics*, **8** (2), 534–44.

Spence, A.M. (1979), 'Investment strategy and growth in a new market', *Bell Journal of Economics*, **10** (1), 1–19.

Sraffa, P. (1925), 'Sulle relazioni fra costo e quantità prodotta', *Annali di economia*, **II**, 15–65.

Sraffa, P. (1926), 'The laws of return under competitive conditions', *Economic Journal*, **36** (144), 535–50.

Sraffa, P. (1960), *Production of Commodities by Means of Commodities. Prelude to a Critique of Economic Theory*, Cambridge: Cambridge University Press.

Steedman, I. (1980), 'A note on the choice of technique under capitalism', *Cambridge Journal of Economics*, **4** (1), 61–4.

Steindl, J. (1976), *Maturity and Stagnation in American Capitalism*, 2nd edn, New York and London: Monthly Review Press.

Steindl, J. (1981), 'Ideas and concepts of long run growth', *Banca Nazionale del Lavoro Quarterly Review*, **34** (136), 35–48.

Stockhammer, E. (2008), 'Is the NAIRU theory a Monetarist, New Keynesian, Post Keynesian or a Marxist theory?', *Metroeconomica*, **59** (3), 479–510.

Sylos Labini, P. (1967), 'Prices, distribution and investment in Italy, 1951–1966: an interpretation', *BNL Quarterly Review*, **20** (83), 316–75.

Sylos Labini, P. (1969), *Oligopoly and Technical Progress*, Cambridge, MA: Harvard University Press.

Sylos Labini, P. (1974), *Trade Unions, Inflation and Productivity*, Lexington, MA: Lexington Books.

Sylos Labini, P. (1988), 'The great debates on the laws of returns and the value of capital: when will economists accept their own logic?', *Banca Nazionale del Lavoro Quarterly Review*, **41** (166), 263–91.

Tamborini, R. (2009), 'Rescuing the LM curve (and the money market) in a modern macro course', in G. Fontana and M. Setterfield (eds), *Macroeconomic Theory and Macroeconomic Pedagogy*, London: Palgrave Macmillan, chapter 4, pp. 76–99.

Tarshis, L. (1939), 'Changes in real and money wages', *Economic Journal*, **49** (193), 150–4.

Weintraub, E.R. (1979), *Microfoundations*, Cambridge: Cambridge University Press.

Weintraub, S. (1978), *Capitalism's Inflation and Unemployment Crisis: Beyond Monetarism and Keynesianism*, Reading, MA: Addison-Wesley.

Wicksell, K. (1936), *Interest and Prices*, London: Macmillan.

Woodford, M. (2003), *Interest and Prices*, Princeton, NJ and Oxford: Princeton University Press.

Index